Testamentary Acts

Browning, Tennyson, James, Hardy

MICHAEL MILLGATE

CLARENDON PRESS · OXFORD

1992

Oxford University Press, Walton Street, Oxford OX2 6DP
Oxford New York Toronto
Delhi Bombay Calcutta Madras Karachi
Petaling Jaya Singapore Hong Kong Tokyo
Nairobi Dar es Salaam Cape Town
Melbourne Auckland
and associated companies in
Berlin Ibadan

Oxford is a trade mark of Oxford University Press

Published in the United States
by Oxford University Press, New York

British Library Cataloguing in Publication Data
Data available

Library of Congress Cataloging in Publication Data
Millgate, Michael.
Testamentary acts: Browning, Tennyson, James, Hardy/by Michael
Millgate.
Includes index.
1. English literature—19th century—Criticism, Textual.
2. Authors, English—Biography—History and criticism. 3. Tennyson,
Alfred Tennyson, Baron, 1809–1892—Authorship. 4. Browning, Robert,
1812–1889—Authorship. 5. Hardy, Thomas, 1940–1928—Authorship.
6. James, Henry, 1843–1916—Authorship. 7. Transmission of texts.
8. Wills—Great Britain. 9. Canon (Literature). 10. Autobiography.
I. Title.
PR468.T48M55 1992 820.9'008—dc20
ISBN 0–19–811276–9

Set by Hope Services, (Abingdon), Ltd.
Printed and bound in
Great Britain by Biddles Ltd.
Guildford and King's Lynn

To
Frederick B. Adams

Contents

Acknowledgements

In preparing this study, touching as it does upon the life and work of several different figures, I have depended upon the resources of numerous institutions, and it is my pleasant duty to thank the following libraries and their staffs for allowing me to see and use relevant materials and for providing advice and assistance of every kind: Balliol College Library, Oxford (especially Penelope Bulloch and Alan Tadiello); BBC Written Archives Centre; Beinecke Rare Book and Manuscript Library, Yale University (especially Ralph Franklin, Vincent Giroud, and Marjorie G. Wynne); Albert A. and Henry W. Berg Collection, New York Public Library, Astor, Lenox and Tilden Foundations (especially the late Lola L. Szladits); British Library (especially Sally Brown, Elizabeth James, and Ian Willison); Colby College Library, Waterville, Maine (especially Patience-Anne W. Lenck); Dartmouth College Library (especially Stephen N. Cronenwett); Dorset County Library, Dorchester, Dorset; Dorset County Museum, Dorchester, Dorset (especially Roger Peers and Paul Ensom); Eton College, School Library (especially Michael Meredith and Helen Garton); Houghton Library, Harvard University; Huntington Library, San Marino, California; King's College Library, Cambridge (especially Michael Halls); Brotherton Collection, Brotherton Library, University of Leeds (especially Christopher Sheppard and Vanessa Hinton); John Murray (Publishers) Ltd (especially Virginia Murray); National Library of Scotland (especially Iain Brown); Manuscripts Division, New York Public Library, Astor, Lenox and Tilden Foundations; Pierpont Morgan Library, New York (especially Herbert Cahoon and Robert E. Parks); Princeton University Library; Queen's College Library, Oxford; Boatwright Memorial Library, University of Richmond (especially James Gwin); Harry Ransom Humanities Research Center, University of Texas (especially Cathy Henderson); Tennyson Research Centre, Lincoln (especially Susan Gates); Trinity College Library, Cambridge (especially David McKitterick); Fisher Rare Book Library, University of Toronto (especially Richard Landon); and the Victoria and Albert Museum.

I am especially grateful to the following collectors and private owners who have allowed me to see and use manuscript materials in their possession: Frederick B. Adams, Celia Barclay, Alan Clodd, Ronald Greenland, David Holmes, the late Revd H. P. Kingdon, Henry Lock, the late Richard Little Purdy, the late Lilian Skinner, and Daphne Wood.

For permission to reproduce previously unpublished material I am greatly indebted to the following: Sir Christopher Cockerell, for diaries and other notes by Sir Sydney Cockerell; the Trustees of Eva Anne Dugdale, for the letters of Florence Hardy; Jennifer Gosse, for reminiscences by Sir Edmund Gosse; Alexander R. James, for the letters of Henry James, Alice James (Mrs William James), and Henry James, junior; and John Murray, for the letters of Robert Browning, Robert Weidemann Barrett Browning, and Sarianna Browning.

Among the many people who have advised and assisted me in various ways I should like to record my particular thanks to the following: Thomas H. Adamowski, Frederick and Marie-Louise Adams, Henry Auster, Christine Bacque, Sabar Balsara, Celia Barclay, Alan Bell, Robin Biswas, Caesar Blake, Adrian Bond, Gertrude Bugler, James Cameron, Michael Collie, Eleanor Cook, Jane Cooper, Graham Dalling, Bernard Dickens, Gillian Fraser, Simon Gatrell, Robert Gittings, Desmond Hawkins, Robert H. Hirst, Heather Jackson, J. R. de J. Jackson, W. J. Keith, Philip Kelley, Kate Lawson, Charles Lock, Lesley Mann, Lawrence Miller, Norman Page, Hershel Parker, Stephen Poulter, Michael Rabiger, J. M. Robson, Barbara Rosenbaum, S. P. Rosenbaum, Hilary Spurling, Lilian Swindall, Brian Thomas, Anthony Thwaite, John Tydeman, Wentworth Walker, Margaret Webster, Judith Wittenberg, Daphne Wood, James Woodress, and Marjorie G. Wynne.

I gladly acknowledge the generous support I have received in the form of a Killam Foundation Research Fellowship and research grants from the Social Sciences and Humanities Research Council of Canada, and take much pleasure in extending my more personal thanks to Catharine Carver, Pamela Dalziel, Michael Meredith, and Ann Thwaite for their thorough, sensitive, and immensely helpful readings of the manuscript itself and to Bill and Vera Jesty for their unfailing friendship and support. To my wife, Jane Millgate, I owe, as always, a unique and ever-accumulating debt, at once personal and professional. I also take this opportunity of celebrating the work and mourning the passing of two great Hardy scholars, Richard Purdy and Henry Reed—and of dedicating this book to a third.

Toronto
November 1991

Introduction

FOR English and American writers of the last two centuries the supreme model of career closure—and, indeed, of noble dying—has been Sir Walter Scott. It's not that Scott was by any means the first writer to give attention in the last years of his life to the view of himself that would be exposed to posterity in the long wake of his impending decease. Nor that he was especially vain. But he was inevitably aware of the immensity of his reputation, of a national and international fascination with the life and person of the Author of Waverley that was all the greater for the Author's identity having been so long concealed. And since the debts he had so gallantly shouldered at the time of the Constable and Ballantyne collapse had still not been cleared away, he was no less sharply and honourably conscious of the possible financial returns upon his popularity even after he had himself departed.

He actively collaborated, therefore, in the production of a final comprehensive edition of his novels, the so-called *magnum opus* edition, which served through its enriching—or, as some would have it, encumbering—combination of new format, textual revision, commissioned illustrations, and specially written authorial introductions and annotations to establish a pattern for collected editions that is still by no means outworn. He gave his approval to a reissue of his poems, in the same format as the novels, and equipped it with a series of specially written introductions. He further envisaged that the completed edition of the fiction, verse, and nonfiction prose should be supplemented—as in the editions of Dryden and Swift he had himself prepared—by a substantial 'life' of the author, prospectively enhancing such a work by keeping a journal and giving a strongly autobiographical emphasis to the new introductions to the novels and the poetry. In his will, finally, he specifically directed that the biography be written by his son-in-law, John Gibson Lockhart, already a distinguished novelist and biographer in his own right.

Lockhart, who had long cherished the prospect of such a task, now undertook it not merely out of a sense of familial duty but with an eagerness and literary purposiveness that made his *Memoirs of the Life of Sir Walter Scott, Bart.* more revelatory of its subject, and even a little more critical, than some contemporaries thought altogether appropriate. Of greater importance in the longer term was Lockhart's success in maintaining the impression that Scott's own recollections and correspondence comprised at once the heart and the substance of the book and that his own role had been as much one of compilation as of authorship—an achievement that effectively established the 'life and letters' format as the dominant biographical mode throughout the remainder of the nineteenth century and even well into the twentieth.

It is not my purpose in this volume to trace the history of Victorian biography or the Victorian collected edition, instructive though it would doubtless prove to set alongside Lockhart and the *magnum opus*—and alongside each other—the official 'lives' and ostensibly 'authorized' editions of such figures as Dickens, Charlotte Brontë, Thackeray, and George Eliot. Nor am I seeking at all directly to extend those speculative enquiries into the beginnings, crystallizations, and conclusions of literary careers so suggestively conducted by Lawrence Lipking in *The Life of the Poet*, published by the University of Chicago Press in 1981. I shall be concerned rather to examine the ways in which writers famous in their own time have sought in old age to exert some degree of posthumous control over their personal and literary reputations—over the extent and nature of future biographical investigation and exposure, and over the interpretation and textual integrity of their published works.

Potentially, of course, a literary career can end at any age—and at any moment: one of the available *OED* definitions of 'career' is 'short gallop at full speed'. Valedictory gestures are not confined to the elderly, and the apprehension of death, even the anticipation of enforced or chosen retirement, can operate very much like old age itself in shaping what may prove, irrespective of age, to be the final phase of a writer's working life. Moral or political censorship, whether directly experienced or merely anticipated, can significantly affect the outward shape of a career, and the same is at least temporarily true of that somewhat shuffling kind of self-censorship which leads (as in the case of Ernest Hemingway) to posthumous publication at the discretion, or indiscretion, of scholars and executors. These present studies, however, have chiefly derived from an interest in questions of evidential authenticity in the writing of biography and of authorial 'intentionality' in the theory and practice of scholarly editing, and are directed towards an essentially biographical exploration of the actual—which is to say practical—processes and consequences of self-conscious career termination. Their focus, therefore, is on writers to whom literary fame, economic security, personal longevity, and continued physical and mental well-being have granted the opportunity not only to reappraise their own past works and deeds but actively to enforce such a reappraisal and seek to ensure its continuation beyond their own lifetimes—to reconstruct, in short, the entire self-construct known as, say, Robert Browning.

Such writers have characteristically looked back to the past with posterity in mind and taken—or signally failed to take—actions that would prove profoundly significant for what was known and said about them and their work in subsequent years. They have, for example, destroyed or selectively preserved such personal papers as diaries, notebooks, manuscripts, and letters; written autobiographies and memoirs; authorized 'official' biographies and even participated in their preparation; revised the texts of their earlier works and provided them with freshly written and highly directive prefaces or annotations; and reissued those newly refurbished titles in so-called 'collected' editions that were often inclusive only of whatever elderly authorial judgement had deemed worthy of canonicity. In recent years it has been possible to watch Graham Greene going through what might almost be called the 'classic' late-career motions of publishing a highly selective 'collected' edition with new prefaces, writing autobiographical reminiscences, submitting to interviews, approving a biographer, and using accumulated fame as a position from which to attack contemporary figures and phenomena—from the mayor of Nice to the foreign policy of the United States—of which he disapproved.

Each of the four authors treated in some detail here—Robert Browning, Alfred Tennyson, Henry James, and Thomas Hardy—enjoyed a high reputation in his own lifetime and survived into what can fairly be reckoned old age, James dying at seventy-two, Browning at seventy-seven, Tennyson at eighty-three, and Hardy at eighty-seven. They were sufficiently contemporary one with another for broadly similar assumptions to be made about the social and intellectual climates within which they lived and died

and about the economic and structural conditions within which
they worked as professional authors—three of the four, indeed,
published extensively, and sometimes contemporaneously, with the
house of Macmillan. In detail, of course, their lives and careers
differed in almost every respect, but it does seem possible to discern
a common if by no means sharply etched pattern of conscious
career conclusion, chiefly characterized by deliberate and sometimes
passionate attempts to ensure the maintenance of personal and
creative privacy up to and beyond the moment of death and to
project forward into the future conceptions of the work and the self
arrived at late in life, and often in extreme old age.

Such projections have necessarily depended for their realization
upon the sympathy, competence, and responsibility with which
testamentary requests—whether explicit or implicit, written, spoken,
or 'understood'—were interpreted and carried out by the relatives,
friends, or functionaries to whom they had been entrusted, and
what strikingly emerges from these particular instances is the way
in which, once a major player has left the stage, it is often a
distinctly minor and previously little regarded figure who comes
forward, Shakespearean fashion, to exercise a substituted intentionality that may, to any external view, prove difficult or even
impossible to distinguish from the author's own. Pen Browning and
Hallam Tennyson, indeed, have demanded and received almost as
much space here as their famous fathers, and Florence Hardy's
unhappy experiences after her husband's death have been given
even more expansive treatment.

It would of course have been possible to invoke more examples.
Since every case would have differed sharply from every other there
was, indeed, no clearly principled limit upon their potential
accumulation. My ambition, however, has been to offer an
exploratory essay rather than a taxonomic treatise, to be suggestive
rather than exhaustive, and for such a purpose four careers and
their aftermaths, treated in some depth, seemed sufficient to prompt
in these and wider contexts a series of pertinent questions about
elderly authors and their conscious and unconscious attempts to
impose upon posterity versions of their works and selves specifically
reflective of the aesthetic perceptions, moral discriminations, and
creative choices they have arrived at late in life—however
profoundly these may differ from those which prevailed earlier in
their careers, at the times of original inscription or commission. We

have been taught to respect and revere the words and actions of the dying, and the legal and ethical significance accorded to last wills and testaments has doubtless had its effect upon the standard editorial privileging of authors' 'final intentions'. But it ought perhaps to trouble us more than it customarily does that we automatically approach a number of major writers—Scott is again an obvious example—by way of the texts, commentaries, and canonical frameworks they established only in late career, and that we unreflectingly depend upon literary biographies that may be largely based on immaculately laundered archival evidence and on uncheckable assertions emanating from the subject's famous but not necessarily scrupulous old age—or from a widow, widower, child, or other dubiously authoritative relict or representative.

Robert and Pen Browning

'HE was always young', wrote Anne Thackeray Ritchie of Robert Browning, 'as his father had been before him.'[1] It might equally be said that the death of Elizabeth Barrett Browning in 1861 had rendered her husband prematurely old. Fixed forever in the popular imagination by the romance of his marriage, originally dependent for his public position upon his wife's far greater fame, emotionally arrested in mid-career by the private and public trauma of her death, Browning seems quite consciously to have entered upon the final phase of his life the moment he became a widower at the age of forty-nine—and to have spent his remaining twenty-eight years settling ever more deeply into the patterns established at that time. The very next day after his wife's death he could write to his sister:

My life is fixed and sure now. I shall live out the remainder in her direct influence, endeavoring to complete mine, miserably imperfect now, but so as to take the good she was meant to give me. I go away from Italy at once, having no longer any business there. I have our child about whom I shall exclusively employ myself, doing her part by him. I shall live in the presence of her, in every sense, I hope and believe—so that so far my loss is not *irreparable*—but the future is nothing to me now, except inasmuch as it confirms and realizes the past.[2]

Browning returned duly and with a certain air of martyrdom to England, ostensibly and to some extent actually centring his life upon his son's education. He bought a house in London for himself and (when not enduring education) Pen, was joined there by his sister Sarianna in 1866, and moved away many years later only because the building seemed doomed to demolition. He drew up the will that was to stand unchanged at the time of his death. And in 1867 he made what proved to be a final change of publisher both for his wife's works and for his own. Although quite distinct in themselves, these actions seem profoundly interconnected as aspects of Browning's painfully achieved personal reconstruction following the grief and disorientation of his bereavement, his deliberate adoption of a style of living that was intended to be settled, circumscribed, permanent, and manageable, and that proved in fact to be so.

Anxious to control the incidence of emotional stress, he avoided extreme and exclusive intimacies in favour of multiple friendships of lesser intensity and more or less equal importance. Determined to simplify and regularize the practical aspects of his life, he adopted a rigid set of domestic habits[3]—dining out a great deal, for example, but entertaining only a small circle of intimates at his own house—and slipped into an increasingly habitual groove of social availability, becoming a familiar figure in London drawing- and dining-rooms and maintaining a wide circle of friends, acquaintances, and admirers through his unwavering affability, his elaborate gallantry towards women, and his brilliantly resourceful small-talk, the latter becoming ever more monologic as his fame grew. A newspaper article of 1881 described him as being 'as far a dandy as a sensible man can be' and 'one of the best and sprightliest of our latter-day *raconteurs*',[4] and Frederic Harrison, the positivist, was to recall the Browning of the 1870s and 1880s as 'the happiest social spirit' he had ever known, 'always ready to meet a congenial company, large or small, at a club, a mansion, or a cottage, to talk with every one on every topic that could interest a man of letters, a man of the world, or a lady of fashion. He was all things to all men and all women, always at his best, always bringing light, happiness, generosity, and sense into every society he entered.'[5] One observer found it appropriate to praise Browning's 'afternoon-tea manner' for being 'as unaffected as that of a bank-chairman contemplating dividends or deposits'.[6]

Many of Browning's contemporaries, however, were troubled by the man they encountered socially during his later years. Thomas Hardy, though irritated by Browning's snobbishness,[7] saw what he called 'The Riddle of Browning' largely in terms of contrasts within and among the published works: 'How could smug Christian optimism worthy of a dissenting grocer [he asked Edmund Gosse] find a place inside a man who was so vast a seer & feeler when on neutral ground?'[8] Gosse, for his part, left a harsh summing up of the social Browning in a note dated from 1876 but not published in his lifetime: 'B. was very affectionate to me, in the uncomfortably self-conscious way he always is, half confidential, half distant and all inscrutable. With all his society manners he has a supreme gift of putting one *not* at one's ease.'[9] Henry James, in particular, who met

Browning on numerous occasions from the late 1870s onwards, reflected in the story 'The Private Life'[10] a sense of him as a deeply divided personality, a poet whose ubiquitous public self—well-dressed, loud-voiced, inexhaustibly talkative, and more than a little overbearing—bore no discernible or even imaginable relation to the invisible private self who demanded to be hypothesized as the author of the poems. Tennyson's dedication of his *Tiresias* volume to Browning's 'genius and geniality' might be said to have recognized the same phenomenon but to have taken it grandly in stride.

The notion of Browning's elusiveness and possible duality has continued to trouble subsequent criticism and biography, especially in the absence of major new sources of information and insight. James in particular struggled with 'the problem of Browning'[11] to the very end of his life: the last completed chapter of the posthumously published *The Middle Years* characterizes Browning's readings from his own work as the reverse of Tennyson's in their self-conscious striving for eloquence, precision, and force—as if 'he had to *prove* himself a poet, almost against all presumptions, and with all the assurance and all the character he could use'. In that same chapter, however, James speaks of having found Tennyson himself distinctly unTennysonian,[12] and it seems at least debatable whether Browning's public persona—grating and even, to some sensibilities, grotesque though it may have been—was significantly more incongruous or impenetrable than, say, Tennyson's bardic panache or Hardy's almost obtrusive self-effacement. Nor is it clear how strictly the public persona was maintained in private exchanges with such closer friends as Carlyle, Jowett, and Joseph Milsand—all deeply attached to him in their very different ways—or with Alexandra Sutherland Orr, intellectually and perhaps emotionally the closest of all his friends in later years.[13]

Browning in these years seems to have sought constant exposure in the interest both of promoting his personal fame and of reassuring himself as to its reality. He gave, from 1880 onwards, many more semipublic readings than the one attended by Henry James, and Michael Meredith has recently spoken of these performances, which sometimes lasted as long as two hours, as part of Browning's deliberate attempt, late in life, to counter the complaints of obscurity still commonly made against his poems and so enhance their—and his own—prospects of acceptance by posterity.[14] The ingratiating social manner permitted him on these and other social occasions to be accessible and agreeable without risking significant self-revelation or personal involvement. 'As a rule,' according to his American friend Katharine de Kay Bronson, 'he seemed purposely to avoid deep and serious topics. If such were broached in his presence he dismissed them with one strong, convincing sentence, and adroitly turned the current of conversation into a shallower channel.' Since he spoke well on all subjects, the loss seemed to her a small one, and she speculated that what led him 'to bring himself down to the ordinary hearer's level' was either simple kindness or a need for 'that repose to the mind which easy talk brings to those who think intensely'.[15] By putting himself on the same level as his hearers, however, Browning did not necessarily engage with them the more directly, and the poem 'Inapprehensive-ness' in the final *Asolando* volume seems to suggest that it was precisely his evasiveness, his inveterate avoidance of the 'serious', which inhibited—deliberately or otherwise—the emotional developments latent in the relationship with Mrs Bronson herself.[16]

But Browning had long recognized that a second marriage would significantly dim the aura of his first, and it is doubtful whether he ever thought of marriage to Katharine Bronson or to any of his other women friends of the 1870s and 1880s as a serious possibility.[17] The presence in *Asolando* of such a poem as 'Now' hints at the sexual repression involved in such a policy but provides no firm basis for estimating its severity. Nor is it possible to get much sense of the other pressures and emotions lurking behind and beyond the public persona, although Browning's capacity for sudden and savage anger was sharply revealed in July 1889 by the violence, disgust, and displaced religiosity with which he too hastily responded, in the pages of the *Athenaeum*, to a flippant reference to his wife's death ('Mrs Browning's Death is rather a relief to me, I must say: no more Aurora Leighs, thank God!')[18] encountered in a posthumously published letter of Edward FitzGerald's:

> I chanced upon a new book yesterday:
> I opened it, and, where my finger lay
>   'Twixt page and uncut page, these words I read
> —Some six or seven at most—and learned thereby
> That you, FitzGerald, whom by ear and eye
>   She never knew, 'thanked God my wife was dead.'

> Ay, dead! and were yourself alive, good Fitz,
> How to return you thanks would task my wits:
>   Kicking you seems the common lot of curs—
> While more appropriate greeting lends you grace:
> Surely to spit there glorifies your face—
>   Spitting—from lips once sanctified by Hers.[19]

Pen Browning evidently did not exaggerate when, in October 1903, he confessed that his temper had been tried by sections of G. K. Chesterton's *Robert Browning*, recently published in the English Men of Letters series, and added, 'How my father would have lost his!'[20]

What the FitzGerald episode above all confirms is the extent to which Browning's social manner was essentially a protective mask and, as such, entirely consistent with other aspects of the carefully managed mode of life, ostensibly open yet in actuality intensely private and self-defensive, that increasingly characterized his final years. Central to the simplification of his professional affairs was his heavy and ever-increasing dependence upon the experience and judgement of George Smith, of Smith, Elder & Co., who had become his publisher as a consequence of one of those determinative decisions of the 1860s. Where Browning had found his previous publishers, Chapman & Hall, to be both inhospitable and inefficient,[21] Smith, Elder was a firm which prided itself on pursuing the interests and retaining the loyalty of its authors and presented, especially through its association with the *Cornhill Magazine*, an established, solid, and distinctly 'literary' image with which Browning felt very much at ease.

In a passage based directly on George Smith's unpublished memoirs, Leonard Huxley's history of Smith, Elder speaks admiringly of Browning as 'not only a man of letters, but a man of affairs, with the amplest knowledge of men and of business',[22] and since Smith once proposed that Browning should succeed Thackeray as editor of the *Cornhill*,[23] he presumably did think well of his practical abilities. But while Browning certainly kept track of what was going on—setting out with lucid scepticism, for example, his understanding of the prevailing arrangements for American editions of his wife's poems[24]—his contemporary reputation for business acumen seems largely to have derived from the absoluteness of his dependence upon Smith. He appears to have been the most complaisant of authors, sensitive indeed to even the most trivial of printing errors but rarely questioning publishing proposals or wavering in the slightest from the position he had adopted at the very beginning of his connection with Smith: 'I agree with you on every point that you mention,—indeed, I must ask you to be good enough always to take the initiative and suggest what may be for the good of our common adventure,—my proper part will be to write as good poetry as I can, to support what is done already.'[25]

Although Browning's deference to his publisher may seem extreme, it was also shrewd. By his insistent expressions and gestures of dependency and trust he was effectively placing Smith under implicit moral obligation and so exploiting to his own advantage the conventions of 'gentlemanly' publishing. When putting himself into Smith's hands so far as print-run sizes and royalty rates were concerned, he was likely to add (as on 29 April 1887), 'I have always been sure that you would deal far more generously by me than I should ask or hope for by any arrangement of my own', or (as on 4 September 1886), 'As to the terms &c. of course, as you need no reminding, I leave all such matters in your hands—and should be foolish indeed if I did otherwise.'[26] He counted upon Smith to publish anything he produced in the form in which it was originally submitted—the curious arrangement by which Smith agreed not to read any new work 'until it was in *corrected* proofs'[27] apparently being designed to render ineffectual, hence forestall, criticism that would have been peculiarly wounding as coming from, so to speak, his own corner. And in referring to Smith, Elder, as he regularly did, such correspondence as related to reprint and translation rights and other business matters, he not only relieved himself of some of the more tedious day-to-day burdens of authorship but gained yet another defensive screen, a means of avoiding personal confrontations and the unpleasantness to which they were liable to lead. Acknowledging in April 1885 that he was on friendly terms with the author of an enclosed request for permission to publish a birthday book of quotations from Elizabeth Barrett Browning's poems, Browning none the less instructed Smith that he must 'absolutely' use his discretion, 'here as in all other circumstances'.[28]

The note of mild concern that enters into a late letter of Browning's suggests that Smith may occasionally have registered awareness of the uses to which he was being put: 'I hope and believe that you do not mistake what you call my "confidence" in your judgment for anything like indifference or laziness, and a wish to turn over the whole business to you.'[29] In fact, Browning thought of himself as engaged with Smith in a campaign of interest and potential profit to them both. He shared Smith's view that to publish poems cheaply was somehow to cheapen the poems themselves and supported, therefore, his resistance to Frederick J. Furnivall's inherently reasonable if immoderately prosecuted campaign for the production of a selected edition priced at one shilling.[30] When a new collected edition was being contemplated in 1887 Browning's first response was not to plead for a grander format but to make the economical suggestion that they might re-use, only slightly corrected, the existing stereotyped plates of the six-volume *Poetical Works*, which he regarded as 'a very good piece of printing and publishing'.[31]

Even when a much enlarged and entirely reset edition had been decided upon, he gave Smith a free hand in manipulating the sequence of poems in order to keep the size of the volumes uniform ('pray—pray take your own course, in which I have every confidence') and wrote to congratulate the printer's proofreader on the accuracy and intelligence of his corrections and interventions.[32] Although his own textual scrutiny of the resulting sixteen volumes of 1888–9 was as close and meticulous as always,[33] it rarely ventured beyond alterations of punctuation and other points of detail. He did, however, on 'a sudden impulse', embark at proof stage upon a thorough refurbishment of 'that unlucky *Pauline*', apparently believing, like Henry James after him, that he could somehow correct 'the most obvious faults of expression, versification and construction' even while 'letting the *thoughts*—such as they are—remain exactly as at first'.[34] That particular ambition was, of course, illusory—the 1833 and 1888 versions of *Pauline* have generally been regarded as distinct and fundamentally irreconcilable[35]—but the attempted rehabilitation in his middle seventies of what he had learned to think of as a youthful indiscretion was very much in line with his determination to represent himself and his work to posterity in the happiest possible light.

One phenomenon of the 1880s on which Browning and Smith did not quite see eye to eye was the development of the Browning Societies. To Smith as a publisher they were a source of irritation, but to Browning they naturally had a more complex significance, and his now well-established system of social relations allowed him to take their occasional eccentricities and extravagances more or less in his stride. The London Browning Society was formed in 1881 by the inveterately energetic and enthusiastic Furnivall and the altogether less obtrusive Emily Hickey, and its members devoted themselves for the next ten years or so to the reading of papers about philosophical and moral issues in Browning's work, to the private performance of his plays, and to the advocacy of his verse and interests as they saw and understood them.[36] Although the Society was founded with Browning's consent, that consent perhaps could scarcely have been withheld, and he seems in fact to have alternated between annoyance at the occasional tactlessness and intrusiveness of the Society's members (particularly Furnivall) and a pleased but essentially passive acceptance of the increased public attention to himself and his works that it undoubtedly generated.

To outsiders the Society often presented a somewhat ludicrous aspect. Three years after its foundation the *Saturday Review* spoke of it as the creation of 'a number of well-meaning but unnecessarily officious persons' who had 'decided upon taking up and patronizing a poet who must surely feel a sense of grim amusement at such patronage',[37] and in the aftermath of Browning's funeral Henry James could still be easily ironical about the dead poet's 'victimisation by societies organised to talk about him'.[38] What rendered it, and hence Browning himself, particularly open to criticism was not merely the cultish exaltation of a writer within his own lifetime but the degree to which the exaltation was focused upon Browning the contemporary comforter and message-giver. Writing for the *Academy* of 11 January 1890 a review of *Asolando* that was also, and inevitably, a reflection on its author's death, Arthur Symons observed that it was Browning, 'of all the poets of our day, . . . whose influence seems to be most vital at the moment, most pregnant for the future'. And he added: 'For the time, he has also an actual sort of church of his own. The churches pass, with the passing away of the worshippers; but the spirit remains, and must remain if it has once been so vivid to men, if it has once been a refuge, a promise of strength, a gift of consolation.'[39] A more recent critic has even suggested that the Society's seriousness made Browning feel that *Jocoseria*, published in 1883, teetered on the edge of frivolity and that he ought rather to 'provide his adoring audience with the reflections on philosophical and religious questions expected of one acclaimed a sage in his own lifetime'.[40]

Browning certainly showed no disposition to ignore or offend the Society. By the summer of 1882 he was already thanking Furnivall for helping to push his poems 'faster than, of their own force, they would have got forward',[41] and gently chiding one of his regular correspondents for assuming that he would naturally disapprove of the Society's activities: 'I feel grateful for it all, for my part—and none the less for a little amusement at the wonder of some of my friends that I do not jump up and denounce the practices which must annoy me so much.'[42] Seven years later his views remained unchanged: 'When all is done—I cannot but be very grateful for the institution of the Society; for to what else but the eight years' persistent calling attention to my works can one attribute the present demand for them?'[43] The Society was thus valued as both an index and a generator of a late-found fame that was plainly of profound importance to him, as if feeding some old and unappeasable hunger, and much of the real importance of the London Browning Society and its counterparts in towns and cities on both sides of the Atlantic[44] consisted in their simultaneously reflecting the high contemporary valuation of the poet as teacher and prophet and confirming, for Browning personally, his public, if belated, elevation to such a role. Asked during a triumphal visit to Edinburgh in April 1884 whether he at all objected to the adulation he was receiving, he is said to have replied, 'Object to it! No; I have waited forty years for it, and now—I like it!'[45]

Despite his adoption of a masking and distancing public persona, Browning increasingly sought in these later years for means of giving discreet circulation to his own matured views of persons, ideas, and events, and especially of his own past work, and in this respect the London Browning Society again proved particularly serviceable. He did not join the Society or attend its meetings, but he corresponded with Furnivall on many questions, returned prompt and courteous responses to enquiries about particular poems and passages, and read—and occasionally corrected—the papers written and delivered by its members.[46] Several of the Society's early publications were known to have been written or compiled with the co-operation of Browning himself, and by actively collaborating with Alexandra Sutherland Orr in the preparation of her immensely influential *Handbook to the Works of Robert Browning*—undertaken (as she explained in the preface to the first edition of 1885) 'at the request of some of the members of the Browning Society'[47]—he achieved a form of public expression at once indirect and authoritative, in that their friendship was well known. In the preface to the second edition of 1886, indeed, his participation was freely and fully acknowledged. This is not to say that Orr was merely Browning's mouthpiece—her later biography of him proved to be a remarkably independent document that caused Browning's sister and son considerable distress. Nor is it possible, given the frequency of their meetings and the apparent non-survival of their correspondence, to say precisely what came from Browning and what did not. But the *Handbook* speaks everywhere with an intimacy and confidence that makes Browning's involvement fully apparent, and there still survive the notes on *Ferishtah's Fancies* which Browning added to Alexandra Orr's set of the revised proofs and which she then drew upon in preparing the *Handbook*'s expanded second edition.[48]

Browning in his later years also spoke with varying degrees of frankness to a number of other contemporary critics—among them Furnivall, Gosse, and William Sharp—and his remarks were reported after his death with varying and now unmeasurable degrees of fidelity. He seems, on at least some of these occasions, to have valued the opportunity to correct existing rumours, misreadings, and biographical misstatements—so Gosse, for one, made a point of claiming[49]—and as he grew older and felt more securely famous he ventured from time to time to make such corrections in direct and public ways.[50] As in the FitzGerald episode, however, such gestures were for the most part chivalric defences of his dead wife. He appeared as a defence witness in Richard Herne Shepherd's 1879 libel action against the *Athenaeum* for the language in which it had condemned Shepherd's unauthorized reprinting of Elizabeth Barrett Browning's early poems, but he found himself embarrassed by the questions raised in court (hence in newspaper reports) about his own role, many years previously, in a similarly unauthorized edition of Shelley letters that had promptly been identified as forgeries.[51] On at least one occasion—the December 1887 composition of a 'Prefatory Note' to his wife's *Poetical Works* that was designed to counter factual errors in John H. Ingram's otherwise inoffensive biographical writings[52]—

he seems to have been stirred to action by a letter from his brother-in-law, George Moulton-Barrett.[53]

For the defence of his own work and reputation Browning continued to prefer the dignity of indirection, relying heavily upon the varied goods offices of George Smith, Alexandra Orr, Furnivall, and friendly—or, at any rate, befriending—critics, and turning the sometimes aggressively pursued self-interest of the latter to his own subtler ends.[54] He also depended, more complexly, upon his own resources as a poet. His verse had always served in some degree as an occasion and opportunity for personal expression and release— in *Of Pacchiarotto, and How He Worked in Distemper* (1876) he had turned upon his critics with scarcely coherent bitterness—and the final volumes added retrospection to these other functions. The Orr *Handbook* says quite straightforwardly of *Ferishtah's Fancies* that 'Ferishtah's opinions are in the main Mr. Browning's own',[55] and its comments on *Parleyings with Certain People of Importance in Their Day,* evidently derived from Browning himself, are similarly specific in their emphasis on the volume's autobiographical character: 'Mr. Browning has summoned his group of men not for the sake of drawing their portraits, but that they might help him to draw his own. . . . And the portrait is in some degree a biography; it is full of reminiscences.'[56]

But this was still the same Browning who steadfastly maintained an intimacy-repelling mask and hated biographical intrusions of every sort,[57] and while *Parleyings* has indeed been drawn upon by subsequent biographers and critics[58] its revelations, such as they are, relate to intellectual debts rather than to personal episodes. It is one thing to see Browning as interested in providing posterity with a fuller and by no means unflattering account of the development of his mind, or in touching up the already established images of his own life and of Elizabeth's that would be projected forward beyond his eventual death. It becomes altogether more difficult to imagine him as embarking upon a formal autobiography—the sheer busyness of his life perhaps having served in part as a technique for keeping introspection at bay—or as wishing through his verse or any other medium to permit, let alone encourage, the promulgation of personal details of any kind, least of all those relating to his marriage.

Browning's deep abhorrence of posthumous intrusions similarly militated against the preservation of papers not absolutely precious, and he seems—especially when moving house in 1887[59]—to have destroyed enormous quantities of letters and other documents, including his unpublished early verse and his working manuscripts from all periods.[60] He made a particular point of reclaiming (or of seeking to reclaim) both his own and his wife's letters from some of their original recipients, and he wrote to George Moulton-Barrett in January 1889 of having, two years previously, 'spent more than a week in destroying my own letters to my family'.[61] On 5 November 1887, sympathizing with Barrett's irritation at Ingram's writings, he declared:

I trust you will never believe for a moment that any species of 'biographical memoir' of our beloved Ba, long or short, important or trifling, can appear 'with my knowledge and sanction'—or rather, 'with my sanction,' for unfortunately I have a quarter of a century's experience of the indelicacy with which the writers, male and female, of such things will in all cases try hard to get information, and, failing that, tell you with the utmost impudence, that, 'after all, such a life is public property and must be given to the public somehow—' this last intimation being in the nature of a threat. I have but one answer to make on these occasions—that my consent is impossible. How otherwise, when I am intimately in possession of my wife's feelings on the subject?[62]

His wife's recorded feelings on the question of privacy were in fact less restrictive than here represented. In 1846 she had been ready to declare that letters were 'the most vital part of biography',[63] and in 1852, following the painful public exposure of some of her own most intimate feelings in Mary Russell Mitford's *Recollections of a Literary Life*, she had protested only that 'one *ought* to be let alone while one's alive—The vultures SHOULD wait a little till the carrion is ready, & not pluck out the living eyes.'[64] Browning's own position, though clear in principle, was less straightforward in practice. He had given permission for the publication, in 1877, of his wife's letters to Richard Hengist Horne;[65] an early statement of his as to the value and importance of biography was aptly cited by Ingram;[66] and in that same 5 November 1887 letter to George Moulton-Barrett he wrote:

While on the subject, let me repeat—for probably the last time—how much it is on my mind that, when I am no longer here to prevent it, some use will be made of the correspondence not in my power: *all in my power* is safe, and will ever remain so: and I shall enjoin on Pen, with whom will remain the property allowed by law in the manuscript letters—*not in the* writings themselves, but in the publication of them,—to hinder this by every possible means.[67]

The correspondence in Browning's power (i.e. his actual possession) at this date of course included all of the courtship letters, and by declaring them to be for ever 'safe' he seems clearly to imply their destruction—even that they had been destroyed already. On 21 January 1889, however, after reacting negatively to a suggestion of George Moulton-Barrett's that the time might be ripe for an edition of Elizabeth's letters, Browning acknowledged that he had not been able to 'bring myself to do away with' the hundreds of her letters to friends that he possessed, let alone those—'so immeasurably superior to any compositions of the kind I have any experience of'—which he had himself received during the months preceding their marriage.[68] Nor in fact did Browning ever resolve the opposition between his passionate desire for privacy and his profound reluctance to destroy documents deemed precious on literary as well as on purely personal grounds. At his death the problem was one of several left for Pen to deal with as best he might.

In the autumn of 1889—famous now in his own right after long years of perceived and to some extent actual neglect, and with his worrisome son Pen apparently settled at last into a satisfactory marriage with Fannie Coddington, a wealthy American devotee of the Browning–Barrett legend—Browning returned once more to Italy, where he had lived throughout his marriage to Elizabeth Barrett but which he had begun to revisit only in 1878, seventeen years after her death. Accompanied, as always in these latter years, by his sister Sarianna, he made his way to Asolo in the hills north-west of Venice. Romantically remembered from earlier years both for its own sake and as the setting for *Pippa Passes*, Asolo was now, by no means unromantically, the summer home of Katharine Bronson, who at other seasons presided so hospitably over Casa (or Ca') Alvisi near the entrance to the Grand Canal—'holding out her hand', as Henry James later put it, 'with endless good-nature, patience, charity, to all decently accredited petitioners, the incessant troop of those either bewilderedly making or fondly renewing acquaintance with the dazzling city'.[69] Thomas Hardy had briefly become one such petitioner two years earlier, little though his hostess appears to have admired his work,[70] but Browning stood with her on an altogether more intimate footing and seems, in his sufficiently hale and certainly hearty middle seventies, to have come very close to making her an open declaration of love.

When Browning went on to Venice that November, however, it was to stay not at Ca' Alvisi but at the vast Palazzo Rezzonico, also on the Grand Canal, which Pen had recently purchased with his wife's money and was now in the process of restoring to something like its original splendour. All seemed well both with the marriage and with the work of renovation; Fannie was admiring and attentive; friends came to call and stay; and Browning took pleasure in reading aloud from the proofs of *Asolando*, his new volume of mostly recent poems, and in renewing his old delight in Venice itself. But early in December he developed one of the heavy colds that had of recent years increasingly impaired his customary vigour;[71] bronchitis soon set in, and during the evening of 12 December he died—in the midst of the Rezzonico's richly restored yet distinctly domesticated magnificence,[72] with his devoted sister, loyal son, and adoring daughter-in-law at his bedside, and after having received the telegraphed news of that very day's critically and financially successful publication of *Asolando*. His last intelligible words, Pen wrote immediately to Katharine Bronson, were in response to George Smith's telegram: 'How gratifying.'[73] A somewhat more elaborate version is given in the diary of a family friend who was also at the Palazzo Rezzonico that day: 'More than satisfied. I am dying. My dear boy. My dear boy.'[74] It appears from the same source that Alexandra Orr arrived in Venice on 13 December, the morning after Browning's death, and that there was much indecision at the Rezzonico as to the place of his burial—Sarianna Browning arguing strongly in favour of Florence—until matters were effectively resolved, late on the 14th, by the arrival of another telegram in which Smith announced that the Dean of Westminster (George Granville Bradley) had agreed to offer interment in the Abbey.[75] There seems to have been little public objection to the Dean's decision—apart from a published letter in which a former sanitary engineer warned against indoor burial as 'a practice dangerous to the health of the living'[76]—but that Bradley himself felt it to be potentially controversial is suggested by his giving publicity to a supportive 'memorial' bearing the signatures of Tennyson, Swinburne, the Archbishop of Canterbury, and twenty-four other leading figures.[77]

Although it has been pointed out[78] that Browning's famously fortunate death was almost certainly more painful, more prolonged, and more predictable than was generally acknowledged by contemporary report or early biographers, he does seem, even so, to have died quietly, fairly quickly, without great suffering—and with an impeccable sense of timing. Not only had the principal threads of his emotional life been drawn together in Venice—Italy was supremely associated with his wife, and their son was restoring the chapel in the Palazzo Rezzonico as a memorial to her—but he was finally famous, commanding the affection and admiration of a world-wide readership and ranking alongside Tennyson as a presiding genius of the age, and had already achieved a fitting conclusion to his life's work in and through the 1888–9 collected edition and his essentially retrospective and summative final volumes, *Parleyings*, *Ferishtah's Fancies*, and *Asolando* itself.

A certain incongruity may have marked the progress of his body from the Rezzonico to the island of San Michele on a highly decorated municipal funeral barge guarded 'by four "Uscieri" in gala dress, two sergeants of the Municipal Guard, and two firemen bearing torches',[79] but the burial service in Westminster Abbey on the last day of 1889 was a well-managed success on a national scale, marred only by a fog so thick that it was difficult inside the Abbey 'to distinguish the features of even the most eminent men, save when accident brought one into close contact with them'.[80] A proposal to bring back Elizabeth Barrett Browning's remains from Florence for re-interment in the Abbey alongside her husband's had finally been abandoned,[81] but the Browning–Barrett romance was none the less invoked in terms of the singing of her poem, 'What would we give to our beloved?', to a setting by the Abbey organist, Frederick Bridge.[82] The pall-bearers—including Jowett, Leighton, George Smith, Sir James Fitzjames Stephen, Sir George Grove, and Hallam Tennyson (standing in for his father)—not only represented, as *The Times* duly noted, 'Art, music, law, literature, philosophy, and the two Universities',[83] but were also numbered among Browning's friends, as indeed were many more of those present on an occasion that Edmund Gosse summed up as 'impressive and without vulgarity. It was the last and by far the finest of all the Private Views which R. B. has graced with his presence.'[84]

Browning's will, witnessed by Alfred Tennyson and Francis Palgrave on 12 February 1864, was complex in its wording but essentially simple in its intentions. Provision was made for the financial security of Browning's sister Sarianna and his son Pen, should the latter not have attained the age of twenty-one at the time of his father's death, and for the possibility that Pen might himself die before his twenty-first birthday, either with or without 'lawful issue'—a point unfortunately obscured in the incomplete text inserted by Furnivall into the *Browning Society's Papers* for 1889–90.[85] Since Browning did not die until more than a quarter of a century later, the operative section of the (entirely unaltered) will became that which effectively left everything to Pen, subject only to the payment of a modest annual allowance to Sarianna during her lifetime. No reference was made anywhere in the will to the retention, disposition, or destruction of either Browning's or Elizabeth Barrett Browning's papers and literary remains, nor to any exercise of the duties and responsibilities of a literary executor in respect of those properties: Browning simply bequeathed to Pen 'all my copyrights' along with everything else.[86]

What seems surprising is not so much that Browning should have made such a will in 1864 as that he should have let it stand without addition or revision throughout the succeeding years, so striking is the contrast between the self-consciously managed character of his later life and the prospective posthumous dependence upon the loyalty and good sense of the often wayward and unsatisfactory Pen. Browning had, after all, been intimately involved in the settlement of William Savage Landor's affairs as well as of his own father's; he had accepted responsibility for the rescued manuscripts of Thomas Lovell Beddoes; he had embraced the role of protector of his own wife's works, papers, and reputation—indeed, of the entire Browning–Barrett legend; and he had found the conduct of his personal career ever more complex and demanding as his reputation grew. He could have had no doubt, therefore, as to the nature and extent of the responsibilities Pen would have to bear, but he seems—whether optimistically or fatalistically—to have given little if any consideration to the possible long-term consequences of imposing such a burden on shoulders not previously noted for their breadth or reliability.

It is of course possible that Browning may simply have postponed too long any formal confrontation with the earthly consequences of his death. Such an avoidance, such an illusion of dateless suspension, would have been consistent with his always sanguine view of his personal health—even after the onset of his fatal illness he was still insisting to Pen, 'My dear boy, I never catch cold'[87]— with the pervasively optimistic tenor of his verse, and with those highly regulated habits of life and thought he had so consistently maintained over the years since Elizabeth's death. During his last days in the Palazzo Rezzonico he made a point of identifying himself with the speaker of the 'Epilogue' to *Asolando*—'One who never turned his back but marched breast forward, | Never doubted clouds would break'[88]—and his faith in Fannie's dispersal of the particular clouds that had hung so long over the head of his beloved son doubtless allowed him to believe that he had indeed done well in leaving so many matters to Pen's discretion in his impending role as guardian of the Browning–Barrett legend, the Browning– Barrett papers, and the Browning–Barrett literary estate.

It is at the moment of Browning's death on 12 December 1889, therefore, that Robert Weidemann Barrett Browning—'Pen' as a consequence of early mispronunciations, doubtless reinforced by a touch of fond but unfortunate parental humour—re-emerges as a central character in the Browning–Barrett story. Remarkable chiefly for having been born at all, associated always with the written and photographic records of his cossetted childhood, his very nickname inviting risibility, Pen has cut an unimpressive figure in literary history—a far lesser one, indeed, than even his mother's dog Flush. It was Henry James who declared that Pen, as 'a poet's double child (or a double poets')', was 'singularly prosy',[89] and the familiar, deprecating 'poor Pen' of Browning's own letters seems at once descriptive, predictive, and complexly exculpatory.

Pen was short—when he 'rowed' at Oxford it was not as an oarsman but as a cox[90]—and became decidedly stocky, capable of being described at the age of thirty-one as 'quite a droll little figure in knickerbockers, with short, fat legs, and a ruddy countenance', almost unimaginable as the son of Elizabeth Barrett Browning.[91] As the years passed his physical appearance became less and less prepossessing—William Lyon Phelps in 1904 encountered 'a short man, like his father, rotund and red-faced', whose 'red veins traced patterns on his cheeks and brow'[92]—and while his own infidelities, real or imagined, may have been a major source of the difficulties in his marriage,[93] there are indications enough that Fannie Coddington was from the first less infatuated with her husband than with the romance of his parentage. Little is in fact known about the course of Pen's marriage, however, most of the available references to it seeming too contradictory and gossip-laden to command much credence, and the same obscurity extends to many other aspects of his life, even though his death in July 1912, at the age of sixty-three, fell well within the lifetime of people now living.[94] He is of course frequently mentioned in letters written by his parents, but his mother died when he was twelve and his father's references to him in later years give little sense of what Pen can have been actually thinking, feeling, or even doing as a boy, youth, and young man. His own letters to his father appear to have been included in the latter's destruction of family correspondence not long before his death.[95]

Genuinely as Browning seems to have embraced the proposition that Pen was Elizabeth's principal legacy to himself, his education and the fostering of his prospective genius nothing less than a sacred trust, he seems to have determined almost immediately after her death—at that time when he was deciding upon so many other aspects of his life—that it was his duty to transform the boy from an indulged, slightly feminized, but entirely happy young Italian into a budding English gentleman of standard tastes and ambitions, capable in due course of going to Balliol and pursuing a diplomatic career. The problems created for Pen by these violent revolutions in his life, by awareness of his parents' extravagant expectations, and by the pressure in particular of his father's relentless devotion—described by George Smith as 'almost painful in its intensity and absorption'[96]—can readily be imagined. Even at the last, when Pen, married and already in his fortieth year, announced his purchase of the Rezzonico, Browning was still capable of combining indulgence with exhortation, and both with a touch of emotional blackmail. Only by hard work, he warned, could Pen disprove

the ordinary notion, too often shown correct by one's everyday experience, that too much prosperity is a hindrance to an artist's career: don't be the little man in the big house. I know very well you want to excel quite as much as I want it—but time flies, and youth with it: so, make me happy before I die by proving yourself the son of your wonderful mother,—and you, dearest Fannie, make him show himself worthy of *you!*[97]

Pen's marriage to Fannie Coddington and purchase of the Rezzonico seem both to have taken Browning somewhat by surprise—even in the face of such open declarations of independence and self-exile he still persuaded himself that Pen would settle down again in London—and he was somewhat grudging ('I never thought it was in him')[98] in his praise of Pen's restoration of the palace, probably the most remarkable single achievement of his life. Pen's work on the Rezzonico, exclaimed Henry James in 1890, 'transcends description for the beauty, and, as Ruskin would say, "wisdom and rightness" of it'[99]—a judgement not altogether cancelled out by a later reference, coloured by disapproval of Pen's apparent desertion of his wife, to the 'bloated Rezzonico' and 'all Pen Browning's hideous luxuries'.[100]

Despite all the problems and pressures attributable to his parentage and upbringing,[101] Pen appears to have subscribed wholeheartedly to the Browning–Barrett legend, to have been devoted to his mother's memory, and to have accommodated himself as best he could to the overwhelming fact of a famous, indulgent, yet essentially uncomprehending father whose expectations he knew himself to be doomed always to disappoint. He resorted early to passivity and inaction, defeating by simple failure his father's many and mostly inappropriate plans on his behalf, and eventually slipped away to the Continent and a more congenially bohemian career as a painter and sculptor—with few illusions, probably, as to his own abilities but not unwilling that his strenuously promotional father should bully the London art world into treating him as a modest success. Pen, though trained in styles and techniques soon to be outmoded, did show a considerable talent in both painting and sculpture, and although almost all of his work has unfortunately vanished from public view, a few pieces can still be located, notably the portrait of his father that hangs in the library of Balliol College.[102] But the eye trouble which finally resulted in near blindness was already painfully present by 1890[103] and he was always liable to failures of application of the kind nicely suggested by the rapid petering out of a notebook in which he had begun to record the titles, newspaper reviews, and occasional sales of his finished pieces—and especially by the designation of the other end of the same notebook as a repository of 'Shooting information'.[104]

But Pen, unprepared and ill-equipped though he may have been (Mabel Dodge Luhan remembered him as 'absolutely inarticulate', with 'no articulation of any kind, not even in his joints'),[105] was by no means a failure in his role as Browning's literary executor and as the guardian during his lifetime of his parents' reputations and discernible intentions. It may have been Fannie Browning who took the initiative in filling one floor of the Rezzonico with those displays of books, manuscripts, pictures, and other memorabilia that made it, in Lilian Whiting's characteristically extravagant phrase, 'a very Valhalla of the wedded poets'.[106] But it was Pen who carried through his father's project of building a house ('Pippa's Tower') in Asolo, who sought to revive there the silk mill memorialized in *Pippa Passes* and, failing, founded a lace factory in its stead, who cared for his father's sister, Sarianna, and for his mother's servant, Wilson, until the ends of their days,[107] and who purchased, in Florence, his own birthplace, the first-floor apartment within the Palazzo Guidi to which his parents had given the since famous name of Casa Guidi.[108] Above all, it was Pen who had to take the responsibility of presiding over his parents' literary remains and of dealing with the enquiries and requests of publishers, journalists, and academics, of gossiping friends, potential biographers, and would-be editors—all without benefit of testamentary directions beyond whatever words his father had been able to speak to him after realizing that he was actually dying.

Pen's inherited role as defender of his parents' interests and privacies was undoubtedly simplified by his dislike of English society and London winters, reinforced as it was by his devotion to the manners and climate of his native Italy. He was not precisely inaccessible in Italy—he was even hospitable to his father's friends and to those who displayed a serious interest in his parents and their work—but he was sufficiently remote from London (if not from Venetian) gossip and from the book-making of littérateurs to remain relatively untouched by the kinds of pressures to which his father had increasingly felt impelled to respond. That Pen had sometimes been made uncomfortable by such responses and wished that his father had remained silent is abundantly clear from both the tone and the content of Browning's self-justifying letters to him about the FitzGerald episode: writing on 13 July 1889 about his reply to 'FitzGerald's brutality', Browning sustained the contemptuous language of the poem with a reference to FitzGerald as Tennyson's 'adulatory lick-spittle';[109] four days later, in response to Pen's deprecating suggestion that expressions such as FitzGerald's 'recoil sufficiently on those who use them', he continued to insist that not to have protested would have been to display indifference.[110]

Where Pen did wholeheartedly follow his father's example was in developing an almost unquestioning dependence on the experience and judgement of George Smith, of Smith, Elder. Pen had no difficulty in recognizing the advantages of maintaining the existing arrangements, especially in light of his intention to continue living in Italy, and when he came to England for his father's funeral (which Smith had organized) he made it clear that he wished to work with Smith, Elder no less closely than his father had done: 'I was deeply touched', wrote Smith in his memoirs, 'when [Pen] related that, on his death-bed, his father told him that if he was ever in any difficulty he was to go to me and act exactly on my advice; and that all matters of business in regard to his works were to be left absolutely in my hands.'[111] The relationship, as amicable as it was mutually convenient, prospered over the succeeding years: Smith, Elder kept close watch over a valuable publishing property and Pen was able to refer to them all requests for permissions and other enquiries of a business nature. 'In doing so', he told Hall Griffin, 'I have simply acted as my father did',[112] and by early 1896—writing as usual on slate-grey stationery strikingly similar to that used by Browning himself—he could echo his father's words when assuring Smith that 'I am, indeed, more than content to leave my interests entirely to you, as always:—full knowing that they are safest in your hands!'[113] George Smith went into semi-retirement in the early 1890s and died in 1901, but by that time Pen had established an equally congenial relationship with the then head of the firm, Smith's son-in-law, Reginald John Smith, who seems to have visited him in Italy on several occasions.[114] It was, however, at George Smith's instigation[115] that Pen gave permission for Smith, Elder's publication of Frederic G. Kenyon's two-volume edition of Elizabeth Barrett Browning's letters (excluding those to Browning himself) and then made the courageous decision to publish, two years later, that extraordinary courtship correspondence which his father had dreaded to reveal yet could never quite bring himself to destroy.

Kenyon's 1897 preface to the Barrett–Browning letters had argued the case for their publication on the grounds—adopted, with varying degrees of justification, by so many other executors, editors, biographers, and publishers—that the Brownings' well-known objections to invasions of their privacy had not extended to posthumous publication: 'there is evidence that they recognised that the public has some claims with regard to writers who have appealed to, and partly lived by, its favour. They only claimed that during their own lifetime their feelings should be consulted first; when they should have passed away, the rights of the public would begin.'[116] Pen must directly or indirectly have given his approval to these arguments—his consent to publication of the letters is acknowledged in the same preface—but he did not repeat them, perhaps feeling that they had already made their due impact, in the 'Note' prefaced to *The Letters of Robert Browning and Elizabeth Barrett Barrett 1845–1846*, published in two volumes by Smith, Elder in 1899. He confined himself instead to a clear and dignified statement of the situation in which he had found himself:

In considering the question of publishing these letters, which are all that ever passed between my father and mother, for after their marriage they were never separated, it seemed to me that my only alternatives were to allow them to be published or to destroy them. I might, indeed, have left the matter to the decision of others after my death, but that would be evading a responsibility which I felt that I ought to accept.

Ever since my mother's death these letters were kept by my father in a certain inlaid box, into which they exactly fitted, and where they have always rested, letter beside letter, each in its consecutive order and numbered on the envelope by his own hand.

My father destroyed all the rest of his correspondence, and not long before his death he said, referring to these letters: 'There they are, do with them as you please when I am dead and gone!'[117]

Pen, as might and indeed must have been expected, was strongly and publicly criticized—and not only by members of his mother's family—for what was widely perceived as an act of filial betrayal.[118] But if he had received no parental authorization to publish the letters, neither had be been instructed to take what he rightly claimed to be the logically alternative step of destroying them, and Thomas Hardy for one seems to have assured him that in such circumstances he should feel free to deal with them as he thought best.[119] That Browning had indeed decided to trust to Pen's judgement in all such matters appears to be confirmed by his 5 November 1887 letter to George Moulton-Barrett and by a remark of Furnivall's that may well have derived from conversation with the poet himself: 'What is or is not to be said of his wife,

Browning left to his son's discretion.'[120] And even had Browning
not spoken the words quoted by Pen, his meticulous (not to say
religious) preservation of the letters while destroying so many other
personal documents would have carried its own sufficient message.

The choice facing Pen was fundamentally the same as the one his
father had been unable to resolve—their situations differing chiefly
in Pen's lack of an obvious heir through whom the responsibility
might have been passed on to yet another generation—and it seems
difficult in retrospect to find serious fault with Pen's action,
especially since the actual editing of the letters was performed with
considerable care and respect. Although Elvan Kintner's introduction
to his own 1969 edition of the same correspondence speaks of the
'serious inadequacies' of its predecessor as a consequence of there
having been 'no editor in 1899 and apparently only the most casual
supervision', the letters were in fact published in their entirety and
with errors, as Kintner allows, 'rather more notable for their
naïveté than their numbers'.[121] The work of initial transcription
may indeed have been delegated to cheaply paid clerical assistants,
but it is clear from the Smith, Elder records that Frederic Kenyon
and Roger Ingpen (both mentioned in the 'Advertisement' to the
1899 edition) received substantial sums for their work on the
proofs and, in Ingpen's case, the index.[122]

Pen did of course profit considerably from such publishing
ventures. By the end of 1899 the courtship letters had already gone
into three editions, and his resulting royalties (totalling £725)[123]
added significantly to those still arising, however modestly, from
the 1897 edition of his mother's letters, from the various editions of
the works of both his parents, from the Orr *Life and Letters*, and
from minor items of Browningiana published on both sides of the
Atlantic. Since he earned little or nothing as an artist now—though
a local photographic business seems to have been run out of the
Asolo house in the mid-1890s[124]—and had sunk so much of his
own and his wife's money into his various Italian properties, such
supplementation of his income was undoubtedly welcome. But
nothing in his correspondence with the Smiths suggests that he ever
attempted to hurry projects forward, urge larger print-runs, or
demand higher fees or royalties. 'With regard to my mother's
letters', he told George Smith early in 1896, 'pray take your leisure
over them. I feel myself how delicate the ground is!'[125] And when
W. Hall Griffin's biography of Browning had been completed after

his death by H. Cotton Minchin, Pen recommended that no fees be charged for its use of either published or unpublished materials, Griffin—'a bold man, not afraid even of Furnivall'—having shown himself to be 'really anxious to correct some of the errors which have been published'.[126] He gave his blessing to the suggestion, originating with Reginald Smith, that the centenary of his mother's birth in 1906 should be marked by the publication of Percy Lubbock's compilation, *Elizabeth Barrett Browning in Her Letters*, in which the love-letters were selectively absorbed into an overall biographical sequence, and to the appearance in 1912, the one hundredth anniversary of his father's birth, of the handsome (if textually unimportant) ten-volume Centenary Edition of his works.[127]

The actual date of the centenary, 7 May 1912, was multiply observed in England, most notably by the meeting of the Royal Society of Literature addressed by Sir Arthur Pinero and Henry James, and by a Westminster Abbey service and subsequent programme of papers organized by Professor William Knight and 'a committee of sympathisers'—including Emily Hickey, one of the founders of the London Browning Society, who herself spoke on the phrase 'We fall to rise' from the 'Epilogue' to *Asolando*.[128] In Italy that same day Pen, though seriously ill, lent himself loyally to the celebrations in Asolo at least to the extent of being driven through the streets in a carriage.[129] He died just two months later, on 8 July 1912, at the age of sixty-three.

Pen seems also to have conducted himself with moderation and good sense in most of his dealings with potential biographers, although he was least at ease in dealing with his father's friend Alexandra Orr, who had long figured imposingly in his own life and imagination and whose collaboration with Browning in the writing of the widely respected *Handbook* had given her an irresistible claim to undertake for Smith, Elder a similarly authorized *Life and Letters*. Pen and Sarianna assented to the project—'in self-defence', as Sarianna told 'Michael Field', 'so many inaccurate statements being afloat'[130]—letters and other family documents were made available, and Orr herself later claimed that the proofs of the book had been 'minutely gone through' by both Pen and his aunt prior to its first publication in 1891.[131] But a surviving letter from Pen to Alexandra Orr, undated but written soon after Browning's death, indicates that there were already profound differences between them ('I despair of our arriving at a clear understanding of each other's views by correspondence'),[132] and in 1904 Pen told William Lyon Phelps that the *Life and Letters* was 'a very bad book', that neither he nor Sarianna had seen it until it was already in proof, and that its author had then refused to make the changes necessary to accommodate the corrections they believed to be essential.[133]

Pen's distress seems to have been chiefly provoked by the frankness and austerity of some of Alexandra Orr's judgements and by her references to Browning's having suffered minor illnesses and occasional failures of memory in his last years—to the detriment, Pen may have thought, of the standard image (and self-image) of his father as a supreme embodiment of physical, mental, and spiritual health.[134] If so, it seems very much to Pen's credit that Kenyon's revised edition of the *Life and Letters*, published by Smith, Elder in 1908 (five years after Orr's death), should have incorporated much fresh material and yet stopped short of altering Orr's statements on such matters as Browning's health and religious views, Kenyon in his preface simply observing that Orr had a right to the expression of her own opinions in what remained essentially her book, but that those opinions 'did not commend themselves to others who were in a good position to judge'.[135] One feature of the revised edition was the replacement of the original account of Browning's death by one written by Pen himself—on the grounds, as Kenyon explained, that he had been present throughout and could therefore 'correct with authority the various inexactnesses which have appeared in previous narratives'. Curiously, however, Pen's eagerness to assert his father's vigour almost to the very moment of his death led him to conduct a kind of running argument with that earlier account which was now no longer present: 'He was not carried up. . . . It is not the case that he suffered from attacks of faintness. . . . There was no pain.'[136]

Later biographers who acknowledged Pen's assistance tended to be less controversial than Alexandra Orr and more uniformly positive in tone. William Sharp, indeed, sidestepped Pen's sensitivity on such matters as his father's health by dealing almost exclusively with the period preceding Elizabeth Barrett Browning's death, although this manoeuvre did not prevent Pen from writing in December 1905: 'I see that W. Sharp is dead. Alas: his blunders survive.'[137] Lilian Whiting, for her part, did not shrink from direct flattery of Pen himself, dedicating her book to him in fulsome terms and praising him within the text itself as a comprehensively gifted connoisseur of literature, painting, and sculpture, 'a true child of the gods'.[138] But Pen also helped Edmund Gosse with his article on Browning for the *Dictionary of National Biography*[139] and actively co-operated with the substantial and independent biographical work of W. Hall Griffin, entertaining him at La Torre all'Antella, the estate he had purchased outside Florence, writing full and carefully considered letters about specific points Griffin had raised, encouraging him to point out in print the errors in Chesterton's English Men of Letters volume, and even trying to assist him in evading restrictions placed by Reginald Smith on the use of certain Browning letters.[140] The published biography did not fail to stress the excellence of Browning's health in old age, quoting Pen himself to the effect that his father was 'the healthiest man I ever knew',[141] but it provides no basis for concluding that Pen made serious attempts to control or influence what was eventually written by those who called to ask him questions, see his treasures, or simply to gaze upon the unlikely product and sole surviving representative of the Casa Guidi romance.

After his wife's final departure, indeed, Pen seems largely to have abandoned Venice (he finally sold the Rezzonico in 1906) in favour of a bucolic, quasi-squirearchal, occasionally embattled,[142] and somewhat isolated life on his estates in Asolo and Florence, and he was doubtless glad to welcome visitors of almost any sort. When Henry James was staying with Katharine Bronson in Asolo in May 1899 he was taken to see all Pen's 'wondrous property including the boa-constrictor, the new mountain (he *has* literally bought one,) & the husband of Ginevra',[143] and Freya Stark, another source for tales of Pen's fondness for snakes, happily includes in *Traveller's Prelude* a photograph of him standing, natty in boater, waistcoat, and watch-chain, in front of the thoroughly agricultural background provided by a pair of tethered cattle.[144]

The complexity, irregularity, and occasional imprudence of Pen's style of living could scarcely have been more distinct from the style his father had so deliberately adopted in his later years, and it was to doom him to an indifferent performance in the role of long-term guardian and eventual transmitter of the Browning relics, the actual documents and physical objects passed down from his parents and his aunt Sarianna. It is not clear, however, that a great deal was actually lost, destroyed, or misdirected during the period of his stewardship.[145] Nor can he be fairly accused of having ignored a wish of his father's that the printer's copy manuscript of *Asolando* should join the corresponding manuscripts of earlier volumes at Balliol, of which Browning's friend Benjamin Jowett had been master and Browning himself an honorary fellow—but against which Pen, once denied admission there, could conceivably have borne a lasting grudge. The manuscripts prior to *Asolando* were all faithfully delivered to Balliol shortly after Browning's death,[146] and in a letter to Kenyon of 31 October 1907 Pen explained that although his father had apparently thought of Balliol as the eventual repository of his manuscripts, he had never given any specific instructions to that effect, either orally or in writing. Believing, therefore, that 'my father had not intended to deprive me of every line of his writing', and knowing that *Asolando* had in any case been written 'long after I had heard him speak about his intentions to others in my presence, and quite casually', Pen had felt entitled to retain the *Asolando* manuscript during his own lifetime, 'after which Balliol would have it along with "Aurora Leigh", which was undoubtedly mine'.[147]

After Pen Browning's death in July 1912 Reginald Smith tried but failed to have *Asolando* assigned to Balliol,[148] and the manuscript, together with that of *Aurora Leigh*, formed instead part of the great mass of Browning and Barrett Browning material, formerly in Pen's possession, that was catalogued by the London auctioneers Sotheby, Wilkinson & Hodge and then dispersed in the famous six-day sale of 1–8 May 1913. Whether or not this essentially bathetic conclusion—so deeply regretted by succeeding generations of Browning scholars—was in fact the result of Pen's indecision and procrastination will probably never be known. As Philip Kelley and Betty A. Coley make clear,[149] he was ill, confused, and almost blind for some time before his death, and his affairs were left in a wholly unsatisfactory state. Two wills were found— the first, of 1889, in favour of his widow, the second, of 1900, in favour of his aunt Sarianna, who had herself died in 1903—as well as what appeared to be a detached codicil, dated in early 1912, directing that a sum of money be paid to a young field-woman living near Asolo (as his *Athenaeum* obituary put it, Pen was always 'on the friendliest of terms' with 'the Italian peasantry').[150] Kelley and Coley, unravelling the resulting complexities, point to the indications (including the codicil itself) of Pen's having made a third will of much more recent date than the first two and to the possibility of its having been found and destroyed by Pen's servants, by his widow (who now reappeared and strongly reasserted herself), or even by his life-long friend the Marchesa Peruzzi (born Edith Story, daughter of the American sculptor William Wetmore Story), who had been with him during his last days. Accusations of this nature were freely traded at the time, though never proved. Fannie Browning would seem to have had the most obvious motive—in the form of a possible reinstatement of the will of 1889—but if, as Kelley and Coley speculate, Pen had made a subsequent will directed largely towards the establishment of Casa Guidi as a Browning memorial,[151] then any of the potentially interested parties might have wished to keep its contents unrevealed.

One of Pen's cousins came to Italy to represent the Moulton-Barrett family interests (there were no close relatives on the Browning side), and after long and difficult Anglo–American–Italian negotiations Pen was officially declared to have died effectively intestate,[152] administration granted to Fannie and to lawyers representing the Moulton-Barretts, and an agreement reached by which all Pen's property would be sold, his debts settled, and the residue divided between his widow (as to one-third of the total) and sixteen of his Moulton-Barrett cousins (as to the other two-thirds). The property in Florence (including Casa Guidi) and Asolo (including the lace school) was offered for sale in Italy, as were such things as his two hundred pigeons, twelve peacocks, and four cockatoos, while some items, chiefly silver and plate deemed to have been originally Barrett property, were privately distributed to current Moulton-Barrett family members.[153] The Browning copy-rights also formed part of Pen's estate and these were sold to Smith, Elder, & Co. in May 1913 for the sum of one thousand pounds—to pass, four years later, to the house of John Murray, purchaser of Smith, Elder following the death of Reginald Smith in December 1916.[154]

In the immediate aftermath of Pen's death both Fannie Browning and Edith Peruzzi seem simply to have commandeered letters found amongst his possessions, Fannie in particular taking it upon herself to destroy or return to their authors some of the letters written to Pen and to Browning himself.[155] Apart from this further depletion

—and some additional items retained by Fannie or stolen by others—all the Browning manuscripts, letters, books, portraits, furniture, and memorabilia went, together with many of Pen's own paintings and sculptures, to the Sotheby sale, proceeding thence, either directly or indirectly, to private and public collections in all parts of the world—though chiefly, of course, in Britain and the United States.[156] The love-letters, the particular focus of the enormous public interest the sale provoked, eventually found their way to Wellesley College, Massachusetts, as did the manuscript of *Aurora Leigh*. The *Asolando* manuscript was purchased by, and remains in, the Pierpont Morgan Library of New York. Fannie Browning bought a total of forty lots at the sale, added these to the things she already had, and in later years created friends and an occupation for herself by distributing her collection in almost random fashion to a whole series of individuals and institutions—sending Browning's Doctor of Civil Law gown to Balliol, for example, and making the Browning Settlement (devoted to social work in a working-class district of London) a frequent object of her charity.[157] All of the letters she and Pen had received either from Browning or from Sarianna she gave to T. J. Wise, receiving in return the dedication of *A Browning Library*.[158] Included among Fannie Browning's purchases at the sale—perhaps out of a belated sense of loyalty—were a number of her late husband's works, but for the most part these went for derisory sums to unknown and no doubt unpropitious destinations: in 1961 a portrait of Browning's French friend Joseph Milsand was discovered, 'shrouded in a thick fog of grey deposit', in the back room of a Sussex public house.[159]

Although the sale included relatively few manuscripts of major importance, it did contain, segregated into numerous distinct correspondences, a large proportion of the surviving letters written by the Brownings, as well as a great many of the books that had been on their shelves. The resulting dispersal of these and other important materials has had a profound effect upon the subsequent development of Browning studies. It has certainly hampered Browning textual and biographical scholarship, and it has resulted, even more noticeably, in the proliferation of editions of letters addressed to a single correspondent and in a consequent, or at any rate associated, delay in the appearance of complete editions of the letters of either poet. The comprehensive edition of *The Brownings' Correspondence* now in progress may to some extent be perceived as suffering from the prior publication of so many of the more important documents; its editors can nevertheless claim that 'fewer than a third of all known letters' have been printed, often in incomplete texts,[160] and they are in the advantageous position of being able to include within a single chronological sequence all the available letters written by both the poets, even from the years before they met.

It was, in any case, precisely the radical and largely random scattering of the Brownings' papers that stimulated the imaginative detective work involved in Kelley and Coley's systematic attempt, in *The Browning Collections*, to describe and track down to its current or last known location not only every item in the Sotheby catalogue of 1913 (even those grouped into large and inadequately analysed lots) but also 'any article which might have influenced Robert or Elizabeth Barrett Browning; any work which they created, possessed or presented; and items which indicated the breadth of their influence on others'.[161] Only letters, separately covered by *The Brownings' Correspondence: A Checklist*, were omitted from the purview of this remarkable undertaking, which thus constitutes, together with the checklist of letters, an incomparable resource—its usefulness enhanced by intricate indexing—for the identification and location of every kind of research material relating to the Brownings. It is true that the information about the Browning and Barrett Browning manuscripts largely overlaps with the previously published listings in the magisterial *Index of English Literary Manuscripts*[162] and that the inclusion of such items as locks of hair and other memorabilia, and of those long disregarded paintings and sculptures of Pen's, ventures some way beyond the normal limits of such compilations. It is also true that many items have remained untraced. But neither qualification can be said to render the work less remarkable, to deprive it of its appropriately romantic character, or to negate its exemplification of the way in which the unique difficulties of a given scholarly field can serve to stimulate the particular energies and methodologies necessary to their resolution.

Above all, perhaps, the causes and consequences of the great Browning sale can conveniently serve as a powerful and still unconcluded morality on the dangers of testamentary casualness—on the risks of indecision and delay, and even of the inadequate safeguarding of documents. It is hard to believe that Browning, who had felt compelled to act so vehemently in defence of his dead wife, can have felt confident that his own reputation could be safely left in the hands of 'poor Pen'. That mask of relentless geniality, however, seems to have left him with no male intimate on whom he could prospectively rely—even George Smith having been only rarely consulted on other than business matters—nor did loyalty to his wife allow, either in principle or in practice, of any real alternative to continuing investment in their son. He had, in any case, made extended trial of Pen's loyalty over the years, knew the profundity of his devotion to the memory of his mother and to all that he had been taught to believe of her, and perhaps imagined that Pen's inheritance of productive literary properties would serve to keep him financially dependent still, a pensioner whose sense of perpetual obligation could be expected to translate into a general willingness to oblige.

Pen did, on the whole, quite competently oblige, displaying a conscientiousness and even, at times, an enthusiasm that seem perfectly unforced. In January 1890 he faithfully distributed copies of *Asolando* to those friends of his father's who might in happier circumstances have expected to receive one from the author himself, adding to Tennyson's the inscription: 'To | Lord Tennyson | This copy of "Asolando" | would have been given by his ever | loving and deeply attached friend | my Father.'[163] He contributed a brief biographical 'Note' to an elaborate if diminutive edition of his mother's *Sonnets from the Portuguese* published in Venice in 1906.[164] He wrote to *The Times* in December 1902 to offer a mild correction to a recently published reference of Hardy's to Browning's 'The Statue and the Bust'.[165] He twice accepted with grace and occupied with more than mere perfunctoriness the presidency of the Browning Settlement.[166] Remaining, however, what he had always been, and experiencing no less than his father the oppression of an extravagantly romanticized past, Pen was perpetually in need of more personal, and far more specific, guidance than his father seems ever to have given him or than he could expect to obtain from the Smiths or from those who cultivated his acquaintance solely for the sake of the historic associations he seemed so incongruously to embody. It can have been of little comfort to him—as it has since been of little comfort to Browning scholars, whose needs he tried but in the end so lamentably failed to meet— to be so often reminded of the rousing 'Epilogue' to *Asolando*

('One who never turned his back but marched breast forward, | ...
Held we fall to rise, are baffled to fight better, | Sleep to wake'),[167]
or of the quotation attributed to Browning by the dubiously reliable William Sharp: 'Without death, which is our crapelike church-
yardy word for change, for growth, there could be no prolongation
of that which we call life. Pshaw! it is foolish to argue upon such a
thing even. For myself, I deny death as an end of everything. Never
say of me that I am dead!'[168]

Alfred and Hallam Tennyson

'I CAN so well realise Pen's loving pride in his parents' history', wrote Anne Thackeray Ritchie to Reginald Smith upon receiving a copy of the Browning–Barrett letters, '—never was there such a story, except my dear Tennysons indeed, and she too was a poet in her life and fervent feeling, though she did not write it down.'[1] But while Emily Sellwood, whom Tennyson married in 1850, was certainly as central to her husband's life and work as Elizabeth Barrett to Browning's, there are as many differences as similarities between the story of the Brownings and their son Pen and that of the Tennysons and their son Hallam. Where, for example, Elizabeth Barrett Browning played so prominent, if tragically brief, a role in her family's drama, Emily Tennyson seems always to have sought self-effacement, a life of service to her husband's genius: 'She valued perhaps in an exaggerated degree', said Benjamin Jowett, 'the spirit of order and subordination.'[2]

Throughout her married life, from 1850 to 1892, Emily Tennyson was almost invariably seen by friends and visitors as the poet's devoted and untiring helper, adviser, protector, supporter, and promoter, as the mother of two adored and adoring sons, and as the unobtrusively efficient chatelaine and hostess of two substantial houses—Farringford, in the Isle of Wight, the family's home from 1853, and Aldworth, near Haslemere, built later as a more private retreat for occupation during the summer and early autumn of each year. Jowett, as one of the most reverent of Emily Tennyson's many reverential admirers, very reasonably believed that Tennyson 'could never have been what he was without her';[3] he also believed, rather more questionably, that she had been 'probably her husband's best critic, and certainly the one whose authority he would most willingly have recognized'.[4] Emily Tennyson did indeed read and comment upon her husband's work at every stage and even seek to provide him with poetically usable images and ideas,[5] but her surviving writings are for the most part unremarkable and Edward FitzGerald, for one, saw her as a largely negative influence on Tennyson, 'who *quoad* Artist, would have done better to remain single in Lincolnshire, or married a jolly Woman who would have laughed and cried without any reason why'.[6]

Emily Tennyson was always frail—to Carlyle, meeting her for the first time shortly after her marriage, she already seemed 'very delicate in health, "sick *without* a disorder"'[7]—but she learned, like Elizabeth Barrett Browning, to exploit physical weakness as an instrument of domestic power. She was late in marrying and having children, and in 1874 she became mysteriously, probably psycho-somatically, perhaps self-protectively, and in any case permanently ill, hence no longer able to perform her repertoire of domestic and secretarial roles. Tennyson's dependence upon such support now seemed absolute, and although he had been receiving assistance in business matters from James Knowles, the architect of Aldworth,[8] his deep sense of privacy evidently ruled out the intimate installation of a confidant from outside the family. In this crisis the burden of service and responsibility fell almost inevitably upon the elder son, Hallam, born in 1852 when his mother was thirty-nine (an earlier son had been stillborn) and his father forty-three—and Pen Browning, whose own father held Hallam at the christening, not quite three and a half. A second son, Lionel, was born two years later, more charming and imaginative but altogether less dutiful and dependable than his doggedly conformist and infinitely accommodating older brother. After receiving his early education from a series of tutors—one of whom, Graham Dakyns, became his lifelong friend—and at a small preparatory school conducted by the Revd Charles Kegan Paul (later Tennyson's publisher) in his Dorset parish of Sturminster Marshall,[9] Hallam Tennyson went on to Marlborough and finally, as his father had done, to Trinity College, Cambridge, from which he was withdrawn in the summer of 1874 without taking his degree.[10]

Charles (later Sir Charles) Tennyson, one of Lionel Tennyson's children, recalled as always hovering in the background of his childhood visits to Farringford and Aldworth 'the tall, blond discreet figure' of his uncle Hallam,[11] and indeed Hallam was almost permanently at his father's side, conducting the greater part of his correspondence, dealing with editors and publishers, over-seeing the affairs of the two family estates, determining who should and who should not be admitted to his father's presence, watchfully orchestrating the content and pacing of such visits,[12] and—by no means least—keeping track of day-to-day events and conversations. One visitor, reporting that Tennyson 'did not like an unfavourable criticism to be left about for his servants to see', added, with a subtle shift from the servants to the poet himself, that 'his son carefully shielded him from the sight of these depreciations in later life'.[13]

Some sense of Hallam Tennyson's persistent and even pugnacious activity on his father's behalf can be gathered from his surviving correspondence with publishers, first of all with Charles Kegan Paul, his former schoolmaster, and then with the house of Macmillan, to which Tennyson made a permanent transfer of his works in 1884.[14] In an April 1885 letter to Alexander Macmillan he expressed his anger at an 'ungentlemanly attack' on his father in the *Spectator* and insisted that the late poems, far from showing signs of decline, were in fact 'as fine as any thing that he has done'.[15] In December 1886 Hallam wrote about the reception of *Tiresias and Other Poems*: 'Best thanks for the Daily Papers. They are not bad saving the spiteful "Times". The Editor ought to be ashamed to allow an old hero like my Father to be so shamefully attacked in his columns by one of those "disappointed authors" who frequent the "Times" staff nowadays. The Editor will not get any new poems like "The Fleet", if I can help it, in the future.' In a postscript prominently inserted at the head of the letter he added: 'Do Let *Mowbray Morris* be civil to my Father in "Macmillan's Magazine".'[16]

'Hallam is, as you know, more to us than we can say', Emily Tennyson wrote to Edward Lear on 14 August 1883. 'He has become more & more necessary to us as I have been very ill during the winter & spring & I still lose my voice & such strength as I have with a very little talking so the care of our numerous guests devolves on Hallam.'[17] But while the care of his ailing mother increasingly became yet another of Hallam's responsibilities,[18] she was none the less capable, even from her perpetual sofa—Thomas Hardy, in 1880, arrived to find her 'lying as if in a coffin'[19]—of retaining overall direction of the family's domestic life, keeping abreast of publishing arrangements,[20] writing some letters that would otherwise have fallen to Hallam, and, above all, conspiring with her son to maintain the poet's health, contentment, productivity, and reputation. If Browning, after his wife's death, can be said to have managed his own life with peculiar care and deliberation, then

Tennyson was in the position of having his life managed for him—
to the point of being kept in ignorance of what the co-conspirators
considered to be the indiscreet publication of some letters of Arthur
Henry Hallam's, the beloved friend of Tennyson's younger days for
whom his own son had been named.[21]

It was with good reason, clearly, that Hallam Tennyson
was described in his obituary as having acted as his father's
'general manager'.[22] At the same time, the conspiracy—precisely
because conspiratorial—tended to strengthen maternal possession
of Hallamee, as Emily Tennyson was accustomed to call her
favourite son, and his marriage to Audrey Boyle in 1884 must
therefore be reckoned a minor miracle. But the disruption of order
was brief and contained: the newly married couple returned to
Aldworth straight from the shortest of honeymoons and Hallam
was immediately reabsorbed into the established rhythms and
rituals of the Tennysonian system. If Audrey Tennyson was initially
viewed as simply a helpmate to her husband, to Tennyson himself
she had the strong recommendation of her beauty, and after five
years of marriage she became the mother of the boy who would in
due course inherit the peerage which Tennyson had accepted—
partly at least for Hallam's sake—in 1883.[23] It was she, too, who
kept the most faithful, hence most moving record of Tennyson's
last days and hours, noting among many other things his dying
recognition of Hallam's life of uncomplaining sacrifice: 'I make a
slave of you.'[24]

The reminiscences of the many friends, acquaintances, and strangers
admitted into Tennyson's presence during the last few years of his
life create an impression of a man deeply wounded by the death of
his younger son, Lionel, in 1886, and physically weakened by the
severe illness he suffered in 1888–9, when he was said to have been
'as near death as a man could be without dying'.[25] Such visitors
were also likely to be struck by the antiquated style of living the
Tennysons kept up. Hubert Parry, the composer, visiting Farringford
at the very beginning of 1892, thought it 'the most old-fashioned
house I ever saw, with dim candle lamps in the passages, four-
poster beds, hundreds of Mrs. Cameron's photographs, ugly
wallpapers and early Victorian furniture'.[26] Tennyson was notorious,
too, for his persistence in wearing to the end of his life the cloak and
sombrero-like 'wide-awake' he had romantically adopted in his

youth: Gladstone, contemplating his old friend's elevation to the peerage, was terrified lest he should appear thus accoutred in the House of Lords.[27] Increasing age also set Tennyson at odds with fashion in more substantial ways—his social and political views, for example, long characterized by a passionate, humane, and often radical toryism, became ever more dogmatically conservative and anti-democratic[28]—and his personal consciousness of physical frailty and of the necessary termination ahead was made abundantly clear by the late inclusion of 'Crossing the Bar', written in October 1889, at the end of *Demeter and Other Poems*.

No one doubted, however, that the Poet Laureate still retained, and to a remarkable degree, his mental faculties and creative powers—that he was proving himself amply 'Ulyssean' in the sense that 'Old age hath yet his honour and his toil'.[29] He kept up as long as possible his established daily routines, including the morning walk and the evening port and tobacco, and he continued, despite his poor eyesight, to read: in May 1885 Hallam told a friend in the United States that his father read 'novels without end. If you ever hear of any American novel that He would like do let me know. I believe that Huxley and he are the largest novel-devourers going.'[30] In June 1891 Tennyson assigned himself a course in Indian history in preparation for the writing of 'Akbar's Dream';[31] later still he was reading—and praising—some modern French poets;[32] and in August of 1892 his desire to re-read *Romola* prompted Hallam to write to Frederick Macmillan in search of a copy in sufficiently large type.[33] Tennyson similarly displayed during those last years a scarcely diminished capacity to cope both physically and mentally with a steady stream of eager visitors, to engage in lively and often highly anecdotal conversation, to read at length and with idio-syncratic precision from his own poems, and to expound, in a more than ever oracular fashion, his matured if not always self-consistent views on life and religion, literature and art.

He kept, above all, continuously active as a poet. His great popularity over many years had provided occasion and need for a long succession of reprints and new editions, including a series of increasingly capacious collected editions, so that his revision of his poems in 1891 in preparation for 'a new single volume edition'[34] constituted a kind of exercise with which he was already thoroughly familiar. He probably moved fairly quickly, therefore, through the already much reconsidered texts of the poems and plays that had been included in the previous one-volume edition of 1889,[35] in order to be able to work more intensively over the new volumes—*Demeter and Other Poems* and the still unpublished *The Death of Oenone* and *The Foresters*—that remained to be added to the *Complete Works* in the one-volume format.[36]

'So much to do, so little done', Tennyson is reported as saying[37] shortly before the onset of his final illness, and he seems, like Browning (whose 'The little done, the undone vast' he could have been faintly remembering),[38] to have continued working until the last possible moment. Almost all the poems in the *Demeter* volume of December 1889 appear to have been of recent composition, even if some of them (for example, 'To the Marquis of Dufferin and Ava' and 'The Ring') incorporated material of much earlier date,[39] and although *The Death of Oenone and Other Poems* was distinctly slimmer, its contents were again for the most part newly written— and showed no sign of senility and very little of failing talent. When Hallam Tennyson, indeed, later referred to *The Death of Oenone* as his father's 'last will and testament',[40] he seems to have had in mind not so much its status as an absolutely final work (one bound and interleaved set of the revised page proofs is identified on its cover by Hallam as 'The last proof my Father corrected October– 1892')[41] but rather its incorporation of the dedicatory 'June Bracken and Heather', a love-poem addressed to Emily Tennyson in her old age ('To you that are seventy-seven'),[42] and of the brief poems of personal affirmation and farewell that are grouped together towards the end of the volume. The closing poem, though ostensibly distanced by its being addressed to those mourning 'The Death of the Duke of Clarence and Avondale', must have carried a sufficiently clear message to those who, by the time of the book's publication, were mourning Tennyson himself:

> The face of Death is toward the Sun of Life,
> His shadow darkens earth: his truer name
> Is 'Onward,' no discordance in the roll
> And march of that Eternal Harmony
> Whereto the worlds beat time, tho' faintly heard
> Until the great Hereafter. Mourn in hope![43]

Another poem in the same group, 'The Silent Voices' ('Call me rather, silent voices, | Forward to the starry track | Glimmering up the heights beyond me | On, and always on!'),[44] was sung as an anthem at Tennyson's funeral to music composed by Lady Tennyson and arranged for four voices by Dr Frederick Bridge, the Abbey organist—who also composed the music for the other anthem, 'Crossing the Bar',[45] as he had earlier supplied for Browning's funeral the setting of Elizabeth Barrett Browning's 'What would we give to our beloved?'[46]

Although the reception of the late verse had not been uniformly positive, there was as Tennyson entered upon his eighty-fourth year in August 1892 no perceptible diminution in the extraordinary public adulation he had continuously and indeed increasingly received ever since the publication of *In Memoriam* in 1850—and his appointment as Poet Laureate—when he was still only forty-one. The laureateship, the peerage, the immense sales of his works, and the popular perception of him as a figure supremely representative of the age had all contributed to an exceptional self-consciousness about his posthumous reputation, and as he saw death approaching he became ever more urgently protective of both his personal and his creative privacy, seeking to secure them even beyond the grave. Fame had not dispelled, had perhaps even inflamed, what appear to have been deeply rooted insecurities: 'I am sick of this publicity [he said on his 80th birthday]—all this fulsome adulation makes me miserable and inclined to vomit morally.'[47] He never ceased to suffer from a fear of journalists and newspapers, an extreme sensitivity to hostile comment from whatever source, and a melancholy conviction that his death would be the occasion for his life and work to become the subject of an intense, intrusive, and ultimately bruising scrutiny: 'Why does one want to know about a man's life?' he asked. 'The less you know about a man's life the better. He gives you his best in his writings. I thank God day and night that we know nothing about Shakespeare.'[48] And when, a few days before his death, the arrival of an anxious telegram from the Queen signalled that the state of his health had become a matter of national concern, there seems to have been genuine terror in his response: 'O, that Press will get hold of me now!'[49]

In an immediate sense, the press would indeed seize upon the opportunity to print obituaries and poetic tributes and long accounts of his death and funeral, and newspapers and magazines continued for several years to publish estimates of his career, reminiscences by his friends, and illustrated articles about the houses and localities with which he was associated. But little of this initial outpouring proved other than adulatory, and Tennyson's paranoiac anticipations of posthumous betrayal must in any case have been hurtful to his devoted son—whose devotion, indeed, they were perhaps in some degree intended to keep up to the mark. If Browning had been ready to trust so absolutely in the wayward Pen, it argues a certain insensitivity and ingratitude on Tennyson's part that he should even have hinted a doubt of his own son's long-proven stability and responsibility. In the event, of course, Hallam Tennyson did not, perhaps could not, fail in his appointed task, and within five years of his father's death any real or imagined dangers of damaging personal exposure had been essentially dissipated by the publication of the two-volume *Alfred Lord Tennyson: A Memoir*, designed, as its Preface declared, to 'preclude the chance of further and unauthentic biographies'.[50]

Tennyson's death, on 6 October 1892, was registered as a national cataclysm. If George Granville Bradley, as Dean of Westminster, had briefly hesitated before approving Browning's interment in the Abbey, he could scarcely have done so before endorsing the presence there of Tennyson, a figure more universally admired—and a personal friend of long standing. *The Times* of 7 October made it clear that the already overcrowded condition of Poets' Corner would not present an obstacle to Tennyson's introduction there, the space next to Browning having been specifically reserved for that purpose,[51] and on 13 October the newspaper opened its report of the previous day's funeral with a paragraph richly expressive of that prevailing national mood which Hallam Tennyson had assisted in creating but which was to place implicit limits on his own freedom of subsequent action:

All that was mortal of the late Poet Laureate has been laid to rest with all honour and simplicity side by side with the dust of Chaucer, Spenser, Jonson, Dryden, Cowley, and Browning. Of the immortal memory which surely belongs to his poetry, instinct with strength, purity, grace, and music, this is not the place to speak. Yet the solemn ceremony in Westminster Abbey yesterday forms the strongest possible testimony of the national belief that the late Lord Tennyson is distinctly and emphatically one of the immortals. Inside the Abbey and without the same testimony was given in different ways. . . . Statesmen of either party stood in common sorrow at the grave-side; medicine, the law, art, the drama, poetry, literature, science, and even the crude socialism of the day were represented by leading men, who shared in one deep feeling of general loss. For the time, doubtless, all of them felt as they stood in mournful silence as Tennyson felt when he wrote of the Duke of Wellington—

The last great Englishman is low.

And their feeling was clearly shared by the seething crowd of men and women without, waiting for the Abbey doors to be opened in the hope, not indeed of catching a passing glimpse of the ceremonial, but of hearing the music of the organ and the singing of the choir or of catching in the distance the solemn sentences of the service. . . . In brief, the occasion was altogether unique in its grandeur and its simplicity; and the day was one deserving to be recorded, not merely by reason of its present and pathetic interest, but also as a piece of English history.[52]

Edmund Gosse, however, privately recorded his impression of the funeral as a much less orderly and reverent occasion, 'enormous, crushing, exceedingly well-done, national, and prosaic', characterized by much initial rushing and pushing for seats and by the presence of 'a crowd of perfectly callous nonentities, treating the thing as a show and rather a poor one'. His conclusion that the ceremony itself was 'a large but by no means an impressive scene . . . not comparable with Browning's funeral in the same place',[53] seems in fact to have been quite widely shared, and some resentment was expressed at the absence of the royal family and of Mr Gladstone and at the poor representation of literature, none of the twelve pall-bearers having any connection with poetry or with any other form of imaginative writing.[54] Although the arrangements in the Abbey and the distribution of tickets had been in the hands of the Macmillans, as Tennyson's publishers—the letters of application they received are now in the British Library—the selection of participants in the service itself seems to have been chiefly in Hallam's hands,[55] and since there had already been speculation as to the vacant poet laureateship, he perhaps deemed it inappropriate to give any individual poet a role that could be interpreted as implying endorsement of a claim to the succession.[56] Walter Besant, the founder of the Society of Authors, shared with Gosse before the service his suspicion that Macmillan & Co. were 'trying to make the thing a mass advertisement for their "shop"',[57] and it was presumably as Macmillan authors that Thomas Hardy and Henry James had received their tickets of admission, James later expressing dismay at the presence of 'too many masters of Balliol, too many Deans and Alfred Austins',[58] and Hardy—unaware of his destiny as the next literary figure to be mourned on a comparable scale—reporting unemotionally to his wife that he had had a good seat and had 'looked into the grave with the rest as we passed it on our way out'.[59]

The departure of a figure of Tennyson's distinction was an obvious occasion for ambitious memorialization. The National Portrait Gallery, it is true, was initially reluctant to accept a marble copy, commissioned by Hallam, of one of Thomas Woolner's busts of Tennyson in his beardless forties,[60] but Hamo Thornycroft's marble statue of the poet in old age, commissioned by Trinity College, Cambridge, was recognized as a more successful statement,[61] with G. F. Watts's massive bronze, sited in the grounds of Lincoln Cathedral, the most powerful of all. Begun when Watts was himself already an octogenarian, cast posthumously from the clay model completed just before his death, and unveiled on 15 July 1905, the project resulted from a local Lincolnshire initiative made realizable only by Watts's willingness to undertake the task as a personal—and prospectively national—gesture of admiration for his dead friend.[62]

Long before the completion of the Watts and Thornycroft statues in 1905 and 1909, however, the popular imagination was caught by the erection of a large stone cross at Freshwater, on the summit of High Down, right above Farringford, as at once a monument to the poet and a beacon to shipping. On 6 August 1897, the poet's birthday, a large crowd toiled uphill[63] to attend a dedication ceremony performed by the Archbishop of Canterbury with the assistance of George Granville Bradley, still Dean of Westminster, and in the presence of Hallam and Audrey Tennyson and of Arthur Tennyson, one of the poet's brothers.[64] The occasion was itself celebrated a fortnight later in some 'Lines on the Tennyson Beacon', written and published by a local resident and former coastguard, which were at once doggedly informative and naively reflective of Tennyson's as yet undiminished appeal:

> This Monument is erected to the memory of the late
>   Lord Tennyson's name,
> Who lived in this locality in the sound of the watery
>   main;
> He was the most famous poet of the Victorian era, no
>   one can this gainsay,

His poems are left behind although he's passed away,
Fond affection has caused this monument to be here
    erected,
Showing how he was universally honoured and
    respected;
This monument has a twofold duty to impart,
Being marked as a Beacon on the Island's chart.
May it boldly stand forth and this duty perform,
Either in the calm and sunshine, or in the raging
    storm;
Its base is embedded in the high down chalk,
The spot and the place where the Poet liked to walk,
It was here the Poet could meditate amid scenery
    superb and grand,
As any to be found in the whole Island;
This monument has been designed by Mr. Joseph
    Pearson, B.A. who is deserving of great praise,
As it stands a real ornament, as it in the air is
    raised;
It is in the form of a tall Iona Cross, 32 feet high
    with the pedestal,
Soaring high into the air, pointing to the celestial.
This cross a beacon to sailors, is raised by the people
    of Freshwater and others who wished to do him
    honour,
Whilst America subscribed over £250, taking this part
    upon her;
  .   .   .   .
That the illustrious Poet himself would have chosen
    this form of monument, there is no kind of doubt,
Especially on this spot he so often was about.[65]

    Biographical interventions of every sort were also anticipated, and Theodore Watts, a family friend, doubtless had prior approval for his pronouncement, in an obituary published within two days of the poet's death, that the writing of Tennyson's biography would be 'a work of incalculable importance' and that Hallam was the only person 'fully equipped' for such a task: 'His son's filial affection', the obituary concluded, 'was so precious to Lord Tennyson that, although the poet's powers remained undimmed to the last day of his life, I do not believe that we should have had all the splendid work of the last ten years without his affectionate and unwearied aid.'[66] Watts's pre-emptive purpose was clear—and anticipatory of the entire exercise that was to follow—and it is equally clear that Hallam had long contemplated and prepared for such an eventuality, his prompt choice of the *Memoir* title suggesting further that he already had Lockhart in mind as his chief precedent and model.

The writing of the *Memoir* must primarily have presented itself to Hallam—now Lord Tennyson in his father's stead and virtually the sole legatee of his father's will—as a logical and even inevitable extension of those habits of devotion and serviceability which had for so long constituted the chief occupation and preoccupation of his life. But it also provided him with an outlet for his own literary aspirations, hitherto chiefly exercised in his *Jack and the Bean-stalk: English Hexameters* of 1886 and in the prose translation of the Sixth Book of the *Iliad* which he had included, together with a personal memoir, when compiling a privately printed memorial volume to his brother Lionel.[67] Hallam later acknowledged that the hexameters of *Jack and the Bean-stalk* had in part been 'made or amended' by his father,[68] and when, in his will, he bequeathed the manuscript of the Homer translation to one of his great-nephews he similarly described it as 'revised for me by my father'. Hallam evidently felt severe constraints, both inner and outer, upon his venturing independently into print, and these emerge poignantly enough from his attempt, in a letter of early 1885, to explain his reluctance to be identified as the author of a poem, 'Orange Blossom: Sonnet', forthcoming in *Macmillan's Magazine*: 'I am shy of doing it—and have only put H. as they will only say "Oh how Tennysonian!" "Oh how closely imitated"! "Oh how personal"! I never have put my name to my things—but just as you like—only then if you put name I should put simple "Sonnet", not "Orange Blossoms" as title.'[69] Just as it seems inevitable that *Jack and the Bean-stalk* should be dedicated principally to his father ('in recognition of what this booklet owes to him'), so it is unsurprising that his authorship of the poem, evidently a romantic gesture to his bride, should indeed be acknowledged only by the initial 'H.'.[70]

It was perhaps, even so, an impulse towards self-fulfilment in addition to the more familiar sense of duty that drove Hallam so rapidly into 'the midst of the Memoir'.[71] By 20 December 1892 he was considering a proposal from the American *Century* magazine for the serialization of 'my work on my Fathers life'.[72] Two days later, writing to George Craik of Macmillan & Co., he confirmed his earlier opposition to further annotated editions of his father's poems and specified that no one other than Craik himself should be allowed to see '*our* Notes', those emanating from the Tennyson household itself. 'This', he added, 'is most important for my book (Life).'[73] On 14 January 1893 he was already able to report to Craik that Jowett had heard him read aloud what he had already written ('in the rough up to 1850') and pronounced it to be 'very interesting & language good'.[74] Letters and other items were publicly solicited, particular friends directly invited to record their memories and impressions, and extracts made from the copious bibliography of published books and articles. Hallam's own records of his father's sayings and doings were also extensively drawn upon: even for the 1870s, when his systematic record-keeping had hardly begun, he had material available, the *Memoir* as published including from that period 'some talks which my father had with Carlyle, jotted down in my note-book'.[75]

Nor did he work alone. As early as 11 October 1892, the day before the funeral, his mother was able to declare that her regret at outliving her husband had been alleviated by Hallam's assurance 'that I can be a help in the work to be done and nothing I can do is too much to be done either for the Father or the devoted Son of our love'.[76] She was in fact assigned the perhaps prudential but curiously perverse task of condensing—which is to say, largely destroying—her surviving journals (covering roughly the period 1850–74) and writing the preserved portions out again in her own hand.[77] Thus irrecoverably abbreviated and rewritten they provided Hallam with the principal biographical thread for at least a quarter-century of his father's life. In a letter of 20 November 1892 Lady Tennyson—now, strictly speaking, the Dowager Lady Tennyson—spoke of working each day on the journal pages that Hallam had read (and presumably marked for retention or deletion) the previous evening: 'The journals are my task after Hallamee has read them at night which makes it easier for me to condense them in the day-time.'[78] In the same letter she described her daughter-in-law as being 'very good in helping Hallam to copy', and the new Lady Tennyson now became a more central figure, chiefly because of her formal status as mistress of Farringford and Aldworth but also because of her ability and willingness to take down her husband's dictation and copy out in her large, rounded hand (so much more legible than his own) whatever documents he needed for *Memoir* use.[79]

The work proceeded with some urgency—Tennyson's contemporaries were rapidly dropping away, Jowett for one dying before his contribution was complete—and the signs of that haste are everywhere evident in the ten manuscript volumes which now represent the *Memoir*'s earliest surviving state.[80] Roughly fastened to the foolscap pages with ordinary dressmaker's pins is an approximately chronological sequence of family records, unpublished poems, correspondence, hand-copied commentaries on Tennyson and his work from both published and unpublished sources, and cuttings and tear-sheets from newspapers and magazines. It had clearly been Hallam's purpose to include, with little or no preliminary editing, any materials that seemed at all likely to be of use, well knowing that final discriminations would be simplified by having everything in print and approximately in sequence. Much that was not included must simply have been destroyed, as were the originals of many of the included items once they had been either completely or selectively transcribed—with errors and modifications at which it is impossible even to guess. Such acts were doubtless taken for granted as necessary and even sanctified acts of protective piety: 'My difficulty in arranging the later chapters [so Hallam declared in the Preface to the published *Memoir*] has been how to choose, and how to throw aside, from the mass of material. I have quoted from many manuscripts never meant for the public eye, many of which I have burnt according to his instructions.' Since two family friends are thanked in a footnote for their help in selecting 'from upwards of 40,000 letters'[81]—mostly, of course, incoming—it would appear that large numbers of such letters were disposed of without their ever passing before Hallam's eyes.[82] Especially to be regretted—from Hallam's point of view, especially to be ensured—was the disappearance of all but a few fragments of the letters that Tennyson wrote to Emily Sellwood prior to their marriage.

The bound manuscript volumes provided the basis for what might be called, by analogy with Tennyson's characteristic method of arriving at final texts of his successive poetry volumes, the 'trial' version of the *Memoir*, privately printed in four volumes under the title *Materials for a Life of A. T.*; the first volume (only) is sub-titled *Collected for My Children*. At least thirty-two copies of each volume appear to have been printed and bound,[83] and this multiplication of copies made it possible for Hallam to seek the advice and assistance of some of his own and his father's closest friends. Because based on the hastily assembled manuscript volumes, the *Materials* were still far from finished work, even by contemporary 'Life and Letters' standards, and the various privately printed stages through which the work passed on the way to its final published form[84] are testimony in themselves to the persistence and strenuousness of Hallam's desire to construct a work that would both possess its own literary integrity and stand as a worthy memorial to the man he loved as a father, revered as a poet-thinker, and felt it his duty to celebrate as an embodiment of national values—not a saint, perhaps, but unmistakably a superior being.

A draft of Hallam's preface to the *Memoir* was included in the first of the ten manuscript volumes, and although it subsequently underwent a good deal of minor revision its central emphases remained essentially unaltered. Acknowledging his father's profound distrust for all forms of biographical investigation—insisting too that the poems alone were capable of revealing 'the innermost sanctuary of his being'—Hallam went on: 'However [Tennyson] wished that, if I deemed it better, the incidents of his life should be given as shortly as might be without comment, but that my notes should be final and full enough to preclude the chance of further and unauthentic biographies.'[85] The angularity of the writing here, the presence of unresolved tensions between editorial and authorial roles, clearly reflects the extreme delicacy of Hallam's task as he sought to establish at one and the same time his loyal deference to his father's wishes and his personal independence ('if I deemed it better') as memoirist—the very choice of title, reinforced by a heavy dependence on the reminiscences of Tennyson's friends, effecting a deft avoidance of such terms as 'biography', 'life', or even the generically more appropriate 'life and letters', and yet at the same time allowing, as in Lockhart's hands, considerable structural and interpretative latitude.

Essentially the same manoeuvre is executed a little later in the same Preface. Recalling his father's expectation that the poem 'Merlin and the Gleam' would probably be 'enough of biography for those friends who urged him to write about himself', Hallam continued: 'However, this has not been their verdict, and I have tried to do what he said that I might do, and have endeavoured to give briefly something of what people naturally wish to know, something about his birth, homes, school, college, friendships, travels, and the leading events of his life, enough to present the sort of insight into his history and pursuits which one wants, if one desires to make a companion of a man.'[86] In the manuscript version of this passage Hallam spoke only of endeavouring 'to give briefly [Tennyson's] every day life, as it is to be found in journals and letters',[87] and the new acknowledgement that people might 'naturally' be interested in such matters appeared to signal a distinct shift in the direction of formal biography, an implicit recognition on Hallam's part of the overall direction of his successive revisions of the book as a whole.[88]

His initial approach to the *Memoir* seems to have been in line with the essentially editorial conception attributed to his father by way of the Preface's solemn, though by no means unambiguous, undertaking: 'According to my father's wish, throughout the memoir my hand will be as seldom seen as may be, and this accounts for the occasionally fragmentary character of my work.'[89] If Hallam became over time less of a mere compiler and more of a shaping presence, that doubtless had much to do with his arriving at a greater distance from his father—and from his mother, who died in August 1896, fourteen months before the *Memoir* finally appeared[90]—and at a heightened sense of the validity and dignity of his project as an independent artefact. And it is precisely upon the convergence of Hallam's earlier and later impulsions that the great strengths of the published *Memoir* can be said to have depended: its constantly evoked sense of the subject's own voice— an effect enhanced by the inclusion of previously unpublished verses—and the emergence of overall coherence from page-by-page miscellaneity as a result of the absolute clarity and essential simplicity of Hallam's vision.

In pursuit of that conceptual goal—of a 'truth' imperious in its demands and allowing of no qualifications—and in the necessary process of reducing the voluminous *Materials* to more manageable size, Hallam did not hesitate to omit, merge, rephrase, decontextualize, and otherwise manipulate the documentary evidence, almost always without any indication that an editorial intervention had occurred. Occasionally, as in the omission of the verses which properly formed part of Tennyson's early (and precocious) letter to his sister's governess,[91] Hallam may have made cuts for the sake of maintaining at least a minimal narrative pace, but for the most part he seems simply to have altered or removed whatever he would have preferred never to have been present in the first place. In a typical, undramatic instance, a letter to Edward FitzGerald of February 1841 presumably lost its 'Damn!' for the latter reason, its final, signing-off sentence for the former, and another, earlier sentence because it alluded to a topic (Dr Allen's wood-carving scheme) with which Hallam was not yet ready to deal.[92] Hallam's determination to impose upon the characterization of his father an almost novelistic or fabular consistency becomes very clear at such moments, pointing to a degree of authorial assertion over the words of others that it is tempting to call patrician—but that was perhaps largely innocent. The freedoms Hallam took were in truth no greater than those taken by many another Victorian biographer, but in combination with the destruction of original documents they have served to render the *Memoir* at once the most indispensable of biographical documents and the least to be trusted, a barrier that must, yet cannot, be overcome.

The prevailing piety of the *Memoir* has also proved somewhat self-defeating in the longer run. As some of the original reviewers complained, the idealizing thrust of Hallam's work was always and inevitably towards the suppression of the darker, wilder, more extravagant aspects of Tennyson's personality and the more outrageous of the improprieties with which his conversation was simultaneously peppered and salted.[93] Hallam does acknowledge and seek to illustrate his father's sense of humour, but his reporting of Tennyson's conversation was undoubtedly tempered, as Charles Tennyson once put it, by 'due allowance for Victorian discretion',[94] and he was backed up—within the *Memoir* itself, in the *Tennyson and His Friends* volume of 1911, and in separately published reminiscences—by the baffles of protective concealment set up around the poet's memory by those who had known him best. Even Henry James was disappointingly unspecific when recalling Tennyson's going 'to the very greatest length imaginable' in speaking of the Marquis de Sade,[95] and James Mangles, who lived near Aldworth, entered into his diary only the briefest notation ('Told of how he had bitten Menken') of his neighbour's lively gossip about Swinburne's unsuccessful sexual transaction with Adah Isaacs Menken.[96]

There is all too much detail, on the other hand, in the notebook in which Hallam Tennyson himself dutifully recorded the astonishing stories his father had found it appropriate to pass on to a schoolboy son: 'The walled up old room found with skeleton of man crawling from under bed & a woman in bed'; 'A chieftain in Dahome[y] I fancy killed young girls to warm his feet in their bowels.'[97] It may be possible to doubt whether Tennyson can in fact have told a story (retailed by Edmund Gosse) about his visiting Clevedon and finding two boys copulating on Arthur Hallam's grave,[98] but there seems little reason to question Gosse's first-hand account, not published in his lifetime, of the distinctly indecorous anecdotes and observations uttered by an 'at times even childishly playful' Tennyson at a private dinner in 1876. In one such story he told of a man who had taken a bet that he could 'successfully chaff' Cora Pearl ('Skittles') and sought to do so by abruptly saying, as she entered the room, ' "Why, Skittles, what a fine a—e you have!" She, affecting modesty, replied "Oh! You shouldn't kiss and tell!" '[99] In a mood more childish and playful still he asked Thomas Hardy to name the first person mentioned in the Bible, to which the required answer was Chap. 1.[100]

Tennyson's troubled and even turbulent family background and rural pre-Victorian upbringing doubtless had much to do with his being, as Archbishop Benson remarked, 'so coarse a talker' even while 'of a life so noble'.[101] But these were precisely the kinds of intimacies, complexities, and franknesses that could not be allowed to disturb the altogether simpler and saintlier image that Hallam had from the first, and even in his father's lifetime, felt committed and determined to present. It is perfectly possible that Hallam had little real understanding of what the conditions of his father's childhood and youth had actually been like[102] and little incentive to challenge or expand upon the versions of such episodes received from his parents,[103] but the revelations about Tennyson's family and the hints about his conversation that have since emerged from other sources have served—rightly or wrongly—to prompt suspicions of other and even darker 'truths' concealed beneath the *Memoir*'s often lively but never unguarded surface.

Hallam's frequent references to his father's wishes for the *Memoir* inevitably prompt speculation as to the encouragement and assistance Tennyson might have given during his lifetime, the extent to which the *Memoir* should properly be considered not merely as an act of filial piety but as in some sense a direct projection of the wishes and self-imaging of its subject. When James Knowles declared in the January 1893 issue of *The Nineteenth Century* that Tennyson had 'recognised that after death a Memoir of him was inevitable, and left the charge of it in its fulness to his son',[104] he clearly opened up, deliberately or otherwise, the possibility that a memoir yet to be realized 'in its fulness' might already have been completed in part, and this implication of active collaboration was doubtless one of the many indiscretions in an article full of quotation and personal detail that was regarded by the bereaved family as a 'gross breach of confidence & of copyright'[105]—Emily Tennyson declaring, with somewhat backhanded charity: 'We dont think that it is *treachery* in Mr Knowles but simply that there are such defects in his character that he is not conscious that it is treachery.'[106]

That Tennyson in his last years deliberately supplied Hallam with biographical material for use after his death there can be no doubt: early in the *Memoir* an account of his poetic beginnings is introduced with the words, 'he wrote the following note for me in 1890'.[107] Again, in the course of a discussion of 'The Palace of Art': 'In 1890 he wrote the following notes.'[108] But Hallam's habitual use of the term 'note' strongly suggests that on at least some of these occasions his father had thought of himself not as yielding up information for a future biography but rather as providing authorial notes to the poems—the jealously regarded '*our* Notes' of Hallam's letters to Craik. It was a process at once obscured and implicitly acknowledged by Hallam's reference to 'my notes' in the Preface to the *Memoir*[109] and by his proffered justification for the inclusion of some stanzas Tennyson had omitted from 'The Palace of Art': 'He allowed me however to print some of them in my notes, otherwise I should have hesitated to quote without his leave lines that he had excised.'[110] For Hallam as biographer the notes to the poems represented a source peculiarly precious—unique, privileged, ready to hand, largely prefabricated, and profoundly interesting to contemporary readers—and he drew heavily upon them for those accounts of Tennyson's successive volumes upon which the *Memoir*'s narrative of a life of such outward uneventfulness was so largely and almost inevitably structured. But Hallam's awareness of his father's more specific intentions in respect of the authorial notes was later to involve him in working repeatedly and to some extent incrementally over essentially the same body of material in preparation for the annotated editions of 1907–8 and 1913.

In June 1885 Hallam Tennyson had offered to supply the Macmillans with annotations to a projected new edition of *In Memoriam*, 'if I can persuade my Father to let me publish his notes given to me from time to time'.[111] Much work was directed during Tennyson's lifetime towards the preparation of notes to all the poems, and it is curious to see Tennyson's concern in honoured old age to counter the trivial criticisms of an earlier—even, in the world's eye, a vanished—day. In March 1848, for example, the *Quarterly Review* notice of *The Princess* had objected to the line, 'That clad her like an April daffodilly', on the grounds that April was too late for daffodils.[112] The form of the note appearing in an interleaved 'trial' printing of authorial annotations some three years before Tennyson's death does not mention the *Quarterly* but reads simply: 'on the 15th of April in Dublin I saw a handful of daffodils'. To which Hallam has added, in what is even for him an unusually clumsy hand, as if he were writing from dictation while balancing the volume on his knee: 'just after reading in the Quarterly an attack on my "*April* daffodilly"'. On the facing interleaf Tennyson's own scrawled-in comment, 'in 1887 I saw them even in May', has again been altered by Hallam to conclude 'saw some blooming in May',[113] and it was presumably Hallam who subsequently refashioned the note into the form in which it was eventually published: 'The *Quarterly Review* objected to "*April* daffodilly." Daffodils in the North of England belong as much to April as to March. On the 15th of April in the streets of Dublin I remember a man presenting me with a handful of daffodils; and in 1887 at Farringford I saw daffodils still in bloom in May.'[114]

It is possible that Tennyson himself enlarged upon the original 'daffodilly' note in one of the other copies of the 'trial' *Notes* that were doubtless circulating in the household, but there is in any case ample evidence that while Hallam regarded the authorial notes as being of the first importance, he none the less saw his editorial role as permitting and even requiring him to intervene with an 'improving' hand. As he put it to George Craik: 'My Father's notes which he wrote with me for his poems want correcting all through. . . . My Father went through them and corrected many things—but there are still many mistakes & some unnecessary notes which need erasing.'[115] Or as George A. Macmillan wrote to the firm's New York office in August 1907: 'The basis of the Notes is the Author's own work, though his son has supplemented it where necessary in consultation with several well known critics and friends of his father.'[116]

The interval between the publication of the *Memoir* in 1897 and the commencement of intensive work on the annotations in 1905 was largely occupied by Hallam's entry into public life. Tennyson's acceptance of a peerage had served, as his wife had said at the time, to provide Hallam with the opportunity for 'an honourable career' once 'his work for his father ha[d] ceased',[117] and as the 2nd Lord Tennyson Hallam did indeed take his seat in the House of Lords in July 1893[118] and serve, over the years, on a variety of governmental and charitable bodies: he became president, for example, of the Royal Literary Fund[119] and the Folk Lore Society and, in later years, Deputy-Governor of the Isle of Wight.[120] From early in 1899 until late in 1903 he was in Australia, first as Governor-General of South Australia and then as Governor-General of the newly federated Commonwealth—an episode from which he seems to have emerged with considerable credit.[121] A speech he made at an Australian Dinner in London some three years after his return is indicative of his political position and perhaps of the grounds of his success: 'I shall not speak as a party man, for I am not a party man. I shall speak as an Imperialist to Imperialists.'[122]

Hallam's responsibilities to his father and to the Tennyson literary estate were largely set aside during these years, but in no sense forgotten, and in June 1905, rather more than a year after his return to England, he wrote to inform Frederick Macmillan that work on the annotations was now in hand. An *In Memoriam* volume would come first—it in fact appeared later that same year—but when the notes to all the poems had been completed they would be '*added as my Father wished at the end of the collected poems*'.[123] The first collected edition to be so annotated was the nine-volume Eversley Edition of 1907–8, and the time, seriousness, and anxiety which Hallam devoted to the project are reflected in his letters to the Macmillans,[124] in his multiple corrections and alterations to proofs,[125] and in his correspondence with his old tutor Graham Dakyns, to whom he often turned for frank criticism and scholarly advice.[126] Five years on the alterations, additions,

and deletions made for the one-volume annotated edition of 1913—
in which the notes were keyed to the (now expanded) one-volume
text—carried still further the process by which Hallam loyally
realized his father's overall wishes for publication of the notes even
while frequently departing from his detailed intentions as textually
inscribed.

Because, however, Tennyson's 'wishes' are again known only
through Hallam's transmission of them, it is conceivable that the
latter's long engagement with the authorial notes, first for the
Memoir and then for the two annotated editions, may have brought
him to the point of regarding them more portentously than the
author himself had done. In both the 1907–8 and 1913 editions the
notes are headed by a Tennysonian quotation: 'I am told that my
young countrymen would like notes to my poems. Shall I write
what dictionaries tell to save some of the idle folk trouble? or am I
to try to fix a moral to each poem? or to add an analysis of
passages? or to give a history of my similes? I do not like the
task.'[127] Hallam had not, however, preserved what stood earlier as
the second sentence of this passage, 'What hope that my prose
should be clearer than my verse?'[128] Nor did he incorporate the
similarly half-humorous, half-rueful insertion after 'trouble?' which
had been made in the trial 'Notes': 'shall I answer all the questions
sent me by letter?'[129] By thus modifying and obscuring his father's
attractively self-irreverent tone, Hallam effectively and perhaps
deliberately diminished any advance deprecation of what had by
this time become so largely his own work.

That Hallam believed his modifications to be in the best interests
of the reader and hence of his father's reputation there seems no
reason to doubt: even Dakyns found the phrasing of some of the
original observations to be confusing or beside the point.[130] But
Hallam's almost lifelong experience of intimate and intensive
participation in the construction of his father as both a public and a
private figure—his realization, at some level, that the Tennyson of
the *Memoir* was in a real sense his own creation—must long since
have eroded such distinctions, and he can scarcely have been
thinking only of the annotations specifically identified as editorial
when suggesting to his publishers that 'Edited by Hallam Lord
Tennyson' should appear on the 1913 title-page: 'As I have written
more than half the Notes—your suggested title wd not be true—
merely "Annotated by the Author".'[131] In such circumstances it

seems reasonable to assume that, where discrepancies occur, the
Memoir's versions of Tennyson's observations are likely to be
closer to what he actually said or wrote than the conscientiously
elaborated 'authorial notes' ultimately published as such. By the
same logic, the 'trial' notes and the printed and manuscript
Materials could well contain versions more nearly authentic still,
and Hallam's successive steps towards the final forms of the notes
and the *Memoir* alike will always need to be retraced by scholars in
search of such authenticity. And yet it is impossible to think of
Hallam as being other than exceptionally well motivated and
qualified for the completion of the tasks explicitly or implicitly
entrusted to him, to imagine anyone better placed to exercise
authority in this father's stead, or to doubt that the substance of the
annotations for whose wording he was partly or wholly responsible
had indeed originated with the poet himself. The 1913 one-volume
edition, including as it did a shorter, rewritten 'Memoir', the
complete works, and the finally elaborated annotations, was at
once the conclusion and the culmination of Hallam's publishing
endeavours, and there were ample grounds for his satisfaction in its
comprehensive representation of 'the grandness, the unity, the
nobility' of his father's life.[132]

Hallam Tennyson necessarily bore a particular responsibility for
the posthumous fate of his father's text and was sharply aware of
Tennyson's often-stated distaste for the publication of rejected
poems and readings. A visitor in 1890 recorded the poet as
speaking vehemently 'of the diseased craving to have all the trifles
of a man of genius preserved, and of the positive crime of
publishing what a poet had himself deliberately suppressed',[133] and
in the *Memoir* itself Hallam wrote of the 'love of bibliomaniacs for
first editions' as filling his father with horror, such editions being
'obviously in many cases the worst editions'.[134] Hallam's emphasis
on these points co-exists somewhat uneasily with his inclusion in
the *Memoir*—as again in the notes to the editions of 1907–8 and
1913—of previously unpublished juvenilia and of those rejected
stanzas from 'The Palace of Art' which had previously appeared
only as footnotes to the edition of 1832. He could, indeed, cite
Jowett as having advised him to print the childhood fragments[135]
and Tennyson himself as having countenanced the reprinting of the
stanzas from 'The Palace of Art',[136] and he must have known that

these latter could not in any case enjoy extended protection under the current copyright laws. It seems remarkable, even so, that he should have recognized no contradiction between his deliberate preservation and publication of juvenilia and rejected readings and his insistence upon Tennyson's desire to be represented only by his authorized final canon in its final form. That he did value, preserve, and print manuscript and notebook materials is now a matter for rejoicing, but it could scarcely have put him in either a legal or a moral position to object, in 1900, to the profusion of variants included in *The Early Poems of Alfred Lord Tennyson*, edited by the despised J. Churton Collins.[137]

The disdain for 'bibliomaniacs' and their obsession with first editions was shared by Hardy, among others, and is not in itself absurd. But within the *Memoir* the position is promptly undercut by the assertion that, in Tennyson's own case,

very often what is published as the latest edition has been the original version in his first manuscript, so that there is no possibility of really tracing the history of what may seem to be a new word or a new passage. 'For instance,' he said, 'in "Maud" a line in the first edition was "I will bury myself in *my books*, and the Devil may pipe to his own," which was afterwards altered to "I will bury myself *in myself*, etc.".': this was highly commended by the critics as an improvement on the *original* reading—but it was actually in the first MS draft of the poem.'[138]

Although no manuscript of *Maud* containing the 'in myself' reading appears to have survived,[139] Tennyson's claim to have made such a late return to an early reading is entirely consistent with his frequent self-borrowings[140] and with his intense but often vacillating attention to the detail of his poems both before and after their initial publication. Edgar F. Shannon and Christopher Ricks have demonstrated Tennyson's return to something close to his earliest conception of 'The Charge of the Light Brigade' even after the poem had been collected into a volume,[141] and recent critical editions of *Maud* and *In Memoriam* reveal lines of textual transmission perfectly capable of looping back to reinstate individual readings or entire stanzas previously abandoned.[142]

Tennyson's habitual retention of his manuscripts and working notebooks was undoubtedly a factor in such returns to his own creative past, but he seems for the most part to have depended on acts of memory rather than on reference to actual documents. He had a profound faith in the eventual retrievability of memories once laid down, reportedly declaring to one visitor: 'I believe that everything which happens to us we remember; it is all stored up somewhere to come forth again upon occasion, though it may seem to be forgotten . . .'[143] And there is ample testimony to the retentiveness of his memory even at the very end of his life: Bram Stoker, consulting with him in April 1892 about Irving's stage production of *Becket*, found that he 'knew every word of the play'.[144] The better Tennyson's memory for his own verse, however, the likelier it seems that his occasions of deliberate textual reconsideration were compromised by the recollection of alternative readings earlier contemplated or even for a time preferred. There is little doubt, in fact, that the continued efficiency of Tennyson's long-term memory—constantly renewed by the revision of successive collected editions and at least potentially reinforceable by reference back to old notebooks—made a considerable contribution to the persistent fluidity and indeterminacy of his texts, right to the end of his career, even while severely limiting the possibilities of a genuine, as opposed to merely imagined, re-entry into the originary experience.

Given Tennyson's combination of restless, unresting textual concern with scarcely diminished creative engagement, there seems something more than usually arbitrary about the (so to speak) externally imposed cessation of Tennyson's work on his texts and his 'notes' at the particular moment of his death. By the same token, there is perhaps a touch of the chimerical about the attempts of modern editors to identify the collective edition with the best claims to be regarded as the final authorial text. It is of course true that the last of his hitherto reversible textual interventions can be said to attain by their very irreversibility something of a testamentary status: 'And sacred is the latest word', he had written of his dead son in 'To the Marquis of Dufferin and Ava', less than five years before his own death.[145] But for the great majority of the poems that status—that steady state—is likely to have been achieved in an edition published long before Tennyson's actual death, and any variant appearing in a later text could conceivably be the result of compositorial error, damage to the stereotype plates, or any of the other hazards that text is heir to.

It is not in itself extraordinary that Tennyson, in addition to providing authorial notes to his poems and authorizing the production of a *Memoir* designed to 'preclude the chance of further and unauthentic biographies', should also have sought the exclusive perpetuation of the final texts of the poems themselves. He had always shown an almost obsessive concern with precision and 'correctness', not merely in word-usage, pronunciation, intonation, and cadence, but also in references to time, distance, geography, astronomy, and a myriad other matters of fact—niceties, minor in themselves, that may nevertheless have signalled the underlying presence of profound insecurities originating in childhood and in subsequent fears of mental instability. Despite the elaborate support system devised and maintained by his wife and son—or perhaps because dependence upon such a system did not prevent him from recognizing it for what it was—Tennyson seems always to have lacked confidence in his work and his eventual fame, and may have genuinely feared that the publication of rejected material might, in some Greshamite fashion, tend to drive out of circulation what he himself had wished to preserve: he was certainly reported as saying, in 1890, that 'If all the contents of a poet's waste-basket were taken out and printed, and issued in a volume, one result would be that the things which he had disowned would be read by many to whom the great things he had written would be unknown.'[146]

It is none the less possible that Tennyson's insistence on the sanctity of his authorized text has been somewhat over-stated. The *Memoir* stands as the principal source for his views on this as on so many other matters, and it is not necessary to challenge the essential accuracy of Hallam's reporting of such statements in order to suspect him of having given them a disproportionate emphasis. Tennyson does indeed appear to have destroyed all his copies of *Poems by Two Brothers* as a gesture of wished-for obliteration,[147] but the legal action he took against Dykes Campbell's *Poems, MDCCCXXX./MDCCCXXXIII.*, a pirated edition of the suppressed poems left stranded in Tennyson's earliest volumes,[148] and against Richard Herne Shepherd's piracies of *The Lover's Tale*[149] needs to be read—like Browning's participation in another action involving Shepherd—as little more than a necessary assertion of his own rights and those of his publishers.

Hallam Tennyson undoubtedly regarded the *Memoir* and the

authorial notes as tasks he was at once obligated and privileged to pursue and complete, the published results as simultaneously acts of memorialization and the means by which his father's work and reputation could be propelled securely forward into an infinite future. The poems themselves, on the other hand, had been so long, so intently, and so repeatedly the object of Tennyson's own scrutiny during his lifetime that Hallam could justifiably think of them as finished business. He remained financially as well as filially interested in keeping Tennyson's works continuously in print in a variety of editions, and he was vigilant in ensuring that his father's intentions, as he understood them, were being faithfully observed— adding, for example, an important line, 'Ideal manhood closed in real man', to the Epilogue to *Idylls of the King* as published in the essentially ceremonial De Luxe edition of 1899,[150] and protesting to George Craik of Macmillan 'in deep *anguish* of spirit' at the placing of *The Foresters* instead of *The Death of Oenone* at the end of the one-volume *Complete Works* of 1894.[151] But, despite his role in the preparation of the Eversley Edition of 1907–8, he seems to have had neither the wish nor, perhaps, the vanity to engage with the existing texts in any extensive fashion.

The nine-volume Eversley Edition was handsomely bound, incorporated the full complement of authorial notes, and was clearly intended to serve as the 'standard' embodiment of Tennyson's final intentions as more fully realized by his son. And the presence on its title-pages of the authenticating 'Edited by Hallam, Lord Tennyson' has caused it to be widely regarded as possessing a uniquely and comprehensively authoritative status. The bulk of the poetic text, however, as distinct from the authorial notes, appears in fact to have been printed—with much renumbering of volumes, some rearrangement (hence repagination) of their contents, and a few additions—from the plates of the so-called New Library Edition, of which eight volumes appeared in 1888 and a ninth, containing the three subsequently published titles, in 1896.[152] George A. Macmillan, writing to George Brett of the firm's New York office on 9 November 1907, was quite explicit as to the use of 'the plates of the existing Library Edition in 9 volumes' and offered, if necessary, to supply a duplicate set.[153] This is not necessarily to say that no alterations were made to the plates or that Hallam Tennyson read proof only on the notes. But it does clearly suggest that his work on the Eversley Edition—as on the one-volume annotated edition of 1913—was overwhelmingly focused on the authorial notes, and that he thought of his claim of editorial participation as applying primarily, and perhaps exclusively, to those notes for whose sake, essentially, the edition existed.[154]

Like Browning, Tennyson in making his will trusted absolutely to the loyalty and discretion of his son, and in bequeathing to Hallam 'all my manuscripts Literary Works and Copyrights' he left no formal testamentary directions as to their future fate.[155] The *Memoir*, therefore, again becomes the primary, though not exclusive, source for knowledge of Tennyson's antipathy to variant readings, chiefly, it would seem, because of their distracting effect upon the reader rather than of any embarrassing revelations of past ineptitudes: 'For himself many passages in Wordsworth and other poets had been entirely spoilt by the modern habit of giving every various reading along with the text.'[156] It was, in any case, Hallam Tennyson who dictated the restrictions which for so long inhibited scholarly use of the Tennyson manuscripts at Trinity College, Cambridge. The first of these, the draft manuscript of *In Memoriam* given by Tennyson to Sir John Simeon, was returned to Hallam by Sir John's widow and then jointly presented to Trinity in January 1898. Lady Simeon's letter of gift of 9 December 1897 simply, if somewhat ambiguously, specified that 'according to Lord Tennyson's wish, no copy of it nor of any part of it is ever made—nor made public'.[157] Hallam's complementary letter, written a day later, was altogether fuller, praising Lady Simeon's generosity and explaining that while his father had wished the manuscript to go eventually to Trinity he had also wanted to place certain limitations on its use: 'My Father however, owing to his hatred of the publication of his "various readings" (which he thought confused the final version of the texts) wished that NO copy of it, or of any part of it should ever be taken and that nothing in it which has not been published, should ever be published.'[158]

These conditions were accepted word-for-word by the College, appearing on the printed notice which long accompanied the *In Memoriam* draft in its glass display-case,[159] and Hallam essentially repeated them when making a larger gift to Trinity in June 1924, specifying in a third-person statement that the manuscripts were being presented 'on the understanding which is in accordance with his Father's objections to variorum readings such as those which had spoilt Wordsworth for him that no one shall be allowed to publish these Manuscripts or use them for the purpose of variorum readings or do more than take short notes of them'.[160] Tennyson's dislike of the publication of variant readings of Wordsworth was again invoked in Hallam's will, and the persistent and, indeed, exclusive repetition of this one instance prompts speculation as to how far Hallam's entire policy may have been based on little more than a single remark by that father whose every word he held sacred: Edward FitzGerald, after all, recorded Tennyson as saying on one occasion, 'I like those old Variorum Classics—all the Notes make the Text look precious.'[161]

There was, of course, an economic element in Hallam Tennyson's position. He had been dismayed by the decline of his father's reputation—he lived to see the publication not only of Lytton Strachey's *Eminent Victorians* in 1918 but also of Harold Nicolson's more specifically unsympathetic *Tennyson* of 1923— and by the correspondingly sharp reductions in those royalties on which the family income so largely depended. By 1903 the annual royalties from Macmillan had already fallen from a peak of £10,370 in the year of Tennyson's death to a relatively modest £2,615,[162] and much of Hallam's correspondence with the firm was taken up with negotiations for higher royalties on both sides of the Atlantic.[163] While, therefore, his insistence upon the integrity of his father's texts remained as dutiful as ever—just as, in his correspondence, he maintained his almost invariable capitalization of 'my Father'—it was reinforced by an entirely understandable desire to retain control over what remained of the Tennysonian publishing empire and to prevent, in particular, the creation of new and textually discrepant editions which might potentially generate new and usurping copyrights and at the same time disturb the tight mesh of texts and 'author's notes' that had been established by the editions of 1907–8 and 1913. The publication around the turn of the century of such volumes as Churton Collins's editions of *The Early Poems* and *In Memoriam, The Princess, and Maud* had been made possible by the then limitation of copyright to forty-two years after the publication of a work or to seven years after the author's death, whichever was the sooner, and while Hallam's immediate anxieties were relieved by the enactment in 1911 of an extension of copyright to a period of fifty years after the author's death, he was perhaps, by the time of his own death, already anticipating for his heirs the eventual expiration date of virtually all the Tennyson copyrights—apart from those pertaining to the posthumously published annotations—in 1942.

Hallam Tennyson lost his two younger sons in action during the First World War.[164] Lionel, the eldest, was wounded three times but survived. Audrey Tennyson also died during the war years, and in 1918, multiply bereft, Hallam married as his second wife May (or Mary) Emily Hichens,[165] intricately associated with the memory of his father, and thus with his own earlier years, as the niece of Thoby Prinsep and the wife and widow of Andrew Hichens, both close family friends. May Prinsep in her youth had been one of her aunt Julia Margaret Cameron's photographic subjects;[166] Hallam and his father had shared a yachting holiday with the Hichenses in 1889;[167] and Andrew Hichens was one of those who walked with Hallam and Audrey alongside Tennyson's body as it was carried by waggon from Aldworth on the first stage of its journey to Westminster.[168] If it seems somehow inevitable that Hallam should have turned in such a direction at such a moment, it is equally unsurprising that the new Lady Tennyson should, like her predecessor, have lent herself to the continuing work of memorialization.[169]

Aldworth was sold, not altogether inappropriately, to an Indian prince, the Gaekwar of Baroda, soon after the First World War,[170] but when Hallam Tennyson died in December 1928 the obituary in *The Times* was able to speak not only of his extraordinary 'filial piety' both before and after Tennyson's death but also of his preservation of Farringford in as nearly as possible the condition (already sufficiently antiquated) in which his father had maintained it: 'To cross the threshold of Farringford was, indeed, like returning as if by some magic into that Victorian age which now seems so remote. Time, in that house in the hollow, seemed to have stood still; within was no anachronism, but everything, pictures, furniture, and family treasures and relics, helped to create the illusion of the past.'[171] Hallam's entire dedication to his parents' memory emerges no less poignantly from his testamentary attempt to secure the future of Farringford as a permanent memorial, establishing a 'Farringford Trust Fund' from the sale of some cottages, identifying most of the significant contents as 'The Farringford Heirlooms', and seeking by all available testamentary means to ensure 'that the estate may not be sold it being my earnest desire that neither the estate nor the articles hereinafter declared to be heirlooms so as to devolve along with the estate should be sold as I wish the same to be kept in the family and to remain intact'.[172]

The 3rd Lord Tennyson's claim to fame, however, was that he had captained England at cricket, and neither his tastes nor his temperament inclined him to live in a house where his father had so long maintained 'an atmosphere of veneration' that was 'almost religious' in its solemnity.[173] Farringford had in any case become, as Charles Tennyson later recalled, a 'dark, rather dilapidated old house' on which a great deal of money needed to be spent,[174] and during the 1930s, inhabited only occasionally by various members of the family,[175] it went steadily downhill. It was eventually sold for use as an hotel, and in some respects, and in the long run, the change of ownership has proved largely beneficial. A substantial dining-room has indeed been built out at the back of the house and small cottages for hotel guests erected among the trees, but the fabric is now well maintained and the front elevation remains essentially unaltered—except that the wellingtonia planted by Garibaldi during his visit in 1864 has become a pitiful sight. In the immediate post-war period, however, the summerhouse in Maiden's Croft, looking out towards High Down, was allowed to deteriorate, collapse, and ultimately perish,[176] and a letter published in *The Times Literary Supplement* in October 1949 complained of the use of the poet's library as a junk-filled hotel box-room, 'his desk and chairs covered with dust, and other relics such as the original tall hat of the "Vanity Fair" cartoon (with hat box), his pipe rack and pipes, the night cap in which he died, the funeral shroud and laurel wreath lying about in disorder'.[177] Most of the Farringford books, including a substantial section from the library of the poet's father, had in fact been removed and stored before the house was sold,[178] but some hundreds remained, many of them early editions of Victorian popular novels, and there can be no doubt that books and perhaps other items were permanently 'borrowed' by hotel guests: four Eversley volumes inscribed by Hallam Tennyson to his nephew Aubrey certainly turned up on the shelves of a bookshop in Ripon in the late 1950s.

Hallam's will had confirmed that the Trinity manuscripts were neither to be removed nor 'used for copying purposes or for recording Variorum readings', and it included the fuller, final manuscript of *In Memoriam* among the 'Farringford Heirlooms' passed on to Lionel Tennyson as the heir of the estate and inheritor of the title. Hallam left the manuscripts of *Queen Mary*, *Harold*, and *Becket* to his nephew Alfred as the 'Alfred Heirlooms', while the important group of manuscripts and notebooks still remaining was similarly entrusted, as the 'Charles Heirlooms', to Alfred's younger brother Charles, in whom Hallam had correctly identified the member of the next generation most likely to uphold the Tennysonian tradition. By attempting to give the manuscripts the status of heirlooms Hallam obviously sought to keep them, like Farringford, within the family, to be handed down, like Farringford, from generation to generation. Superficially, he must be deemed to have failed, in that very few of the documentary and other materials he passed on to his immediate heirs can now be in family hands. But in his historical role as the preserver of those same materials and their transmitter to posterity Hallam has proved to be quite extraordinarily successful. The rich collection of manuscripts and notebooks which once comprised the 'Charles Heirlooms' is now securely in the Houghton Library, having been sold to Harvard by Sir Charles Tennyson (as he had become) in the mid-1950s,[179] and a combination of good fortune, inspired initiatives, the generosity of Tennyson relatives, and the determination of modern scholars and readers has enabled a remarkable proportion of the original Tennysonian archive to find its way, together with much related material, into the attractive and efficient setting of the Tennyson Research Centre at Lincoln. The establishment of the Centre in the early 1960s was made possible by the willingness of the 4th Lord Tennyson (eldest son of Lionel the cricketer) to deposit on 'permanent loan' a great mass of Tennyson material that included the bulk of the books, documents, and other items once numbered among the 'Farringford Heirlooms'. Of particular importance were that final manuscript of *In Memoriam*, the books from Tennyson's library, the several thousand letters that survived the destruction attendant upon the preparation of the *Memoir*, and virtually the entire record of Hallam Tennyson's multi-stage progress towards the *Memoir*'s compilation and publication.

Other significant materials came to the Centre from other members of the Tennyson and Tennyson d'Eyncourt family—especially notable being the deposit by the family of Alfred Browning Tennyson of those manuscripts of *Queen Mary*, *Harold*, and *Becket* once designated by Hallam Tennyson as the 'Alfred

Heirlooms'[180]—and the serried ranks of books and boxed materials on the Centre's shelves became, as Robert Bernard Martin has movingly observed, sufficient by their 'sheer quantity' to 'strike terror into the heart of the Tennyson student seeing [them] for the first time'.[181] A crisis arose in 1980 when financial exigencies obliged Lord Tennyson's Trustees to put up for public auction many of the more important items, headed by the *In Memoriam* manuscript, which had earlier been deposited in the Centre, but energetic and well- and widely supported fundraising efforts made possible the recovery, by purchase, not only of the *In Memoriam* MS but of many (if by no means all) of the other manuscript and archival materials as well.[182]

The editors of *The Letters of Alfred Lord Tennyson* were perhaps a little ungenerous in suggesting that 'the death of Hallam Tennyson did as much for Tennyson scholarship as the death of Arthur Henry Hallam did for Tennyson's poetry'.[183] For all his destruction and misrepresentation of specifically biographical documents, Hallam was a determined preserver of working notebooks, manuscripts, corrected proofs, and other pre-publication stages of textual transmission, and those crowded shelves in the Tennyson Research Centre are an eloquent if indirect memorial to his custodial zeal, and one that he might well have appreciated. And even if some of the thirty volumes of photographic facsimiles from many different collections that make up *The Tennyson Archive*, edited by Christopher Ricks and Aidan Day, could be said to bear witness to Hallam Tennyson's testamentary defeats, he would surely have welcomed so ambitious a scholarly attempt—comparable to that embodied in *The Browning Collections*—to temper the consequences of archival dispersion. Hallam's concern for the preservation and transmission of the documentary record clearly suggests that he foresaw a time—after all copyrights had expired and the immediate reaction against the Victorians had run its course—when such materials would provide the basis for intensive scholarly investigation, hence for a full reinstatement and reprojection of his father's work and reputation. His harsh (though now evaded) restrictions upon the use of the Trinity manuscripts were at least protective both in intent and in their result, and his will, while recalling Tennyson's dislike of variant readings, did not in fact prohibit publication of the manuscripts and notebooks being passed on to the next generation.[184]

In Andrew Wheatcroft's *The Tennyson Album* there is a fine late photograph of Tennyson and his wife sitting side by side on a sofa—he looking somewhat concernedly at her, she gazing fixedly forward as if at some private vision inaccessible to others— and of Hallam standing protectively above and behind them, wearing an overcoat, ready for all contingencies, and looking intently and a little suspiciously out of the picture as if at some potentially troublesome intruder—interviewer, tourist, grandchild, servant, or even the photographer himself.[185] It was a position from which Hallam could be said never to have broken free, unsmiling as he remained in all his photographs, profoundly conservative in his views and instincts, almost pathological in his devotion to his parents' memory,[186] and dutiful rather than ambitious in his acceptance of public positions. The stark practical issues he was forced to confront as a result of changing economic conditions, increased taxation, and the decline in his father's reputation and royalties may have somewhat compromised the purity of Hallam's motives over the longer run, but in the immediate aftermath of his father's death it was clearly in a spirit of the most absolute dedication, and with a zeal born of the long-withheld prospect of independent authorship, that he undertook the tasks of producing a complexly collaborative idealization of the poet's life, securing against all foreseeable futures the poet's preferred texts and their accompanying annotations, and preserving for posterity the objects most closely associated with the poet and at least the more important of his notebooks and manuscripts:

> This is my son, mine own Telemachus,
> To whom I leave the sceptre and the isle—
> Well-loved of me,   *   *   *   *
>
> Most blameless is he, centred in the sphere
> Of common duties, decent not to fail
> In offices of tenderness, and pay
> Meet adoration to my household gods,
> When I am gone. He works his work, I mine.[187]

The spirit of the times has undergone many personality changes since Tennyson's day, and Hallam's acts of destruction and obscurantism have not in practice benefited his father's reputation either as a man or as a poet. Nor can they be readily forgiven by those scholars and readers persistent and sensitive enough to discover in and through the poetry itself a Tennyson altogether stronger in voice and presence than the *Memoir* ever ventured to suggest. Even so, 'Though much is taken, much abides'.[188] Farringford survives, with some at least of its associations still vivid, the resources for the serious study of Tennyson remain richer than those for almost any other of the major Victorians, and Hallam Tennyson must be allowed to have achieved a remarkable degree of success in his pursuit of the ambitions he most deliberately set himself—in that biographers, confronted by the destruction of source materials, have only rarely been able to break free of the patterns established by the *Memoir*, and editors, though well supplied with pre-publication witnesses, have none the less continued to respect the authority of Tennyson's final text, even while disagreeing amongst themselves as to where, precisely, that text most authentically resides.

Henry James

ONE of the last pieces written by Henry James was the essay entitled 'Mr. and Mrs. James T. Fields', dictated and then redictated to his typist, Theodora Bosanquet, and published in the July 1915 issues of both the *Atlantic Monthly* and the *Cornhill*— but with the audience of the Boston-based *Atlantic* principally in view. Looking back on his memories of Boston at the height of its literary efflorescence, James rejoiced in the way in which that distant time now 'all densely foreshortens, it positively all melts beautifully together, and I square myself in the state of mind of an authority not to be questioned. In other words, my impression of the golden age was a first-hand one, not a second or a third; and since those with whom I shared it have dropped off one by one, . . . I fear there is no arrogance of authority that I am not capable of taking on.'[1]

It was entirely characteristic of this late period of James's life that he should be engaged in autobiographical reminiscence within the context, at once genuine and ostensible, of an act of memorialization, celebratory of the personal qualities and historical significances of friends now dead from times now past. No less characteristic— except in the bluntness of the overt acknowledgement—was his assertion of absolute creative authority over the always questionable materials thus thrown up by memory. In recognizing, within the essay itself, that to turn one's attention 'from any present hour to a past that has become distant is always to have to look through overgrowths and reckon with perversions',[2] James displayed an understanding of the fundamental nature and functioning of autobiographical memory that subsequent psychological research has not notably advanced. He knew that recall was never total, that it was always affected by subsequent experience, especially of a repetitious or analogous character, and that it was almost inevitably constructive,[3] impelling conscious or unconscious supplementation of its own necessarily incomplete data.

A few years earlier, in 1910, James's autobiographical fragment 'The Turning Point of My Life' had referred back to the suggestion (originating with his old friend William Dean Howells) that the crucial moment of decision in his career had occurred when he withdrew from the Harvard Law School in 1863 and sent his first literary pieces to the *Atlantic Monthly*: 'Let me say at once [James wrote] that I welcomed the suggestion—for the kindly grace of it, the element of antique charm and bedimmed romance that it placed, straight away, at the disposal of my memory; by which I mean that I wondered whether I mightn't find, on ingenious reflection, that my youth *had* in fact enjoyed that amount of drama.'[4] Memory, made virtually synonymous with 'ingenious reflection', was thus openly acknowledged by James as an active and creative force, capable of exploiting for literary effect or personal satisfaction the associative values retroactively bestowed upon past events by the (often nostalgic) perspectives of the present. Capable, too, of generating coherent images, narratives, and explanations by a process of quasi-archaeological extrapolation— at once evidential, inferential, and imaginative—from the perhaps vivid but probably illusive fragments of the actually remembered.

There is, of course, a substantial sense in which all of James's work—as novelist, critic, and travel-writer—had depended from the beginning upon a constant sounding of the resources of memory. His notebooks consist, precisely, of a series of *aides-mémoire*, many of them already in course of being 'ingeniously' worked up for fictional purposes: they served—though perhaps not to the degree originally envisaged—as 'a record of passing impressions, of all that comes, that goes, that I see, and feel, and observe. To catch and keep something of life—that's what I mean.'[5] His extraordinary output of personal correspondence might similarly be said to have represented a continual seizure of the passing moment, a technique for capturing and verbalizing immediate experience and emotion and so enhancing its permanence in the memory, hence its potential recoverability. Percy Lubbock saw even the notorious deliberateness of James's speech in just such terms:

Henry James never took anything as it came; the thing that happened to him was merely the point of departure for a deliberate, and as time went on a more and more masterly, creative energy, which could never leave a sight or sound of any kind until it had been looked at and listened to with absorbed attention, pondered in thought, linked with its associations, and which did not spend itself until the remembrance had been crystallised in expression, so that it could then be appropriated like a tangible object. To recall his habit of talk is to become aware that he never ceased creating his life in this way as it was lived; he was always engaged in the poetic fashioning of experience, turning his share of impressions into rounded and lasting images.[6]

James's interest in autobiographical writing for its own acknow-ledged sake seems to have been particularly associated with his acceptance of the invitation to write a biography of the American sculptor William Wetmore Story, with the disturbing approach and arrival, on 15 April 1903, of his own sixtieth birthday and seventh decade, and with the onset, largely prompted by that same awareness of advancing age, of a desire to reassert control of his past and present life by making an extended and extensive visit to his native United States. Even ahead of that sixtieth birthday, in a letter that spoke also of a yearning to return once more to Italy 'before I descend into the deep tomb', James on New Year's Day of 1903 told a friend that he remained 'very much where you left me last,—save that I am a great deal older and *plus gros* and *plus pesé* and *plus solitaire*'.[7]

The writing of *William Wetmore Story and His Friends* was for James neither a happy nor an especially satisfying experience. He had little time for Story's sculpture, still less for his verse, and undertook the biography only under pressure from Story's family as reinforced by an advance payment from the publisher and by a certain interest in Story's long years of Roman expatriation: 'I shall live & write it [James declared in 1897]—among many old friends & old ghosts'.[8] It was not until five years later, in the late summer of 1902—after he had completed *The Ambassadors* and *The Wings of the Dove* and was writing some of the stories later included in *The Better Sort*[9]—that James finally turned his attention, first to the documents with which he had been supplied by the Story family, and then to the actual work of composition. The diary of Agnes Weld, James's amanuensis at this date, first mentions the preparatory copying of letters on 25 August 1902; on 27 September she writes, 'Copying finished so really begin W. W. Story'.[10]

James evidently went through the letters available to him—predominantly, of course, letters written *to* Story—and had the more interesting of them typed up. He then used the transcribed letters, essentially in chronological order, as the basis of a dictated

narrative, not hesitating to make extensive excisions from the
original documents (with or without ellipsis points) and minor
adjustments to the wording,[11] but extorting from each item
whatever it could be made to yield in the way of local or period
'colour', personal reminiscence, general reflection, or biographical
insight into either Story himself or, just as frequently, the actual
author of the letter in question. It was a method that he was to
adopt again in his acknowledged autobiographies, and that enabled
him on this occasion to tease out his meagre material[12] to the point
of filling two published volumes rather than the one 'of medium
size' he had originally projected.[13] The resulting structure, however, was inevitably loose, its transitions often tenuous, and since
Story's correspondents tended to be of greater interest to James
than Story himself the whole focus and emphasis of the narrative
was for long stretches directed quite away from its ostensible
subject. Robert Browning, indeed, always a particular obsession of
James's, figures so prominently throughout that a recent critic has
seen him as the book's 'true centre' and 'informing presence'.[14]

Writing to Story's daughter-in-law on 6 January 1903, James
made an embarrassed attempt to justify his transformation of the
commemorative enterprise into something rather different from
what she and the rest of the Story family had not unreasonably
anticipated:

All the material I received from you has been of course highly useful—
indispensable; yet, none the less, all of it put together was not material for
a Biography pure and simple. The subject itself didn't lend itself to *that*, in
the strict sense of the word; and I had to make out, for myself, what my
material *did* lend itself to. . . . I have looked at the picture, as it were, given
me by all your material, *as* a picture—the image or evocation, charming,
heterogeneous, and a little ghostly, of a great cluster of people, a society
practically extinct, with Mr. and Mrs. Story, naturally, all along, the
centre, the pretext, so to speak, and the *point d'appui*. This course was the
only one open to me—it was imposed with absolute logic.[15]

Since Story's 'artistic and literary baggage were of the slightest and
the materials for a biography *nil*', James observed to the Duchess of
Sutherland towards the end of that same year, 'I had really to *invent*
a book, patching the thing together and eking it out with barefaced
irrelevancies—starting above all *any* hare, however small, that
might lurk by the way.'[16]

James's method was in fact rather less random than his imagery suggests: the 'irrelevancies', seen from another angle, reveal themselves as precisely the connections perceived and established between the small matter of Story's life and achievement and the larger issues of expatriation, of pre-Civil War American innocence, and of transatlantic cultural relations. In this respect, clearly, James's appropriation of the Story material, kept marginally within the bounds of 'authorized' biography by its discreet withholding of any ultimate dismissal of Story's talent, can be said to have been conducted in the interests not so much of mere professional book-making as of retrospective self-discovery. One old friend, the historian Henry Adams, certainly saw it in such terms: 'So you have written not Story's life, but your own and mine,' he wrote from Paris on 18 November 1903, '—pure autobiography,—the more keen for what is beneath, implied, intelligible only to me, and half a dozen other people still living; like Frank Boott: who knew our Boston, London and Rome in the fifties and sixties. You make me curl up, like a trodden-on worm. Improvised Europeans, we were, and—Lord God!—how thin!'[17]

James had, of course, known many of the Story circle, even apart from Browning and Story himself, and within so centrifugal a work the transitions were easily made between analogical allusion to the expatriate experience and direct autobiographical recollection and reflection. The actual process of textual construction is frequently referred to—'I only regret', says James at one point, 'that in respect to these liveliest middle years I find few letters or journals at hand'[18]—and at one point a letter of Story's is acknowledged as having been quoted chiefly for the sake of its reference to a figure whom James recalled from his own childhood with an excitement at first inexplicable but eventually revealed by the ferretings of memory to have derived from an association with Edgar Allan Poe: 'Remembrance, I find, clutches at him with an eagerness not explained by the patent facts, so that I wonder at the obsession till there suddenly breaks a light . . .'[19] Through experiences such as this—simultaneously seized upon as material and fascinatedly described as process—the writing of the Story volumes taught James a good deal about both the nature and the uses of memory, especially as stimulated by documentary materials. He had also discovered how to exploit such materials, omitting or altering what was not germane to his purposes and freely filling out the gaps in the surviving documentary record, and he had not hesitated to take deliberate possession of the proffered subject in the name of creative necessity, imperialistically subjugating the rights of the lesser to those of the greater power by imposing a narrative of general interest and implication upon a particular instance initially perceived as distinctly lacking in either.

Further lessons of essentially the same sort were learned during the course of that long-awaited expedition to the United States, begun in August 1904—after the completion of *The Golden Bowl*—and announced as undertaken, like the as yet delayed return to Italy, 'in anticipation of the tomb'.[20] If he did not go soon, James told his brother William in May 1903, he would lose the impulse 'under the mere blight of incipient senile decay. If I go at all I must go before I'm too old, and, above all, before I mind being older.'[21] Ostensibly an exploration of the present, with *The American Scene* and a never-completed companion volume as its anticipated product, it was more profoundly a journey in search of a national and personal past. And if such a journey was by no means risk-free—as is suggested by the ghostly encounter in 'The Jolly Corner' between the visiting expatriate and the American self he might have stayed home and become—it at least provided more substantial occasions for the sounding, in *The American Scene*, of that elegiac note rather artificially sustained in *William Wetmore Story and His Friends*.

While James's travels were actually in progress, his prospective material proved more recalcitrant than anticipated, and he reported back to Edmund Gosse on 16 February 1905 that he was finding it difficult, 'with perpetual movement and perpetual people and very few concrete objects of nature or art to make use of for assimilation', to get any of his impressions written down: 'I see with a kind of despair that I shall be able to do here little more than get my saturation, soak my intellectual sponge—reserving the squeezing-out for the subsequent deep, ah, the so yearned-for peace of Lamb House.'[22] The few notes of James's that do in fact survive from the American visit say essentially the same thing in more positive terms: 'Everything sinks in: nothing is lost', and it will therefore be possible, back home at Lamb House, 'to [plunge] my hand, my arm, *in*, deep and far, and up to the shoulder—into the heavy bag of remembrance—of suggestion—of imagination—of art—and fish out every little figure and felicity, every little fact and fancy that can be to my purpose'.[23] James not only equates memory here both with imagination and with art but his forceful image of simultaneous retrieval and discovery is strongly suggestive of the apparently random procedures which Theodora Bosanquet described him as employing some years later during the dictation of *A Small Boy and Others* and the other autobiographies. For the 'volumes of memories', she recalled shortly after James's death, no preliminary work had been required:

He plunged straight into the stream of the past, without a doubt or an hesitation. The reading over each morning of the pages written the day before was all the stimulus needed to start him on a fresh effort to render adequately the depth and the delicacy of his early impressions. After about an hour of conscious effort he would often be caught on a rising wave of inspiration and would get up from his armchair and pace up and down the room, sounding out his periods in tones of resonant assurance. He was then beyond the reach of unconnected sights or sounds. . . . He was impervious to them. The only thing that could arrest him was the escape of the word he wanted to use.[24]

Just such a rapt absorption into 'the stream of the past' seems also to have characterized much of James's work on the New York Edition of the Novels and Tales of Henry James, the great project that was already under way at the time when Theodora Bosanquet came to do his typing, including typing from his dictation, in the autumn of 1907. Bosanquet noted in her diary that the first morning of her employment by James, 11 October 1907, was given over to what was evidently a re-dictation—'in the tone of a personal reminiscence', as she acutely registered—of a portion of the Preface to *The Tragic Muse*.[25] Three days later, however, when James, reassured as to Bosanquet's skills, began dictating the Preface to *The Awkward Age*, she noted with emphasis that he did so '*not* from previously written matter but straight away'.[26] Exasperatingly unspecific though the Bosanquet diary often becomes in its record of what soon became for its author a series of routine tasks, it leaves no doubt that this was for James a frequent and even standard method of attack. By the time work on *The American Scene* came to an end and James's attention turned squarely to the New York Edition he had become fully accustomed to relying on memory not merely as a source of 'material' but as a generative instrument and structuring principle: an initial plunge into the 'heavy bag of remembrance' could provide the stimulus for

developments whose subsequent direction would be largely determined by the partly unconscious, partly purposive, and finally
selective unlayering of memories either 'nested' in or around the
first or capable of being linked to it in some logical, chronological,
or associative fashion. It is not surprising, therefore, that so many
of the Edition's famous prefaces should find their starting- and
growth-points in James's recollections—accurate or otherwise—of
the circumstances of original composition and publication.

James had already had the gratification of seeing a fourteen-volume
collective edition of his novels and stories brought out by
Macmillan & Co., his regular London publishers, as early as 1883,
just a few years after his work had first begun to appear in England.
In welcoming the proposal his principal concern, characteristically
enough, had been that 'the books be as pretty as possible'. 'Can you
make them really pretty for 18 pence a volume?' he asked Frederick
Macmillan, four days after his fortieth birthday. 'I should like them
to be *charming*, and beg you to spare no effort to make them so.'[27]
But while the volumes were indeed attractively produced, their very
inexpensiveness and diminutive (16.5 × 10.5 cm.) format precluded their matching the kind of statement subsequently made by
Meredith's *édition de luxe*, by Stevenson's Edinburgh Edition, by
the Osgood, McIlvaine Wessex Novels edition of Hardy's fiction,
or by the several Kipling editions, one of them, the Outward
Bound, emanating from James's own American publishers, Charles
Scribner's Sons. During the years intervening between his fortieth
and sixtieth birthdays James had of course published many more
novels and stories and developed an ampler sense of his own
literary consequence; he had also become the increasingly grateful
client of James Brand Pinker, an exceptionally able representative
of the newly emerging profession of literary agent.[28] After finishing
work on *The Golden Bowl*, therefore, and before embarking for the
United States, James asked Pinker to explore more actively with
Charles Scribner's Sons of New York the interest they had earlier
expressed in an up-dated collective edition: 'I recollect our
conversation about the collected edition of Mr. Henry James'
books', wrote Pinker to Edward Burlingame of Scribner's on
3 August 1904, 'and I thought you would like to know that
Mr. James thinks the time for that has come. . . . Mr. James' idea is
to write for each volume a preface of a rather intimate, personal

character, and there is no doubt that such a preface would add greatly to the interest of the books.'[29] To which Burlingame rather ominously replied that while Scribner's remained interested in the project and hoped 'from every point of view of literature' that it could be carried out, 'it is undeniable that the commercial situation is much less favorable than at the time I first made my inquiry of you'.[30] It was an opposition, between authorial ambition and marketplace realism, which would run throughout the edition's history.[31]

Although *The Golden Bowl*, published by Scribner's in November 1904 and by Methuen in London four months later, proved to be the last novel James ever finished, it was also one of the better-selling,[32] and there is no indication that he thought of himself, then or later, as having completed his work in fiction, or that he envisaged the New York Edition as a specifically valedictory gesture. Even so, the timing of his decision to resume negotiations with Scribner's was undoubtedly affected by his sense of having reached—with the completion of the 'major phase' novels—a significant turning-point in his career and by his consciousness of being already in his seventh decade and of approaching, therefore, the limits of those 'middle years' of productive adult life beyond which 'the night cometh, when no man can work'.[33] Precisely relevant here, indeed, is 'The Middle Years', James's obviously self-referential and, to that extent, remarkably prescient story of the 1890s—first collected, appropriately enough, in the *Terminations* volume of 1895 and needing only very minor revision to fit it out for renewed service in the New York Edition armada.

The story's central character, Dencombe, a novelist approaching the end of his life, seems strikingly anticipatory of James's own final years in his dread of a 'surrender to silence, unvindicated and undivined', his yearning for 'a certain splendid "last manner," the very citadel, as it would prove, of his reputation, the stronghold into which his real treasure would be gathered', his frustration at the impossibility of a 'second chance', and his eventual, not altogether countervailing, acceptance of the proposition that no second chance is ever in fact available but only that first chance which is life itself, the span of 'the middle years'.[34] Most obviously and predictively autobiographical is the way in which Dencombe's identity is betrayed to his young admirer by the existence of pencilled revisions in the otherwise pristine pre-publication copy of his latest work, itself entitled (since James was perfectly familiar with the infinite regression of mirror-images) *The Middle Years*. Dencombe is presented, indeed, as 'a passionate corrector, a fingerer of style; the last thing he ever arrived at was a form final for himself. His ideal would have been to publish secretly, and then, on the published text, treat himself to the terrified revise, sacrificing always a first edition and beginning for posterity and even for the collectors, poor dears, with a second.'[35] Such contempt for the rawness of first editions is more often associated with authors such as Tennyson and Hardy whose popularity provided them with more frequent occasions for textual reconsideration, but James had certainly availed himself of his own relatively limited opportunities of that kind, and in the New York Edition he would reveal himself to be the most passionate of 'correctors'—the restlessness of his stylistic fingering emerging with particular vividness from the densely revised pages of his still extant working copy of *The American*.[36]

But James had first to identify the novels and stories whose texts would be thus scrutinized, and while he may once have yearned for a comprehensive reprinting of his works, he was now perfectly clear that he should proceed on the basis of the twin principles of selectivity and integration: the new 'Edition Définitive', he declared, would be 'collective (and *se*lective)',[37] so sifted as to retain 'nothing but fine gold'.[38] To thus project, Dencombe-like, a 'stronghold into which his real treasure would be gathered' was to take it for granted that certain works could and should be excluded. It is true that James did not think of himself as definitively rejecting all of the titles omitted from the New York Edition: he mentioned the possibility of 'a supplementary volume or two—putting quite new books aside' when writing to Scribner's in 1906,[39] and at the very end of his life, after the Edition had proved a financial failure, he could speak of it as 'rather truncated' and as a 'series' that had been arbitrarily 'stopped short . . . when a couple of dozen volumes were out'.[40] But in that same letter he reasserted his satisfaction with his original conception—'the artistic problem involved in my scheme was a deep & exquisite one, & moreover was, as I hold, very effectively solved'[41]—and there can be no doubt that he saw the power of deliberate non-inclusion as crucial to his desire that the Edition should present his achievement in the best possible light.

Although Leon Edel once suggested that James's original scheme for a twenty-three-volume set of the novels and stories had been conceived in conscious emulation of the twenty-three-volume collected Balzac,[42] Michael Anesko has since demonstrated that the New York Edition total was in fact arrived at by a process of negotiation and compromise between author and publisher and largely determined by such practical matters as the lengths of the texts James wished to include and the maximum wordage of the volumes the publishers were prepared to put on the market.[43] Once, however, the prospective complement of volumes had been agreed upon with Scribner's, and their contents at least tentatively decided, James devoted much care and persistence to the attempt to give the entire Edition a coherent and indeed shapely internal structure, although in practice the difficulty of fitting the shorter works into volumes of a pre-determined length eventually enforced the addition of a twenty-fourth volume and a series of related last-minute redistributions of the stories James had selected.[44]

If James's acts of exclusion from the Edition were designed to achieve the banishment or at least the backgrounding of the works concerned, thus identifying for his contemporaries and imposing upon posterity a sharply defined authorial canon, his acts of inclusion could also be accompanied by radical consequences. Especially when engaging with titles from the earlier stages of his career he sought, in effect, to obliterate or render obsolete all previous editions, inscribe on the cleared textual surface the achieved splendours of his late manner, and bestow upon that 'form final for himself' an infinitely pre-emptive textual permanence for all his future readers. It is for these latter reasons that the Edition has become a *locus classicus* for modern editorial theory, and especially for debates as to the point at which extensive revision results in a text so altered as to constitute a distinct 'version', and the degree to which an editor should feel obliged to respect and adopt what are perhaps unfortunately called an author's 'final intentions', those latest textual instructions that can be discovered to have been inscribed, stated, or otherwise signalled on the near side of senility or the grave. Most immediately at issue, perhaps, is the question, sharply raised by Hershel Parker, as to the nature of the 'intentionality' governing the New York Edition texts themselves, the extent to which James succeeded—or believed himself to have succeeded—in regaining access through memory to the motives and emotions which had at once driven and directed the initial conception and composition of each individual work.[45]

By the time he came to write the first of the New York Edition prefaces, that to *Roderick Hudson*, James had already completed the revisions of *The Portrait of a Lady* and of *Roderick Hudson* itself and was somewhere in the middle of *The American*—an especially recalcitrant text on which he worked at intervals over the course of an entire year. As the *Roderick Hudson* preface makes clear, his experience with the Edition thus far had led him to the conclusion that through an actively responsive and preferably pen-in-hand re-reading of an earlier work it might indeed be possible for its creator to 'live back into a forgotten state' and reanimate some at least of 'the buried secrets, the intentions', that had been operative at the time of original composition. But he also recognized that such recovery was never complete, that some intentions always remained 'buried too deep to rise again', and that it was precisely this element of unpredictability that made the process so stimulating to the awakened authorial imagination: 'the very uncertainties themselves yield a thrill'.[46]

It was, of course, a process not merely analogous to but virtually identical with the progressive but never total unlayering of autobiographical memories, and in so far as James—with a finely discriminatory regard to what he believed that he could remember and what he knew that he could not—sought to recover the circumstances in which particular works were written, the New York Edition prefaces can be read as documents relevant to an understanding not only of the evolution of the Edition but of the psychology of memory itself. Of his conception of the central figure of *The American*, James declared: 'I recall sharply the felicity of the first glimpse, though I forget the accident of thought that produced it.'[47] That conception, however, was not immediately taken up but dropped 'for the time into the deep well of unconscious cerebration: not without the hope, doubtless, that it might eventually emerge from that reservoir, as one had already known the buried treasure to come to light, with a firm iridescent surface and a notable increase of weight'.[48] He was similarly frank about his inability to recall the development of the plot complications in *The Portrait of a Lady*: 'They are there, for what they are worth, and as numerous as might be; but my memory, I confess, is a blank as to how and whence they came.'[49] Consultation of his own working notebooks might in this instance have materially facilitated the workings of James's memory, but it appears that for some reason—perhaps a desire for recollective 'purity'—he did not always have recourse to such memoranda even when they were potentially available.[50]

Several of the prefaces record, and with a good deal of specificity, the routes traced by James's stimulated memory in reaching across time to the origins of a given work, and it seems as impossible to believe that he arrived securely back at none of those origins as that he arrived back at them all. The difficulty remains that of determining—or even reasonably guessing—just which of his initial conceptions James managed to recapture, which he wrongly believed himself to have recaptured, and to which in either category he remained at all consistently faithful. Especially in the revisions of the four earliest novels, words, sentences, and even entire paragraphs are omitted, rewritten, elaborated, or replaced; but the nature of a particular change does not in itself appear to indicate whether James felt himself to be reinforcing an intention fully recognized and recovered from the past, stepping gingerly across the troubling conceptual lacuna of a passage whose original purpose and function he could neither disinter from the past nor newly imagine in the present—or pursuing an agenda of an altogether different kind.

As he observed in the preface to *The Reverberator*, once a glimpse had been caught of a 'miraculously recovered' past experience, it became impossible to set any precise limits to the spreading of its 'associational nimbus': 'nothing more complicates and overloads the act of retrospect than to let one's imagination itself work backward as part of the business'. At the same time, such recoveries could be brought to renewed creative life only by a fresh infusion of imaginative energy: 'The musing artist's imagination . . . supplies the link that is missing and makes the whole occasion (the occasion of the glorious birth to him of still another infant motive) comprehensively and richly *one*.'[51] What remains unclear is whether this process should be thought of as the replacement of one creative act or impulse by another, or rather as a collaborative interplay between—or, to adapt James's hesitantly sexual imagery, the productive fusion of—an earlier impulse only partially reactivated and a new impulse somewhat artificially stimulated.

It is of some significance in this respect that work on the Edition, though often intensive, was by no means uninterrupted.[52] James's daily routines were not based on any absolute procedural imperatives but left quite flexible—capable of adjustment to such practical circumstances as illness, holidays, the onset of visitors, or, ecstatically, a belated production of one of his plays. Nor was his attention always—or, indeed, often—focused for extended periods on a single title. Since he normally devoted his morning hours with Theodora Bosanquet to 'inventive' work on the ' prefaces, his evenings to revision of the novels and stories themselves,[53] he must often have found himself dealing with two or more different texts within the course of a single day. On 25 June 1906 he wrote to James Pinker of being more or less simultaneously engaged in revising *The Portrait of a Lady*, correcting the proofs of *Roderick Hudson*, and writing the still outstanding final chapters of *The American Scene*.[54] He completed several unrelated tasks while *The American* remained unfinished,[55] and when the publication of *The Wings of the Dove* was postponed because of a mis-understanding with Scribner's as to the sequence of the New York Edition volumes the composition of the preface actually preceded reconsideration of the text by the best part of a year. It is true that James's memory of the individual texts received constant refresh-ment as revisions were made, prefaces dictated, 'clean' typescripts read over, and proofs corrected, and *The Wings of the Dove*, published as recently as 1902, doubtless remained sufficiently vivid for him not to feel obliged to revisit the text before writing its preface. It seems none the less remarkable—and indicative, so Parker would argue, of a failure to reassert full creative control—that even when dealing with titles of an earlier vintage James would sometimes allow the different stages of his work to be separated not only by substantial periods of time but also by significant diversions of attention to other works, whether themselves part of the Edition or not.

What seems to have enabled James to accommodate such delays and distractions was precisely his perception of the Edition less as a series of individually reconsidered texts than as a single multi-volume construct—ordered and integrated not only by its common format (binding, typeface, etc.) but by its chronology, by its cross-referential prefaces, by its mutually sympathetic photographic frontispieces, and, above all, by the unbroken consistency of its stylistic refinement. Complexly self-deluding though he may now appear to have been, there seems little doubt that James, as he embarked upon the textual revisions for the New York Edition, thought of himself as improving the surface of his past work without affecting what he was accustomed to call its substance or essence—as in the letter he wrote on 12 November 1906 to his Rye friend, Alice Dew-Smith, who had been reading *Roderick Hudson* in its original form and wanted that form preserved:

But we are really both right, for to attempt to retouch the *substance* of the thing would be as foolish as it would be (in a *done* and impenetrable structure) impracticable. What I have tried for is a mere revision of surface and expression, as the thing is positively in many places quite *vilely* written! The essence of the matter is wholly unaltered—save for seeming in places, I think, a little better brought out. At any rate the deed is already perpetrated—and I do continue to wish perversely and sorely that you had waited—to re-peruse—for this prettier and cleaner form.[56]

Although at this point the first volumes of the Edition had not yet appeared, James had already grown sensitive to complaints—from the novelist Robert Herrick,[57] for example, and even from the Edition's publisher[58]—to the effect that his alterations would result only in the alienation of his existing readership, a damaging defamiliarization of texts already published, established, and admired. Similar reservations presumably prompted, somewhat later on, the omission of any reference to textual revision from Macmillan's prospectus for the English issue of the Edition.[59] But the Dew-Smith letter, while self-consciously ingratiating, seems neither defensive nor especially disingenuous. James implies that he fully accepts the reality of previous publication and has no interest in the kind of total 'rewriting' later discussed (and dismissed) in the preface to *The Golden Bowl*. The existing 'substance' or 'essence' of the work (conception, plot, characterization) is regarded as accomplished fact (presented, public, 'done'), hence quasi-historical, hence off-limits ('impenetrable') during the revision process—except in so far as some of its aspects might become, almost incidentally, 'a little better brought out'. But it was evidently James's view that it would nevertheless remain feasible and even indispensable to engage in the close scrutiny and systematic enhancement of textual detail. His working principle, as he had earlier told his publishers, was 'to revise everything carefully, and *to re-touch*, as to expression, turn of sentence, and the question of surface generally, wherever this may strike me as really required'.[60]

By 'revise' James seems here to have meant no more than read over, or reconsider—literally, 're-see'. The crucial term is 're-touch', one that recurs (as 'retouching') in other letters of this period[61] and corresponds to those claims of 'minute revision and beautification'[62] which James increasingly advanced as the Edition itself proceeded. The term of course belongs with the other analogies from painting that were invoked in the preface to *Roderick Hudson* and seized upon by F. O. Matthiessen as crucial to an understanding of James's revision strategy and tactics—his record, set down in the very thick of the engagement, of what he believed himself to be doing.[63] But the suggestiveness of those analogies as metaphors for the operations of memory does not entirely cancel out the apparent triviality of such processes as, precisely, 'beautification', their hint of Tennyson's 'sad mechanic exercise',[64] or, at best, of Turner at a Royal Academy 'Varnishing Day' fettling up his paintings for actual exhibition.

It would in any case appear that—with whatever perceptivity or recognition James may have re-read his original texts, to whatever extent he might be said to have imaginatively re-entered this or that particular novel or story—he subjected all of them, in practice, to essentially the same revisionary procedures. Since the objective was to bring all the selected texts into conformity with those stylistic habits which had developed gradually over the course of his career, it was natural enough that the heaviest revisions should occur in the earliest texts, considered as a group, the lightest in the most recent. But across the board the changes are consistent in direction and kind:[65] the punctuation becomes sparser, the imagery denser and more sustained, the rhythms and word-forms increasingly colloquial, and such standard formulae as 'he said' yield place to more expressive (if sometimes cumbersome) alternatives such as 'he faintly mused'.[66] For James himself this exhaustive process, fundamentally questionable as it was and so demanding of his diminishing energy and time, clearly outranked even the much-cherished prefaces as constituting the most important element both in his task and in his final achievement. Much as he appreciated the handsome appearance of the first two volumes when they reached him on the last day of 1907, his chief satisfaction was in the renewed conviction that he had been 'a thousand times right to revise & retouch them exactly in the manner & in the degree in which I proposed to myself to do it. My effort has taken effect &

borne excellent fruit—I have, I feel sure, surer than ever, *immensely* bettered & benefitted them.'[67]

Earlier in 1907, right in the middle of work on the New York Edition, there had appeared an edition of Shakespeare's *The Tempest* with an introduction by James. Surprising as such a diversion may at first appear, it quickly becomes obvious from the introduction itself that James saw in *The Tempest*—as the supreme product of Shakespeare's maturer years, 'the finest flower of his experience'[68]—a flattering analogue for what he confidently expected to be his own culminating achievement. James celebrates the play as Shakespeare's 'high testimony to this independent, absolute value of Style' and as constituting the occasion when, after 'too much compromise and too much sacrifice', Shakespeare at last 'sinks' profoundly, as an artist, into 'the lucid stillness of his style' and for one 'magnificent moment' permits himself to resolve the career-long conflict 'between his human curiosity and his aesthetic passion' firmly in favour of the latter.[69]

If it seems impossible to resist the autobiographical implications of these assertions, their reflection of James's soaring confidence in the nature and quality of his work on the New York Edition, it is by the same token easy to understand his bewilderment at the fact (since fact it appeared to be) that Prospero's 'surrender of his magic robe and staff' had indeed prefigured Shakespeare's own deliberate cessation of creative activity at a moment when he was still so obviously 'at the zenith of his splendour':[70]

What manner of human being was it who *could* so, at a given moment, announce his intention of capping his divine flame with a twopenny extinguisher, and who then, the announcement made, could serenely succeed in carrying it out? Were it a question of a flame spent or burning thin, we might feel a little more possessed of matter for comprehension; the fact being, on the contrary, one can only repeat, that the value of The Tempest is, exquisitely, in its refinement of power, its renewed artistic freshness and roundness, its mark as of a distinction unequalled, on the whole (though I admit that we here must take subtle measures), in any predecessor.[71]

'Power' is a term invoked more than once in the *Tempest* introduction to express admiration of Shakespeare's absolute control over himself and his art at that late stage of his career, and it seems clear that James's implied unreadiness to

contemplate the early extinction of his own 'divine flame' derived at
least in part from his confident sense (illusory or otherwise) of being
at the height not merely of his personal powers but specifically of
his power, his ability and licence to determine the future perception
of his lifetime's achievement by selecting for the Edition only those
works by which he was now prepared to be judged, by using its
prefaces to direct the ways in which those chosen works should, in
his matured judgement, be read and understood, by helping to
determine the physical appearance of the volumes themselves—
from Alvin Langdon Coburn's photographic frontispieces to the
paper watermarked with a monogrammed 'HJ'[72]—and, above all,
by imposing on the entire series those exquisitely developed stylistic
preferences that had become in these later years inseparable from
his sense of himself as a literary artist.[73]

This had not been James's mood at the time of his sixtieth
birthday, and in later years, when the New York Edition had failed
to bring either the financial rewards or the enhanced reputation he
had once so euphorically anticipated, James sank into depths of
humiliation and despair that made Edith Wharton, for one, see him
as altogether more pitiful than the self-exiled disdainer of popular
opinion she had earlier sketched in her short story 'The Legend',
and even as a proper object for her charity.[74] At such moments
James was accustomed to complain that his profitless preoccupation
with the Edition had prevented him from undertaking other, more
lucrative, work and, in particular, from writing other novels.[75] But
neither *The Sense of the Past* nor *The Ivory Tower* at all obviously
contains the seeds of its own completion, and there is perhaps a
sense in which the Edition was of supreme importance to James
precisely because at a critical moment in his life—marked by the
perceived onset of old age and the much less clearly recognized
conclusion of his career as a novelist—it at once required and
permitted him to devote to it, hence to discover still within himself,
just such reserves of time, taste, and creative energy.

To ask, therefore, whether the acts of creativity contributory to
the New York Edition revived or replaced those embodied in the
original texts is perhaps to miss the main point. It is not necessary
to insist that James was unresponsive to the distinctive qualities of
his own early works in order to argue that the changes made for the
New York Edition were primarily determined by creative priorities
of a wholly different kind. Because of his programmatic ambitions

for the Edition itself as an independent artefact—the *Tempest*-like culmination of his career, his passport to immortality—what he sought were the qualities he so much admired in Shakespeare's last work: its 'refinement of power, its renewed artistic freshness and roundness', its attainment, above all, of 'a distinction unequalled . . . in any predecessor'. What he achieved can be and has been very variously evaluated, but it represented in any case the radical imposition of elderly preferences upon earlier work to a degree that few other novelists have approached, or perhaps even contemplated.

When, in the preface to *The Golden Bowl*, James looked exultantly back over the entire 'taking in hand of my earlier productions' and summed up the experience as 'this infinitely interesting and amusing *act* of re-appropriation',[76] he could equally have been alluding to that process of specifically autobiographical repossession—begun with *William Wetmore Story and His Friends* and entrenched in the New York Edition prefaces—which reached its triumphant conclusion in *A Small Boy and Others*, *Notes of a Son and Brother*, and the completed chapters of *The Middle Years*. The starting-point of these latter volumes, now customarily grouped and published as *Autobiography*,[77] appears to have been James's promise, made to his sister-in-law, Alice James, following his brother William's death in August 1910, to write a 'Family Book', a volume of memories of his parents and siblings that would incorporate a number of the lively, affectionate, anecdotal letters William had as a youth and young man written home from Cambridge, Germany, and elsewhere.[78] William's son, Henry James, junior, was already planning the full-dress edition of his father's letters which he would publish in two volumes in 1920,[79] but he eventually agreed to his uncle's inclusion of some of them in the 'Family Book'.

James had been with his brother throughout the period of his final illness and death and then stayed on in the United States for almost another year, so that it was only in the late autumn of 1911 that he was ready to summon his amanuensis back to work—this time in London rather than in what now seemed the loneliness of Lamb House and Rye. The note he sent to Theodora Bosanquet on 2 November suggests that he meant to proceed with the new project very much as he had done with *William Wetmore Story and His*

Friends, letting the available documents provide the core around which his own evoked and elaborated memories could more or less spontaneously accrete: 'I find the question of the Letters to be copied or dictated baffles *instant* solution, but shall have been able to judge in two or three days.' Before tackling the letters, however, he proposed 'to begin with something that goes very straight so as to get the easier back into harness',[80] and specifically with that direct and, so to speak, preliminary autobiographical exploration of childhood memories which was to result in the volume he called *A Small Boy and Others*. That Christmas he was able to write to his nephew:

I get on, distinctly, with my work—the only trouble is 1st that the whole retrospect & all my material from it come to me, flow vividly in, in *too great* abundance, & 2d that I want it all such a perfectly unique & beautiful thing that the want operates almost as an anguish while I go. But the only thing is to *let* everything, even *make every*thing, come & flow, let my whole consciousness & memory play in to the past as it will, & then see afterwards about reducing & eliminating—though I feel I shall lose some more or less exquisite stuff *whatever* I shuffle off.[81]

The experience James so remarkably evokes obviously corresponded —in its emphasis on coming and flowing, on the play and interplay of consciousness and memory, on stages of reduction and revision still lying ahead—to what Theodora Bosanquet called his plunges into 'the stream of the past',[82] and at this early point in the composition of *A Small Boy* he evidently thought of the book as emerging, like previous autobiographical exercises, from an act of voluntary surrender to the progressively generated associative imperatives of recollection itself.

Work on the book did not always go so smoothly,[83] and its final submission was delayed by the severe attack of shingles which he suffered in the autumn of 1912.[84] By late September, however, he could tell Henry James, junior, that he had not yet reached 'the "letters" portion' of the Family Book but proposed to go ahead with separate volume publication of those still earlier reminiscences into which he had been ineluctably drawn: 'This whole record of early childhood simply *grew* so as one came to write it that one could but let it take its way.' He added that he had *A Small Boy and Others* in mind as a title for this first volume and perhaps *A Big Boy and Others* or, better, *Notes of a Son and a Brother* for its successor, his earlier idea of paired titles, *Earliest Memories:*

Egotistic and *Earliest Memories: Altruistic,* having been abandoned on the grounds that the second of these was less good than the first.[85] Nor, indeed, would 'altruistic' have been an especially appropriate term to associate with a work in which James revealed himself as in certain crucial respects a monster of egotistical voracity, treating the letters written by his father and his recently deceased elder brother even more cavalierly than those early texts of his own that he had incorporated into the New York Edition, nowhere scrupling (to adapt one of his own phrases) to omit or rewrite a sentence or entire paragraph 'on judging it susceptible of a better turn'.[86]

It seems clear from both the 2 November 1911 letter to Bosanquet and a long letter he wrote to his nephew in November 1913 that the first and crucial stage in James's processing of the family letters for *Notes of a Son and Brother* was to 'redictate' them, making omissions and alterations as he went. That he should leave out whole sentences and even paragraphs was not particularly surprising: such excisions were standard practice in contemporary editions of letters and it is not, in any case, clear that the transcriptions supplied by his brother's family (he never saw the original documents) invariably reproduced the texts in their entirety. Much more striking, however, is James's restless and pervasive 'improvement' of William's prose, even at the cost of deadening that very vitality and spontaneity which had presumably made him so eager to use the letters in the first place. Writing from Cambridge to his 'Dearly beloved Family', for example, in November 1861, William James had referred to a recent visit of Henry's and then gone on to talk about their brother Wilkinson:

[Harry] is a good soul though in his way too, much more so than the light fantastic Wilky who has been doing nothing but disaster since he has been here, breaking down my good resolutions about eating keeping me from any intellectual exercise, ruining my best hat wearing it while dressing, while in his nightgown, wishing to wash his face with it on, insisting on sleeping in my bed inflicting on me thereby the pains of crucifixion and hardly to be prevented from taking the said hat to bed with him.[87]

In *Notes of a Son and Brother* this became:

[Harry] is a good soul, though, in his way, too; and less fatal than the light fantastic and ever-sociable Wilky, who has wrought little but disaster during his stay with me; breaking down my good resolutions about food,

keeping me from all intellectual exercise, working havoc on my best hat by
wearing it while dressing, while in his nightgown, while washing his face,
and all but going to bed with it.[88]

In an earlier letter, written from Bonn in the summer of 1860,
William described to his parents the kind of life he was currently
living:

My room is very comfortable now that I have got used to it and got a pair
of slippers of green plush heavy and strong enough to last all my life and
then be worn by my children. My bed is all right and it will please Aunt
Kate to hear that I have had two FLEAS, (my first) which have bitten my
skin off of me nearly. Now I can sympathise with her sufferings, which I
never rightly respected before. The Zofingian photograph has come. I had
hard work to get it out of the post Office. It is perfectly laughable though a
better picture than I expected. They have given me a moustache big enough
to furnish 3 horse guards. Tell Nelly that her letter was an unexpected
pleasure and I will answer it if I can get time. How long does she expect to
stay abroad? Tell us something about her. Who is this Doctor Adams? the
man she was engaged to? She tells me to address any letter for her to
Munroe, care of Dr. Adams. Ask her if I shall still address her as Miss
James. She hopes to meet me. Tell her it would of course be painful, but I
think I could do it if the Doctor were not present. However as I do not
know her real relation to him perhaps it would not be proper to
communicate these messages. So use your discretion.[89]

In *Notes of a Son and Brother* James adopted the initial, pleasantly
humorous, sentence essentially as it stood but freely exercised his
own 'discretion' in cutting and rewriting the remainder:

My room is very comfortable now I've got used to it, and I have a pair of
slippers of green plush heavy and strong enough to last all my life and then
be worn by my children. The photograph of our Zoffingen group has come,
which gives me a moustache big enough for three lifeguardsmen. Tell us
something more about Mary Helen. How long does she expect to stay in
Europe, and who is this Dr. Adams—the man she is engaged to? She directs
me to write to her in his care—so that I wish you would ask her, as she says
she hopes to meet me, whether I shall still address her as Miss James? Of
course it would be painful, but I think I could do it if Adams weren't
there.[90]

Criticized by an indignant Henry James, junior, for these
extravagantly doctored transcriptions of his father's letters, James
responded in mid-November 1913 with a letter of mingled

explanation, apology, and defiance. It was above all, he insisted, 'an *atmosphere*' that he wanted as an artist to evoke, and it was therefore necessary to 'work' William's letters 'into the whole harmony' of a text designed 'to show us all at our best for characteristic expression & colour & variety & everything that would be charming'. He continued, with a revealing turn of phrase:

And when I laid my hands upon the letters to use as so many touches & tones in the picture I frankly confess I seemed to see them in a better, or at all events in another light, here & there, than those rough & rather illiterate copies I had from you showed as their face value. I found myself again in such close relation with your Father, such a revival of relation as I hadn't known since his death, & which was a passion of tenderness for doing the best thing by him that the material allowed & which I seemed to feel him in the room & at my elbow asking me for as I worked and as he listened. It was as if he had said to me on seeing me lay my hands on those weak little relics of our common youth, 'Oh but you're not going to give me away, to hand me over, in my raggedness & my poor accidents, quite unhelped & unfriended, you're going to do the very best for me you *can*, aren't you, & since you appear to be making such claims for me you're going to let me seem to justify them as much as I possibly may?' And it was as if I kept spiritually replying to this that he might indeed trust me to handle him with the last tact & devotion—that is do with him everything I seemed to feel him *like*, for being kept up to the amenity pitch.[91]

Academic editors have sometimes sought to justify on similar grounds their more modest interventions into the imperfectly spelled and punctuated texts with which they have found themselves confronted: Leon Edel, for one, believes that 'when letters are translated from handwriting to print, they should be edited to read as one reads books', and that 'all abbreviations and shortcuts of hasty writing deserve to be spelled out'.[92] And since James, elsewhere in *Notes of a Son and Brother*, works over with the same freely excising, 'improving', and transforming hand a number of his father's letters[93] as well as several written by his adored cousin Minny Temple,[94] it is not easy to discount his insistence that in smoothing out the 'raggedness' of William's prose he was merely seeking to display him in the best possible light—to render him 'more easily & engagingly readable & thereby more tasted & liked'.[95] The foregrounding of William's humour was undoubtedly consistent with such a purpose—even his son later acknowledged that the 'intimate raillery' of the early letters was best appreciated

within the context of *Notes of a Son and Brother*, 'where the whole
family has been made to live again'[96]—as was the omission of
material that would have needed extensive explanation to make it
accessible to James's audience of 1914. At the same time, the frank
aesthetic disdain audible in James's references to his brother's early
prose points clearly towards a determination not to allow its
rawness to disturb the finished surface, the 'whole harmony', of a
text that was ultimately—as an autobiography, peculiarly—his
own.

Although James's increasing creative and emotional dependence
upon the survival of documentary witnesses from the past might
seem suggestive of growing age and declining powers, his unhesitat-
ing and often radical adjustments of the texts of his brother's,
his father's, and Minny Temple's letters remain fully reflective
of the characteristic imperiousness of his irresistibly expansive
imagination—what Adeline Tintner, borrowing a phrase from
the preface to *The Tragic Muse*, aptly calls his 'usurping consciousness'.[97] James's less than repentant confession in that mid-
November 1913 letter to Henry James, junior ('I daresay I did
instinctively regard it at last as all *my* truth, to do what I would
with')[98] could equally have referred to his public appropriation of
Browning's *The Ring and the Book* as a Jamesian fiction *manqué* in
the paper he delivered before the Royal Society of Literature on the
occasion of its Browning Centenary celebrations in May 1912[99]—
or, for that matter, to that comprehensive '*act* of re-appropriation'
of his own earlier productions constituted by the New York Edition
itself.

James during these final years was not always capable of such
heights of assurance and command. The arrival of his seventieth
birthday, it is true, was anticipated with rueful bravado—'I hate
having it bruited abroad that I'm a fabulous age when I'm trying to
put forth some further exhibition of my powers!'[100]—and his
satisfaction at its public celebration is suggested by the confident
pose of the Sargent portrait his friends commissioned as a birthday
gift.[101] More gratifying still was the warm British reception of both
A Small Boy and Others and *Notes of a Son and Brother*: 'The two
books together', he told Henry James, junior, in April 1914,
'appear to have made me (vulgarly speaking,) famous, & to be
greeted as a new departure, a new form & manner struck out in my

70th year.'[102] But such moments only relieved without dissipating his profound discouragement at the commercial failure of the New York Edition, and on 25 August 1915 he complained to Gosse: 'I am past all praying for anywhere; I remain at my age (which you know,) & after my long career, utterly, insurmountably, unsaleable.'[103] He became depressed, ill, and fearful of death,[104] and the outbreak of war in August 1914 brought him to a dangerous pitch of excitement as both an immediate, passionate, and undeviating advocate of the Allied cause and a horror-stricken observer of the entire ongoing slaughter: according to Logan Pearsall Smith, by the second year of the war James 'had no courage or desire to make an effort to live—age and isolation and the war had made him indifferent to everything'.[105]

James did find some relief from depression in his active support of wartime charities and, above all, in literary engagement itself. Theodora Bosanquet records how remarkably he was invigorated simply by the act of narrating to her the details of William's death: 'dreadful as was the tale he unfolded his cheek took on a healthier tint while he did so, and by the end he was quite blooming.'[106] But his attempts to finish *The Ivory Tower* petered out in bafflement in July 1914—'I do so hate crude elementary narrative', he declared[107]—and when, two months into the war, he began re-dictating *The Sense of the Past*—set aside several years earlier but now deemed 'sufficiently fantastic and divorced from present day conditions to be taken up and worked at'[108]—he seemed to his amanuensis to become ever more inextricably involved in the difficulties and, as she feared, the impossibilities of his basic idea: 'I don't see [she wrote on 13 January 1915] how he *can*, with all his ingenuity, bring it to a really triumphant conclusion. But I'm coming more and more to the conviction that he doesn't really face and solve his problems, anyway not his problems of possibility, he trusts to his technique to obscure the fact that they are there at all.'[109] The need to remain financially productive as a writer also told upon him—it seemed 'rather a strange fate to be committed to "earning" at 71 even (relatively) as one was so committed at 25'[110]—and so, according to Percy Lubbock, did the daily burden of authorship itself: 'Not long before his death he confessed that at last he found himself too much exhausted for the "wear and tear of discrimination"; and the phrase indicates the strain upon him of the mere act of living.'[111]

Despite all pressures and setbacks, James remained unremittingly vigilant in the assertion and defence of his authorial authority, and correspondingly distressed by indications that it had in any way been weakened or evaded. In June 1912, dismayed by the way his paragraphing had been altered in the proofs of the *Quarterly Review* version of 'The Novel in *The Ring and the Book*', James lamented to George Prothero, the editor, the prospective sacrifice of his 'fond ideal of paragraphs of a sufficiently equal length & rhythm to suggest rather stanzas'.[112] When Prothero gracefully yielded the point, James wrote back at once to express his appreciation of the concession:

And for *this* reason—that it seems to me the only way one can proceed with a system or a feeling of that sort is by being absolutely *consistent* & regular about it & not giving it away save for some altogether rare or extraordinary reason; for so it may finally glimmer upon readers that one has reasons for one's paragraphs as one has them, or ought to have them, for everything connected with one's style. I don't see how any such matter can decently pretend not to be rhythmic, as it were; at any rate the more or less equal or stanza-like length of my parts between breaks is for me almost the apple of the eye of form—or *one* of the apples at least, for I have a whole bushel of them; whereby you will see with what sentiments I do welcome your reprieve.[113]

Characteristically, even inevitably, James took advantage of the revised proof sent by Prothero to make yet further additions and revisions to his original text,[114] and it was with the same admirable but sometimes infuriating insistence that he gave an interview to the *New York Times* early in 1915 about his involvement with the work of the American Ambulance Corps, demanded to see copy, and then refused to sanction publication until after he had spent four days re-dictating the interview to the interviewer himself. It was fortunate, as Theodora Bosanquet noted in her diary, that the young man was a good typist.[115] And in early November of that same year James found himself deploring to his nephew the 'sad infelicity' of his having been sent no proof of the *New York Times* printing of his appeal for Belgian refugee relief, the article consequently 'bristling with certain dire misprints that sicken me, though I try to think of most of them as so obvious as not to contribute to the last disfigurement'.[116]

Within a month of writing that November 1915 letter James suffered the first of the strokes that rendered him immediately powerless to influence even the course of his own remaining days. Mentally as well as physically incapacitated, he could no longer determine the fate of the few but significant pieces of recent work that were being typed by Theodora Bosanquet. Nor could he retain control over the completed preface to Rupert Brooke's *Letters from America*, re-dictated, retyped, and sent off to Edward Marsh just before the onset of his final illness—although it was 'the most immense relief' to his mind, Bosanquet told Marsh, that the preface had indeed been finished.[117] The proofs of the book arrived not long afterwards, and when the editor of the *Westminster Gazette* objected to an implication in the preface that his paper had gone back upon an agreement to publish Brooke's contributions, Theodora Bosanquet sought and obtained the permission of Alice James—not James's sister, dead since 1892, but his sister-in-law, William's widow, just arrived from America—to remove the offending passage and patch over the gap, a task she performed with a skill deemed to be worthy of the Master himself.[118] It is hard to imagine what James would have made of this intervention, could he ever have become aware of it. Theodora Bosanquet, as shown by her diary and by her subsequent career,[119] was no ordinary amanuensis, and James had learned to place a very high value on her loyalty and intelligence as well as on her practical skills as a typist. It would have been one thing, however, for James, as a practising professional author, to revise his piece in light of the *Westminster Gazette*'s objections, quite another for him to countenance a compromise made in his name but without his participation.

In the event, of course, he remained ignorant of the transaction, pathetic in his helplessness, and only flickeringly aware of either the fact or the significance of his appointment to the exclusivity of the Order of Merit on the first day of 1916. Devotedly but somewhat sternly watched over by Alice James (who had firmly displaced Theodora Bosanquet from her central position), James hung on to life, distressed and increasingly confused, for two months longer, dying at last in his sister-in-law's presence[120] on 28 February 1916, six weeks short of his seventy-third birthday. Percy Lubbock, acknowledging that James's body 'was too tired and spent to live longer', nevertheless insisted that he carried away with him at the time of his death 'the power of his spirit still in its prime',[121] and his famous adoption of a specifically Napoleonic persona when dictating to Theodora Bosanquet during the sad bewilderment of his last illness[122] suggests that he was at some level still seeking to assert that authority into which he had, of recent years, so imperially grown.

During one of his more lucid moments, Alice James later reported to Edmund Gosse, James had directed her to 'tell the boys to *follow*, to *be faithful*, to *take me seriously*',[123] and many of his friends did at least pay him the tribute of their presence at his funeral, in Chelsea Old Church, on 3 March 1916. In a letter written to *The Times* immediately the service was over, Gosse at once lamented and celebrated the recently naturalized James as an 'English hero', a 'volunteer' in his adopted country's wartime cause, but it was chiefly because of the prevailing mood and condition of national crisis that James's death attracted no great attention, let alone the recognition of a service in Westminster Abbey: approached by some of James's friends, the Dean appears to have replied that the necessary request from either the Crown or the government had not been forthcoming.[124] Sixty years later, however, a stone to his memory was laid in Poets' Corner—between T. S. Eliot's and, less congruously, Dylan Thomas's—and James, who died within a few yards of Chelsea Old Church, might have taken satisfaction in knowing that although the (somewhat grandiloquent) memorial placed there by his friends suffered serious damage during an air raid in 1941 it was subsequently restored, along with the church itself and its many other monuments, largely as a result of the determination of the parishioners themselves.[125] James's body was cremated, as his will had directed, and the ashes taken back to the United States—smuggled in, according to Leon Edel[126]—by Alice James, to be interred in the family plot in Cambridge Cemetery, close to his parents, his brother William, and his sister Alice, and within less than fifty yards of his old friend William Dean Howells. His stone records—as his death certificate had done[127]—his specifically British distinction as a member of the Order of Merit and adds some words that succinctly reinforce what he would perhaps have called the international theme:

NOVELIST-CITIZEN
OF TWO COUNTRIES
INTERPRETER OF HIS
GENERATION ON BOTH
SIDES OF THE SEA

Suddenly though James was struck down and deprived of authority, his sustained autobiographical engagement during his last years was only one among several ways in which he sought, as Henry Adams had recommended, to 'take [his] own life'[128] and enhance or, at the very least, protect the image of himself that would be handed down to posterity. In 1909 he had made in the garden of Lamb House 'a gigantic bonfire' of incoming correspondence and other papers in compliance with 'the law that I have made tolerably absolute these last years . . . of not leaving personal and private documents at the mercy of any accidents, or even of my executors!'[129] He seems to have burned still more material during a visit to Lamb House in the autumn of 1915[130]—his recent naturalization as a British citizen having exempted him from the wartime travel restrictions on resident aliens—and, indeed, to have destroyed at one time or another the vast bulk not only of his personal papers but also of such working papers as manuscripts, typescripts, proofs, and corrected copies of his own books. There remained, however, the thousands of letters he had written to other people, and in April 1914, when he was in his early seventies, he shared with Henry James, junior, his anxieties about possible biographies or posthumous editions of his letters:

My sole wish is to frustrate as utterly as possible the postmortem exploiter—which, I know, is but so imperfectly possible. Still, one can do something, & I have long thought of launching, by a provision in my will, a curse not less explicit than Shakespeare's own on any such as try to move my bones. Your question determines me definitely to advert to the matter in my will—that is to declare my utter & absolute abhorrence of any attempted biography or the giving to the world by 'the family,' or by any person for whom my disapproval has any sanctity, of any part or parts of my private correspondence. One can discredit & dishonour such enterprises even if one can't prevent them, & as you are my sole & exclusive literary heir & executor you will doubtless be able to serve in some degree as a check & a frustrator.[131]

If James feared that he might become the victim of the kind of biographical intrusion he had so intimately portrayed in *The Aspern Papers*, he also had the discomfort of knowing that there was no one obviously suited to become the custodian of his literary remains. Not only did he lack the wife and children who might classically be expected to perform such a protective function, but his famous sociability had always co-existed with a personal privacy that did not encourage discipleship or even any exceptional intimacy. Lamb House served in his later years as an efficient domestic and professional castle with its distance from London as its modest moat, and that immense Jamesian correspondence has the look at times of a deterrent barrage, a means of keeping people at least a letter's-length away. He might conceivably have chosen as his literary executor someone such as Edith Wharton, who could be expected to handle matters with an affection and respect enhanced by the intelligent understanding of a fellow-artist, but James perhaps did not sufficiently trust her or any other writer to be entirely disinterested in such a situation, to have the restraint and discretion to place a higher valuation on his testamentary requests than on her own natural desire to celebrate, publicly and in print, the memory of a dead friend. Theodora Bosanquet, as an employee, was presumably never thought of in such a capacity, although when the time of James's last illness actually arrived it was she who showed—until her virtual exclusion by Alice James—the greatest sensitivity to what he himself would have 'wanted',[132] and who later worked with Pinker to ensure the preservation of the work he had left unfinished at his death.[133]

But it probably never occurred to James to look so far afield. Although he had become, when William died, the sole surviving representative of 'the family' as he had always known it, he was also, by that same token, the head of the Jameses who remained, and while it is hard to believe that he saw his authority as other than symbolic[134] he doubtless saw it as his duty to make a family-centred will. In the actual document drawn up and signed in December 1910, while he was still in the United States following his brother's death, he had indeed appointed Henry James, junior, as the sole *executor* of the will—and as the inheritor of Lamb House and its contents—but it was his sister-in-law, Alice James, who was nominated as his literary *heir*, the recipient of 'all my copyrights dramatic rights and other rights and interests whatever in any and all publications of which I am author or editor and in any and all dramatic compositions manuscript or type-copied matter and letters'.[135] James effected a codicil to this will in August 1915, but although, as a newly naturalized British citizen, he sensibly inserted his London solicitor as his nephew's co-executor, he neither added any stipulation as to the handling of his correspondence and other papers nor altered the blanket bequest of literary rights to his sister-in-law. It had perhaps been his intention to make the latter the financial beneficiary of his literary property and yet leave all decisions as to the publication of unpublished materials in the hands of her son, but it was Alice James to whom he assigned a general power of attorney early in January 1916[136] and when he died it was she who took the initiative in seeking an editor for precisely that edition of letters James himself had been so anxious to prevent. Her choice seems first to have fallen on her own daughter, Margaret (Peggy) James, but she was eventually persuaded by concerted representations from James's friends[137] that the task might be more appropriately assigned to Percy Lubbock, then in his mid-thirties, whom James had known and liked and who had already published a life-in-letters of Elizabeth Barrett Browning and, still more relevantly, an intelligent and entirely positive review of the New York Edition.[138]

James's literary standing and importance seem never to have been quite grasped by his brother's family, and while Henry James, junior, was prepared to take his executorial duties seriously, even a little portentously, as a matter of family obligation, he clearly did not think of himself as acting in the service of genius.[139] Many years later he confessed to Maxwell Perkins of Scribner's that his very intimacy with his uncle had prevented him from ever becoming a good judge of his writings.[140] James may, of course, have taken some opportunity other than the April 1914 letter to tell his nephew how he wanted his papers handled, but in the absence of more specific instructions it seems unlikely that the latter would have felt at all tightly bound by a vague plea for privacy uttered in the midst of a voluminous correspondence and at a time when he was still irritated by his uncle's elaborate attempts to justify those outrageous reworkings of family letters in *Notes of a Son and Brother*: 'Of course this is not feasible' is one of the exasperated comments pencilled by the younger man in the margins of James's long, self-justifying letter of 15–18 November 1913.[141] Any blocking or frustrating action he might have contemplated following James's death had in any case been compromised by his mother's early intervention—which may, indeed, have received his approval—and he doubtless concluded that some such publication of his uncle's correspondence was in the long run inevitable, hence best anticipated by an edition whose scope could be partly controlled by the family's co-operation—and whose discretion could be guaranteed by the ultimate granting or withholding of permission for publication.

Percy Lubbock, obliged to work very largely from transcriptions supplied by the various recipients of James's letters and to submit his text to the James family for its collective approval, did not have an altogether easy task,[142] but he showed sensitivity and independence enough for *The Letters of Henry James*, published in two volumes in 1920, to be seen as a positive memorializing gesture in which James's family and friends, generally rather at odds, for once collaboratively shared. It is true that Alice James did not sign the contract with Scribner's for the American edition until 1 April 1920, only eight days before the date of publication,[143] and that Lubbock had earlier been pressed by Henry James, junior, to omit certain letters and moderate James's more extravagant protestations of male friendship and affection.[144] But on this latter question Edmund Gosse, for one, seems to have shared and perhaps even helped to formulate the family's point of view. Sending Gosse a copy of what he had written to Lubbock, Henry James, junior, remarked: 'On the whole I agree more and more with your suggestion that terms of endearment had better be omitted in a fair number of letters.'[145] Neither the dignity of the two volumes, however, nor the good intentions of those responsible could alter the fact that James had not wanted such an edition, and had indeed sought specifically to prevent it: at least one of James's friends, Margaret Brooke, the Ranee of Sarawak, declined to make her letters available on the grounds that she remembered his saying how 'unutterably horrible' it would be to see one's private correspondence in print.[146]

James was more successful, at least on the face of it and in the short run, in escaping the attentions of biographers. Unlike Tennyson, Browning and, later, Hardy, he was never made the subject of an 'official' or 'authorized' biography—a 'memoir', 'life', or 'life and letters'. Partly, perhaps, this was because there was again no self-evident candidate for the task, partly because he had taken the deliberately evasive action of engaging in an extensive destruction of such documentary materials as remained in his possession, and partly because he had managed to die at a moment when his popularity was still relatively low and when the world was preoccupied with a war of unprecedented scale and ferocity which had not yet run half its course. Percy Lubbock's obituary in the

Quarterly Review spoke of James's art as having filled his life, so that it was his work, 'in its rounded completeness', that must be regarded as constituting 'his portrait',[147] and this was certainly true, in an unintended sense, of those early years which were to prove largely unapproachable other than by way of those dubiously reliable, infinitely manipulated, and luminously impenetrable auto-biographies in which James had at least begun the process of taking his own life.

Four years later, in his Introduction to *The Letters of Henry James*, Lubbock went so far as to suggest that a biography was in any case a virtual impossibility, the absolute inextricability of the practical, emotional, and creative strands in James's life rendering it wholly inaccessible to external investigation:

When Henry James wrote the reminiscences of his youth he shewed conclusively, what indeed could be doubtful to none who knew him, that it would be impossible for anyone else to write his life. His life was no mere succession of facts, such as could be compiled and recorded by another hand; it was a densely knit cluster of emotions and memories, each one steeped in lights and colours thrown out by the rest, the whole making up a picture that no one but himself could dream of undertaking to paint. . . . Looked at from without his life was uneventful enough, the even career of a man of letters, singularly fortunate in all his circumstances. Within, it was a cycle of vivid and incessant adventure, known only to himself except in so far as he himself put it into words. So much as he left unexpressed is lost, therefore, like a novel that he might have written, but of which there can now be no question, since its only possible writer is gone.[148]

Lubbock went on to argue that much that James left unexpressed in his work did in fact survive in his correspondence and that it was therefore of the letters 'that his biography must be composed': 'They give as complete a portrait of him as we can now hope to possess.'[149] Macmillan & Co., as the London publishers of the *Letters*, carried through the logic of this argument by bringing out the two volumes in a format identical with that used in James's lifetime for the autobiographical *A Small Boy and Others* and *Notes of a Son and Brother*,[150] and Lubbock began his first volume with letters dating from early in 1869, the moment of arrival in England at which James's own reminiscences had broken off.[151]

Less consistently—though perhaps with a glance back at his Elizabeth Barrett Browning volume—Lubbock provided in the *Letters*, section by section, a narrative sketch of James's life, as if implicitly recognizing that a biography-in-letters, especially one so selectively realized, could not in practice be wholly self-sustaining. Lubbock was a shrewd reader of James, capable of challenging not only the chronology of the autobiographies ('in evoking his youth it was no part of Henry James's design to write a consecutive tale, and the order of dates and events is constantly obscured in the abundance of his memories')[152] but also their reliability,[153] and perhaps recognized the paradoxical aspects of his own position: he admitted, for example, that the letters he was publishing provided only limited insights into the 'daily drama'[154] of James's creativity. But when the two volumes of the *Letters* stood matched on the shelf with *A Small Boy and Others* and *Notes of a Son and Brother* he may not have appreciated the extent to which they constituted a kind of composite 'Early Life and Later Letters' that might have distressed James, could he have known of it, even more than a simple gathering of correspondence would have done.

James would certainly have disapproved of Lubbock's editing and publishing *The Ivory Tower* and *The Sense of the Past*, both left incomplete at his death, and especially of their subsequent appearance (in the United States only) as supplementary volumes of that New York Edition whose contents he had so deliberately chosen and whose texts he had sought to render so exquisitely 'finished'. Somewhat absurdly, perhaps, both novels were excluded from the much more comprehensively collective edition, *The Novels and Stories of Henry James*, published in London by Macmillan in 1921–3—either for the purely practical reason that they had been published by another firm just a few years previously or because, as unfinished works, they failed to meet eligibility criteria which also excluded items (notably *The Outcry* and *The Other House*) adapted from plays.[155] The new edition, overseen by Percy Lubbock and issued in both a standard and a 'pocket' format, would presumably have been welcomed by James as making the bulk of his fiction available at reasonable prices, and while he might have been aesthetically offended by the juxtaposition of revised with unrevised texts he would surely have endorsed Lubbock's rejection of the suggestion, originating with Henry James, junior, that the titles previously included in the New York Edition should appear without their prefaces.[156] It seems altogether less clear what James would have made of Lubbock's critical study, *The Craft of Fiction*, which did much to enhance his posthumous reputation but perhaps at the cost of simplifying, hence vulgarizing, some of his central perceptions and critical propositions.[157]

Because James had engaged in pre-emptive destruction on so large a scale, there remained after his death only a very few—from a scholarly viewpoint, a pitifully few—documentary witnesses of the immense literary labours of his lifetime.[158] His notebooks happily survived, presumably because he was making occasional entries in them as late as 1911 and still thought of them as potential sources of usable 'material'; prudence, abetted by an unquenched ambition for theatrical success, similarly ensured the survival of the typescripts of his unpublished plays, some of them in multiple versions.[159] Those pre-publication materials that came into the possession of the family were given by Henry James, junior, to the Houghton Library at Harvard in 1941 as part of a far larger 'Collection of James Family Papers', subject to conditions designed to 'facilitate the work of mature and competent scholars' while preventing the exploitation of the materials by 'immature and unscholarly persons'.[160] Always beyond the range of James's zeal for obliteration had been the letters sent out in such profusion to friends and professional colleagues on both sides of the Atlantic, and these, with their characteristic vitality, intelligence, and flourish, were not surprisingly preserved by their recipients in enormous numbers. Letters to family members were included from the first in the James Collection in the Houghton, and numerous other correspondences have since been gathered around these, either by purchase or by gift, and there are extensive holdings of letters in the Berg Collection, the British Library, the libraries of Leeds, Princeton, and Yale universities, and elsewhere—their vast totality a sometimes doubtful boon to the biographer and an as yet unconfronted challenge to full-scale editorial attention.

As James's will had specified, the approximately five thousand books in Lamb House passed with the building itself to Henry James, junior, who seems, however, to have had a limited appreciation of their interest and importance as a Jamesian collection. He soon removed a substantial number of the more obviously valuable items to the United States, most of them going to his own home, the rest to the homes of other family members, and the remaining four thousand or so volumes later suffered a more widespread dispersal when his widow, Dorothea James, sold them for £200 to the Rye bookseller who had taken them into storage following the bombing of the Garden Room at Lamb House during the Second World War.[161] A few of James's books have been returned to Lamb House itself, which Dorothea James, in a happier moment and in pursuance of her husband's testamentary instructions, presented to the National Trust as a gesture of Anglo–American friendship. The Trust, for its part, has made a point over the years of letting the house to custodians with literary interests who would accept the responsibility of allowing public access to the garden and one or two of the downstairs rooms for a few hours each week. Proposals for the rebuilding of the Garden Room—the separate building which James used for much of his writing and dictating—have not as yet materialized.

The control of Henry James's papers and literary estate has remained with the descendants of William James. The latest (single-volume) version of Leon Edel's massive five-volume biography acknowledges its indebtedness 'to Alexander R. James, grandson of William James, and to various members of the James family for certain priorities given me long ago in the family papers',[162] and a similar phrase appears in the first volume of Edel's four-volume but radically incomplete *Henry James Letters*.[163] The impact on James scholarship of that long-standing reservation of materials to Edel's use has obviously been considerable, and while it would be unreasonable to begrudge a biographer a position of privilege obtained by virtue of his own energies and pioneering initiatives (a prospective biographer of Yeats, after all, threw up the task some years ago precisely because he could not obtain exclusive publication rights to important documents) there is certainly a sense in which Edel's domination of the field might be seen as making its own sufficiently obvious point about the unforeseeable consequences of testamentary action and inaction alike.

What factors determined James's final absolute dependence upon his own family—what hopes or fears of posterity, what delicacies of considerateness or terrors of rejection, what braveries of confidence or depths of insecurity—it seems impossible now to recover or even guess at. Henry James, junior, took his executorial responsibilities with all due seriousness and even sought—in ignorance of the copy or perhaps copies already in existence[164]—to destroy those distressing 'deathbed' dictations which reflected their author's incapacity in the very extravagance of his assertions of power. But what James seems not to have allowed for was the incomprehension on the part of the family of what it could have meant to be Henry James, or even one of his readers, its lack, judged by his own high standards, of the fullest imaginative and even intellectual sympathy—its failure, in short, to *be* any longer the family he had in his own exceptional generation known.[165] It is of course conceivable that James had intended to leave more specific instructions for his executor, only to be prevented by the sudden debilitating onset of his final illness. On the other hand, he had already written a number of formal and informal auto-biographical volumes and destroyed a great deal of what he did not wish preserved, and his realistic perception of the difficulty of frustrating 'the postmortem exploiter' had perhaps generated a profound scepticism as to the usefulness of further anticipatory measures other than those represented by the explicit epistolary appeal to family loyalty, the implicit testamentary appeal to family solidarity, and the twenty-four volumes of the New York Edition.

Thomas Hardy

THOMAS HARDY assumed the mantle of old age like a destiny, settling into longevity as into a role for which he had spent his entire life preparing. As early as 1906 he was expressing a strong preference for late Wagner over early Wagner and for late over early Turner, 'the idiosyncrasies of each master being more strongly shown in these strains'. He continued: 'When a man not contented with the grounds of his success goes on and on, and tries to achieve the impossible, then he gets profoundly interesting to me.'[1] He praised Verdi for his 'modulation from one style into another' in late career, and would unblushingly cite Homer, Aeschylus, Sophocles, and Euripides as happy precedents for his own creativity in old age, adding in his poem, 'An Ancient to Ancients', the names of still other figures from antiquity who 'Burnt brightlier towards their setting-day'.[2] In 1920, at the beginning of his ninth decade, he roundly declared: 'The value of old age depends upon the person who reaches it. To some men of early performance it is useless. To others, who are late to develop, it just enables them to complete their job.'[3] Hardy clearly had no doubt as to the category within which he personally fell, and nothing in his career is more remarkable than the job-completion of his extreme old age, the combination of his late productivity as a poet and his painstaking attention to the posthumous survival of his work and reputation.

Hardy's life-span, extending from June 1840 to January 1928, was significantly greater than James's, or even Tennyson's. When he spoke of Wagner in 1906 he had more than twenty productive years still ahead of him, even though, at sixty-six, he was already old enough to have retired from the kind of architectural career in which he had first started out. Eight years earlier, indeed, he had already effected an elaborate public closure of his second career, as a novelist, and embarked rather more tentatively upon his third, as a poet. His turning from architecture to novel-writing in the early 1870s had simultaneously involved a conscious deferral of his ambitions as a poet, and while it seems reasonable to accept his insistence that a return to poetry had long been envisaged ('I have been going to publish it for years', he said of *Wessex Poems* at the time of its first appearance in December 1898),[4] it is evident that the feasibility of such a return remained dependent upon a fortunate financial outcome of the laborious novel-writing decades— assured in the event by the immense popularity of *Tess of the d'Urbervilles*, the changes in the American copyright laws, and the resulting prospect of continuing royalties on the fiction from both sides of the Atlantic. Whether the precise timing of the publication of *Wessex Poems* was at all affected by Hardy's response to hostile criticisms of his last novels, it is difficult to judge: that he was prompt in threatening to abandon fiction certainly does not diminish the likelihood of a prior decision to precisely that effect. What clearly was a factor, on the other hand, was his intense and prolonged engagement with the 'Wessex Novels' collected edition of 1895–7, published by the American-owned but London-based firm of Osgood, McIlvaine.[5]

Hardy's previous publishers, Sampson Low, had brought out several of the novels in cheap reprint editions with matching formats, but the Osgood, McIlvaine edition was the first to combine uniformity with comprehensiveness. No attempt was made to gather in the non-fiction prose or those few short stories which had not already achieved volume publication, but the edition was otherwise complete—to the point of including *Under the Greenwood Tree*, the only book whose copyright Hardy had sold outright. It spoke resoundingly, in fact, to his achieved status as a major novelist and displayed the standard characteristics, at once cumulative and implicitly celebratory, to be found in the collected editions of successful novelists from Scott onwards—of Lytton, Dickens, and George Eliot, for example, and more recently of Robert Louis Stevenson, whose Edinburgh Edition had begun to appear in 1894, shortly before his death. Each of the 'Wessex Novels' volumes—the very title of the edition distantly but distinctly echoing Scott's Waverley series—was handsomely bound in dark green ribbed cloth, with the author's elaborately decorated monogram blocked in gold on the front cover, and its contents included, in addition to the actual text, a specially commissioned etched frontispiece with a facsimile of the author's signature on the facing page, a newly written authorial introduction, and a map of the fictional Wessex, also designed if not actually drawn by the author himself.[6]

The first volume, containing *Tess of the d'Urbervilles*, had a portrait of Hardy as its frontispiece, but the frontispieces to the other volumes all showed relevant Wessex scenes—chosen by Hardy himself in active collaboration with the illustrator[7]—and these combined with the map and the occasional footnotes on topographical and dialectal matters to demonstrate and indeed firmly register Hardy's claim to be both the originator of Wessex and its only legitimate exploiter. The prominently displayed authorial signature harked back, consciously or otherwise, to the devices of the so-called Charles Dickens Edition, the last to appear during Dickens's lifetime, whose purchasers were assured—in the prospectus Dickens himself wrote—that the title of the edition, as endorsed by his facsimile signature, was a guarantee of 'the Author's . . . present watchfulness over his own Edition, and his hopes that it may remain a favourite with them when he shall have left their service for ever'.[8]

These assertions of authority, though important in themselves, were not the aspects of the edition which chiefly preoccupied Hardy, whose authorial 'watchfulness' was directed rather to the composition of the retrospective, justificatory, and, at times, distinctly valedictory prefaces, and to the meticulous revision of the texts of the novels and stories themselves. He had developed through long experience as a professional author a keen and almost moralistic eye for both the technical and aesthetic aspects of typography and book production. His handwriting was clear and even elegant (it was later to be featured in a Society for Pure English Tract on *English Handwriting*);[9] he prepared his manuscripts and corrected his proofs with care; and he had almost always taken the opportunity offered by new editions, especially the earliest one-volume editions, to re-read the text and correct at least the more egregious errors, particularly those pointed out by reviewers.[10] In preparing the volumes of the 'Wessex Novels' edition he attended as usual to such matters—most notably by restoring to *The Mayor of Casterbridge* a few pages omitted from previous editions—but he was especially and indeed systematically concerned to achieve both an ampler realization of his conception of a fictional-yet-recognizable Wessex and a sharper and more consistent definition of its topographical details, independently introduced in successive novels and stories over the years. He did not, however, make any fundamental alterations of structure, story, characterization, or theme, nor attempt any shifts of emphasis beyond increasing or decreasing the use of dialect by certain characters and introducing, here and there, a slightly greater degree of sexual explicitness.[11]

An unusual feature of the edition was the November 1895 appearance of the first edition of *Jude the Obscure* as its eighth volume, already so numbered, already accoutred with the paraphernalia of collectivity—including a frontispiece engraving of a 'Christminster' scene that was readily identifiable as Oxford High Street—and with its principal settings already located on the Wessex map that was standard to the edition as a whole. It is not clear what, if any, effect the novel's format had upon its original readers and (often hostile) reviewers, but the mode of publication chosen seems in retrospect a confirmation of the closural aspects of the entire Osgood, McIlvaine project, a Hardyan signal (however unreadable at the time) that the outspokenness of *Jude*, the intransigence of its social criticism, reflected a determination to speak out, once and for all, on issues that his past dependence on public and especially editorial favour had made it politic to avoid. But even if the reception of *Jude* had in a sense been discounted in advance by Hardy's decision that it was in any case to be his last novel, the sheer brutality of some of the criticism must at the very least have confirmed him in the wisdom of that choice. Nor is he likely to have received a different message in March 1897 from the mixed response to *The Well-Beloved*, whose late addition to the Osgood, McIlvaine series seems to have been essentially a tidying-up gesture, delayed by the extensiveness of the revisions to the earlier serial which he had felt to be indispensable to its publishability in volume form.[12]

A few short stories apart, Hardy published no new fiction after *The Well-Beloved*. His Preface to it is dated January 1897; a notebook entry dated 4 February 1897 reads simply: 'Title: "Wessex Poems: With Sketches of their Scenes by the Author."'[13] Despite the self-assurance of this private memorandum, Hardy's earliest comments about *Wessex Poems* are sufficiently hesitant to suggest that he was by no means confident of being able to establish himself as a poet: he seems, for example, to have offered to guarantee his publishers against possible financial loss.[14] The very title of the volume hinted at a dependence upon the established public acceptance of the 'Wessex Novels', and both *Wessex Poems* and its successor of 1901, *Poems of the Past and the Present*, were published in bindings uniform with those of the seventeen prose volumes of the Osgood, McIlvaine edition—as, in effect, an extension of that edition, claiming the shelter of its dark green umbrella.

Osgood, McIlvaine & Co. and its existing contracts, however, had in the meantime been absorbed by the much larger New York house of Harper & Brothers, for which it had formerly acted as London agent, and while there is no evidence of Hardy's having objected to the specific publishing arrangements for *Poems of the Past and the Present* he was clearly dissatisfied at finding himself 'carried by currents, & against my intentions, into the position of having only a subsidiary branch of an American house as my English publishers'.[15] Writing to Clarence McIlvaine, now Harper's London representative, on 28 February 1902, Hardy explained his feeling 'that my publisher for England in the future ought to be one whose head office is London & not abroad: since, for one thing, if Messrs Harper were by any chance to abandon their London branch or change their representative here, it might be inconvenient for me in conceivable cases, now that I am getting old & begin to find publishing matters irksome. And if, moreover, anything were to happen to me, it would be better that my publisher's head house should not be across the Atlantic.'[16] Glossing that last statement a few days later, Hardy explained to McIlvaine that there were 'family reasons—which I am scarcely at liberty to enter into—that bear upon the matter & make my situation rather different from that of most other writers',[17] an apparent implication that in the event of his death neither his widow nor any member of his own family would be capable of looking after his literary estate.

McIlvaine protested that the departure of so well-known an author would reflect negatively on Harper & Brothers, even though they were to remain his American publishers; but Hardy persisted in his purpose, made terms with McIlvaine, and took the initiative in transferring British publication of all his books, both past and future, to the highly successful London house of Macmillan, publishers of Tennyson, Kipling, Henry James, and many other notable writers in all areas of literature and scholarship. For Hardy, however, the question of the firm's standing was probably secondary to his first-hand experience of its operations (it had published *The Woodlanders* and *Wessex Tales* and was currently issuing a Colonial Edition of his fiction) and to his personal respect for individual members of the Macmillan family. Frederick Macmillan, the head of the firm at this period, responded warmly to Hardy's overtures, and arrangements were quickly entered into for a modestly priced English reissue (with minor revisions) of all the existing volumes from the Osgood, McIlvaine and Harper plates—the so-called 'Uniform Edition'—and for the publication of future volumes as they appeared. 'The kind of agreement that occurs to me', Hardy wrote, 'is one under which, if nothing subsequently be done by either party, it will continue in force till the end of copyright',[18] and in the years that followed he depended increasingly on Frederick Macmillan's advice and settled ever more comfortably into a stable and efficient publishing relationship that persisted to the time of his death, and beyond.

The Osgood, McIlvaine edition, the composition and publication of *Jude*, the shift to poetry, and the change of publishers were major events that seem, in a long perspective, to have clustered together at the time of the century's turn and of Hardy's own sixtieth birthday as elements in a profound reassessment of his past achievements, current situation, and future prospects. At the time when, aged sixty-one, he signed the comprehensive agreement with Macmillan in April 1902 the Boer War was finally winding down, Queen Victoria had died, and a new century and a new reign were jointly under way. In the final stages of his own career as a novelist he had been outspoken on issues about which he cared deeply. In the Osgood, McIlvaine 'Wessex Novels' edition he had provided both himself and the readers of his fiction with a satisfying and potentially permanent act of culmination and closure. He had enacted with at least modest success the shift to poetry that had been so long in contemplation. And he had acquired a new publisher of whose standing there could be no doubt and on whose sympathetic co-operation he believed he could rely. Although the unhappy state of his twenty-eight-year-old marriage might offer few prospects of domestic comfort and personal happiness, the way seemed open to a full realization of his long-standing ambitions as a poet.

In the first decade of the twentieth century Hardy did indeed establish himself as a significant poetic voice, publishing two more collective volumes, *Poems of the Past and the Present* and *Time's Laughingstocks*, in 1901 and 1909 respectively.[19] During the same decade he might be said to have at once confirmed and compromised his new status by emerging as a specifically national if dubiously eloquent voice in the three separately published volumes of *The Dynasts* (1904, 1906, 1908), a long verse-drama ambitious in its historical scope and compelling at least in terms of its essentially narrative exploration of Britain's struggle with Napoleonic France. Given so strong a commitment to verse, reinforced by an insistence that verse had always been his preferred mode of expression[20]— given, too, the changes he had been able to make to the Osgood, McIlvaine edition when the plates were taken over by Macmillan in 1902—it is somewhat surprising to find Hardy, in 1911, engaged in detailed preparation for another collective edition. But the new project, an American-inspired *édition de luxe* limited to 750 sets, had been designed from the first to incorporate the verse as well as the prose, and the proposed *de luxe* format seemed to promise an enhanced status for both. Hardy was well aware that Macmillan had published such an edition of Kipling's works and applied the term to its English issue of Henry James's New York Edition, and early in 1909, while the James volumes were appearing, he had exclaimed to Frederick Macmillan, 'I suppose I shall never reach the dignity of an edition-de-luxe!'[21] The hint could scarcely have been broader, and although Macmillan's awareness of his firm's losses over *The Dynasts* perhaps deterred him from returning an immediate response he was ready, in October 1910, to give a cautious welcome to the American proposal.

Hardy had suffered much in the past from the scorn directed by reviewers at what were in fact printer's errors—'To think that *you*, of all people, can't see that "road" . . . is a misprint for "load"', he complained to Edward Clodd after the publication of *Tess of the d'Urbervilles*[22]—and evidently concurred with James in thinking of such disfigurements as a kind of public disgrace. His principal non-financial concerns when agreeing to the *de luxe* edition proposal had been that the proofs would be sent to him for correction and that the spelling would not be American,[23] and in June 1911, when the transatlantic negotiations had been completed and a working set of the in-print Macmillan (ex-Osgood, McIlvaine) texts was in his hands, Hardy again expressed to Sir Frederick Macmillan (as he had now become) the sleep-defying anxieties he still felt about the new edition's being produced in the United States: 'unless I correct those proofs myself there will be errors in the text—of a minute (the worst) kind—that will endanger the reception of the edition by [British] reviewers, & by impairing its value in a literary point of view, injure its commercial success'. Even the best printers, he added, were capable of making grievous errors, and it was clear that 'the literary insight of America cannot be depended on'.[24] In the event, the American arrangements fell through, to be replaced in January 1912 by an alternative scheme for a collected (but not limited) edition which Macmillan would publish for the English market, with or without American co-publication. Hardy, readily agreeing to this revised conception of the edition, referred to it for the first time as 'definitive', while it was Macmillan who suggested that it be called the Wessex Edition.[25]

Hardy had meanwhile been reading and revising each of his books in turn. It was a process he referred to in a letter of July 1911 as 'the drudgery of reprinting',[26] but in writing to a more intimate correspondent, Florence Henniker, he acknowledged that while the exercise involved 're-reading old books of mine, written when my spirits were brisker than they are now, & full of artistic errors which cannot be altered', it might in some respects prove to be 'a good thing'.[27] The self-criticism, as so often with Hardy, was perhaps more formal than felt, and his standard deprecation of the quality of the novels—especially by comparison with the greater maturity of the verse—by no means precluded a clear recognition of the financial as well as aesthetic importance of their republication in a handsome format and with an improved text. At the same time, the stress on the unalterability of 'artistic errors' effectively defined the limits of Hardy's revisionary impulse—he did not, for example, displace the 'happy' ending of *The Return of the Native*[28] or reconstruct, as he once spoke of doing, his abandoned and dismembered first novel, *The Poor Man and the Lady*[29]—and implicitly acknowledged that his work on the new edition was being conducted along lines essentially similar to those he had followed in the Osgood, McIlvaine edition some fifteen years earlier. Sexual specificity was again mildly enhanced; typographical errors and minor stylistic infelicities were again corrected or removed; the incidence of dialect forms in the speech of certain characters was once more adjusted, though sometimes in the reverse direction; Wessex place-names and the distances between places were further altered in the interests of consistency and of fidelity to the 'actual' topography of south-western England; and there was again a tendency to so modify the descriptions of Wessex locations as to make their 'originals' more plainly identifiable.[30]

Hardy's approach to both his major editions thus remained much more conservative than James's approach to the New York Edition. Rejecting wholesale reconceptualizations of existing texts and recognizing that fundamental 'artistic' weaknesses could not be made good at the level of the individual sentence, he essentially concurred in the position Scott had taken in respect of his '*magnum opus*' edition—that the processes of revision and correction would not extend to 'the tenor of the stories, the character of the actors, or the spirit of the dialogue. There is no doubt ample room for emendation in all these points—but where the tree falls it must lie.'[31] It was in the Wessex Edition preface to *Tess of the d'Urbervilles* that Hardy declared of his earlier attacks on the novel's reviewers: 'The pages are allowed to stand for what they are worth, as something once said; but probably they would not have been written now.'[32] Two paragraphs later Hardy's characteristically combative 'apology' for his retention of the novel's much-criticized subtitle—'*Melius fuerat non scribere*. But there it stands'[33]—expressed still more forcefully the same realistic and responsible acceptance of the indelibility of the already published, the 'something once said'.

The Wessex Edition none the less differed from its predecessor in many respects—most notably, of course, in its inclusion of the verse—and Hardy was now much further away from his novel-writing career and in a better position to survey and appraise it as a whole. Several of the existing Osgood, McIlvaine prefaces were revised and enlarged—the new 'postscript' to the *Jude the Obscure* preface was almost three times the length of the statement it ostensibly supplemented—and the entirely new General Preface to the Edition as a whole was perhaps Hardy's most substantial piece of critical writing, at once a description of his methods and a justification of his literary ambitions. Within the individual texts he was particularly concerned to restore bowdlerizing deletions, reincorporating for the first time the full text of the 'Saturday Night in Arcady' episode that he had deleted from the manuscript of *Tess of the d'Urbervilles* before the novel was serialized,[34] and he was later to add to the Edition not only the subsequently published volumes of his verse—*Satires of Circumstance* with *Moments of Vision* in 1919, *Late Lyrics and Earlier* with *The Famous Tragedy of the Queen of Cornwall* in 1926, and *Human Shows* with *Winter Words* in 1931—but also, if much more reluctantly, *A Changed Man*, a gathering of miscellaneous stories which he claimed to have left deliberately uncollected until 'frequent reprints of some of them in America and elsewhere . . . set many readers inquiring for them in a volume'.[35]

The Edition was not, even so, absolutely complete: a few stories and poems remained uncollected and, the prefaces apart, none of Hardy's non-fiction prose was included. But it had every claim to stand as the embodiment of Hardy's authorized text of the works of fiction and verse by which he wished to be remembered, and it possessed other features that marked it as a culminative authorial statement. The consolidation of his reputation during the intervening years, signally recognized in his appointment to the Order of Merit in 1910, was perhaps reflected in the absence of the assertive authorial signature that had been a feature of the Osgood, McIlvaine edition. At the same time, the renewed process of textual Wessexization was endorsed by the enlarged and elaborated map, prepared by Hardy himself and then professionally redrawn, which was inserted at the back of each volume; by the photographic frontispieces, taken by the Dorset photographer Hermann Lea in accordance with Hardy's specific instructions, which served to demonstrate even more directly than the Osgood, McIlvaine etchings the correspondences between fictional locations and their visitable originals; and by the Hardy-approved text and illustrations of Hermann Lea's guidebook, *Thomas Hardy's Wessex*, which covered the verse as well as the prose and was published by Macmillan in a format matching that of the volumes in the Edition proper.

Most significant of all, perhaps, was the division of the fiction volumes into separate categories, ostensibly descriptive but effectively judgemental—an obviously descending order of 'Novels of Character and Environment' (including all novels now conventionally identified as 'major'), 'Romances and Fantasies', and 'Novels of Ingenuity' (comprising *Desperate Remedies*, *The Hand of Ethelberta*, and *A Laodicean*).[36] It is true that Hardy once told Sir Frederick Macmillan that he had devised the system in order to give journalists and reviewers 'something to discuss',[37] but the act of classification, with the discriminations it so clearly implied, obviously constituted a conscious gesture of canon-formation—

comparable to the more absolute selectivity of Henry James's New York Edition—that was very much in line with Hardy's determination to use this occasion to set his literary house finally and definitively in order. It was evidently a similar impulse which led him to agree so readily, even eagerly, to the suggestions made by Sydney Cockerell in the early autumn of 1911, while work on the Wessex Edition was still in progress, for the distribution of most of his surviving manuscripts to selected institutional libraries, *Tess* and *The Dynasts*, for example, going to the British Museum, *A Group of Noble Dames* to the Library of Congress, and a particularly handsome couple, *Jude the Obscure* and *Time's Laughingstocks*, to the Fitzwilliam Museum, Cambridge, of which Cockerell was himself the director.[38] Characteristically, Hardy felt that it would 'not be quite becoming for a writer to send his MSS. to a museum on his own judgment', and therefore wanted the distribution to be made as far as possible in Cockerell's name rather than his own.[39]

As the proofs of the later and implicitly deprecated prose titles in the Edition continued to arrive for correction during the summer and autumn of 1912, Hardy wrote to Edward Clodd of the tediousness of the experience ('Proofs are still passing mechanically through my consciousness as through a mill') and of a yearning to 'annihilate half the volumes'.[40] In the years that followed he consistently affected to hold the fiction in low esteem, declaring in October 1925 that it was 'difficult, of course, for one who has been occupied during the last thirty years in the production of more mature works, good or bad, than the novels, to enter into questions concerning his now nearly forgotten art in fiction, the writing of which came to an end last century, in the reign of Queen Victoria'.[41] But this was essentially a public strategy designed to downplay the prose, which could well take care of itself, in order to emphasize the importance of the verse, which had by no means gained such wide acceptance. In practice, Hardy retained a strong sense of both the literary and the economic importance of his novels and stories, maintaining a vigilant eye on their textual health and on their continuing availability to the public in a range of variously priced editions. He kept notes of late-discovered misprints in his own study copies of the Wessex Edition, prose and poetry alike, reminding Macmillan every now and then of the need to bring the texts of the cheaper editions up to the Wessex standard, and although there was another collected edition, the Mellstock, in 1919–20—limited, signed, handsomely bound, virtually the *édition de luxe* he had hoped for a decade earlier—he did not regard it as qualifying the Wessex Edition's essential 'finality' but sought rather to ensure that the relatively few textual alterations made to the Mellstock were incorporated—authoritatively, as it were—into later Wessex printings.[42]

The astonishing poetic achievement of Hardy's late career was the 'harvest' of his novels in more ways than Ezra Pound perhaps had in mind.[43] The experience of gathering material for his fiction and struggling with the problems and vicissitudes of composition, publication, and revision had left him older and wiser, better informed and verbally more adept, and engaged him in an urgent search for social and philosophical values and a sustained contemplation of the tragi-comic patterning of individual human lives. The sheer intensity of his commitment to the writing of *Jude*, reinforced by its painful quasi-autobiographical re-enactments of his most fundamental hopes, decisions, disappointments, and defeats, had not only reinstated more powerfully and directly than ever before the socio-political positions and passions of the never-published *The Poor Man and the Lady* but simultaneously prepared the intellectual ground for the return to poetry itself, and specifically for those comprehensively interrogatory, philosophically querulous poems—'The Lacking Sense', 'The Sleep-Worker', 'God-Forgotten', 'To an Unborn Pauper Child', and so on—which figure so notably in *Poems of the Past and the Present*. What Hardy's insistence on the greater maturity and deliberateness of his verse chiefly reflected was his sense of being no longer restricted by the formal and quantitative demands of fiction, especially as artificially imposed by the conditions of contemporary publishing, and of possessing a correspondingly greater freedom to determine length, subject, and point of view and to draw freely on his accumulated emotional and intellectual reserves. Because he was not dependent on his poetry as a source of income he could even make a virtue of the limitation of his audience and combine directness of expression with the enjoyment of a kind of privacy and exemption from controversy that had regularly eluded him during his final years as a novelist: 'If Galileo had said in verse that the world moved, the Inquisition might have left him alone.'[44]

In late November 1912—just as proof-correction for the Wessex
Edition was coming to an end—Hardy's wife, born Emma Lavinia
Gifford, suddenly died, and Hardy himself, after years of marital
discord, was plunged with equal suddenness into depths of remorse
and regret. Precisely for that reason, however, the event provided—
as the 'Poems of 1912–13' so eloquently show—an immense and
wholly unexpected stimulus to his creativity at a time when it might
otherwise have been threatened by advancing age, by the profoundly
depressive experience of living through the First World War, and by
the continuation of domestic unhappiness. Fourteen months after
his first wife's death, Hardy, now aged seventy-three, married as his
second wife Florence Emily Dugdale, thirty-eight years his junior.
One of the five daughters of a somewhat authoritarian elementary
school headmaster, she had been making a living for herself as a
teacher and writer of children's stories and possessed excellent
secretarial skills that Hardy, after the manner of literary husbands,
was to draw upon heavily—not to say, exploit outrageously—in
the years ahead. Recognizing that his future wife possessed a
temperament even more melancholy than his own, Hardy pushed
his capacity for optimism to the point of hoping (so he told a friend)
that the junction of two negatives would prove, as with electricity,
to form a positive,[45] but the new Mrs Hardy found Max Gate cold,
isolated, and depressing—hemmed in as it then was by dark pines
that her husband could not bear to have trimmed or cut down—
and although she found deep satisfaction in her conscientious
devotion to her husband's genius, it seems rarely to have been a
source of active happiness.

   To Hardy the marriage brought levels of comfort and security
such as he had scarcely known, and the productivity of his last
years was significantly enhanced not only by Florence Hardy's
unstinting—though by no means uncomplaining—attention to his
personal needs but also by the specifically professional assistance
she was able to offer. Her presence, indeed, as an able and willing
collaborator was crucial to the most elaborate—and most notorious
—of Hardy's attempts to anticipate and even outwit the intrusive
inquisitiveness of future generations: it was her name alone that
was from the first intended to appear as author of that official
biography of Thomas Hardy which Hardy himself secretly composed for posthumous publication, and it was as Florence Emily
Hardy's *The Early Life of Thomas Hardy 1840–1891* and *The*

Later Years of Thomas Hardy 1892–1928 that the work was brought out by Macmillan in 1928 and 1930 respectively. The composition of the 'Life'—originally called 'The Life and Work of Thomas Hardy'[46]—seems to have got seriously under way in 1917–18, prompted by Hardy's loss of his sister Mary late in 1915, by his fear of biographical exposure both before and after his death, and by the insistence of Sydney Cockerell that he should 'write down something about yourself—& especially about that youthful figure whose photograph I have got, & of whom you told me that you could think with almost complete detachment'.[47]

Even as he urged Hardy to the task, Cockerell seems simultaneously to have been pointing him towards the possible adoption of a third-person point of view—along the lines of the third-person auto-biography of Thomas Hardy, the early nineteenth-century radical, of which he had given him a copy two years earlier.[48] But it was Hardy's own decision, encouraged by a 'Hardyan' concatenation of circumstances, which led to the essentially fictional assignment of that third-person voice to his wife, whose modest reputation as a writer of children's stories lent a little colour to a deception that otherwise depended upon the well-established literary tradition of memorialization by way of a family-generated 'Life and Letters'. Florence Hardy herself evidently saw the task as engaging her own literary energies to a degree which would validate the appearance of her name on the title-page, and it is certainly clear that her typing skills were fundamental to the project and that she was, in the final event, to play a larger part in determining the text than Hardy had perhaps envisaged.

Florence Hardy may have begun by writing down her husband's remarks and reminiscences as he talked, but by early 1918 they had settled upon a method which Hardy at least found more efficient and congenial: 'I am in the midst of reading Colvins "Keats" to *Him*', Florence Hardy told Cockerell on 2 February, '& working hard at notes, which he corrects & adds to daily, as I go along'.[49] Since Hardy found Colvin lacked 'the knack of lighting up his subject',[50] the Keats biography presumably proved of little value to him as a biographical model, even though its itemizing sub-title— *His Life and Poetry, His Friends, Critics, and After-Fame*—could have struck him as curiously anticipatory of his own central concerns in the 'Life'. The rest of Florence Hardy's comment, however, clearly evokes the process, then ongoing, by which she was daily typing up for her husband's reconsideration and possible revision the pages of manuscript that he was daily producing in the privacy of his study, sliding the pages under the blotter whenever he was threatened by intrusion.[51] A typescript draft covering the earliest period of Hardy's life is still in existence,[52] and there may have been other preliminary typescripts along the way, but the crucial textual document was the version typed by Florence Hardy in three copies—the ribbon or 'top' copy, eventually destined for the printer; the first carbon, intended to serve as the copy of record for the Hardys themselves; and the second carbon, designated as the 'rough' or working copy.[53]

Once the typing was done, the basic procedure was for Hardy to make his corrections, revisions, and additions on the rough copy and for his wife then to transfer them on to the file copy; when he had considered the changes further and given them his final approval, it would again be her job to transfer them on to the top copy. Sometimes, it appears, changes would be inscribed on to the file copy in pencil, to be inked over or erased once Hardy's final decision had been made. Some of these discreet and admirably systematic procedures suffered erosion as a result of Hardy's almost obsessive revision and supplementation of the 'Life' over the subsequent years, but he was reasonably consistent in using a stiffly calligraphic hand that he had learned in his architectural days. The same concern to avoid self-betrayal through the appearance of his normal hand on documents that would eventually be seen by printers and other outsiders also sealed the fate of his manuscript once his wife had finished typing from it: on 27 June 1918, shortly after Hardy's seventy-eighth birthday, she reported to Sydney Cockerell that a bonfire in the Max Gate garden had consumed 'the first draft of the notes—1840 to 1892. T. H. insisted.'[54] The impossibility, however, of finishing and publishing the work until after its subject's death left Hardy powerless to control either those final production stages or the destruction of the working typescripts, and it was the incomplete but still substantial survival of the latter which in course of time enabled Richard Purdy to determine the actual processes of composition.[55]

What can scarcely ever be determined is the degree of Hardy's fidelity to the source materials for the 'Life'. The references to public events and the datings of private events are for the most part correct enough, and such inaccuracies as do occur appear to result from simple carelessness rather than from any deliberate mis-representation of what would, in most instances, be readily checkable from other sources.[56] More problematic are the many quotations from Hardy's notebooks and diaries, for the destruction of the original documents has left no possibility of corroborating the accuracy either of the transcriptions themselves or of the dates to which they are assigned. It is sufficiently clear, however, that when transferring his old notes into their new contexts Hardy did not hesitate to cut, expand, or simply rewrite them in accordance with his current—that is to say, his elderly and hindsighted—notions of how they should ideally read. Fortuitously preserved on the back of a pencil sketch Hardy made in 1866 from the window of his London lodgings is an almost uniquely surviving leaf from one of his early working notebooks which happens to contain—heavily overscored, in his usual manner, to indicate that it has been used in some way—the original version of one of the earliest notes that he chose for publication, and while the central idea of the printed version does not significantly differ, stylistic revision during the transcription process did indeed occur.[57] Internal evidence makes it obvious that other quoted extracts must have been reworked to some degree—among them the 'Life's' one (indirect) allusion to Hardy's cousin Tryphena Sparks—and when the originals of letters included in the 'Life' happen to have survived substantial discrepancies can often be detected.[58]

It is true that such discrepancies may sometimes have resulted from Hardy's having been obliged to work with the retained drafts of letters rather than with the (perhaps modified) versions that were actually sent, but the broad implication of such evidence is, again, that Hardy—like Hallam Tennyson and Henry James—had no compunction about revising documents that seemed to need refurbishing in the light of matured judgement or subsequent events. An oversight of Florence Hardy's allowed one of her husband's letters to the eugenicist Caleb Saleeby to appear twice in *Later Years*, once on the basis of a transcript supplied by Saleeby himself, and earlier in the form of an extract revised by Hardy from the draft he had found in his files. Made aware of the error and of the differences between the two versions, Florence Hardy added a justificatory footnote which perhaps served only to raise still sharper questions: 'Both versions are printed [the footnote read in part] in order to illustrate Hardy's artistic inability to rest content with anything that he wrote until he had brought the expression as near to his thought as language would allow.'[59]

An unauthorized biography by Ernest Brennecke, Jr,[60] appeared in the United States early in 1925, and Hardy, angered and alarmed by its 'quizzing impertinence',[61] prompted Macmillan & Co. to threaten an action for breach of copyright against any publisher or bookseller who introduced the book into England.[62] When a member of the firm, alerted to the pre-emptive purpose of the 'Life', suggested that it should be set up in type ahead of Hardy's death, Florence Hardy was obliged to relay her husband's fear that information as to its contents 'would leak out, through the printers'. She added that he was currently 'going over the MS. & correcting it very carefully. This may be wise, or the reverse. However he is greatly interested.'[63] Since the 'Life' had now been a major preoccupation at Max Gate for something like ten years, the hint of weariness in these words is perhaps understandable. At the same time, allowance must be made for Hardy's no less natural perception that while he lived his 'Life' remained at least potentially in process. It was, in the event, only Hardy's death, on 11 January 1928, which brought the book's reconsideration by its subject finally to an end: in a letter written a week later Florence Hardy spoke of her husband as 'going through his biography with me a few days before he went to bed with this last illness'.[64]

Florence Hardy's phrase, 'his biography', was nicely ambiguous, in that the work she was shortly to publish was at once a biography of Hardy and a biography by Hardy, a life of himself. That she should not refer to it as an autobiography was, of course, indispensable to the maintenance of the fiction of her own authorship, but it was an avoidance in which she was already well practised: Hardy had so often declared he would never write such a work, she told Cockerell as early as 1918, that she was sure he would destroy all the 'notes' he had already completed if the word was ever used in his hearing.[65] The extent to which it seems appropriate to categorize as an autobiography the altered version of the 'Life' finally published by Florence Hardy is a question best considered in relation to the broader fate of Hardy's explicit and implicit testamentary dispositions, but that Hardy's personal rejection of the term was not merely disingenuous is suggested by that earlier claim to be able to write objectively and dispassionately about his own younger self. As Mary Jacobus has observed,[66] Hardy never

found it difficult to imagine himself as dead, as a posthumous
visitant to the world he was still in fact inhabiting,[67] and on this
occasion his remarkably successful projective impersonation of his
own widow—one reviewer of the 1984 edition of the 'Life'
suggested that it ought really to be called *The Life and Work of
Thomas Hardy by Florence Hardy*, by Thomas Hardy[68]—seems to
have answered to something deeply if mysteriously rooted in his
personality and self-image. It is rather as if he found himself
insufficiently substantial to serve as an autobiographical subject but
was none the less capable of imagining how he might, as the author
of his novels and poems, appear mildly interesting to an external
retrospective view.

When Hardy was eighty-two the publisher John Lane sent him a
book his firm had just brought out, *How to be Useful and Happy
from Sixty to Ninety*. Lane evidently intended it as a good-
humoured birthday gift; the degree of Hardy's amusement is not
recorded, but if he did in fact dip into the volume he would have
found it full of generally sensible advice on how to stay physically
healthy and mentally active—advice, however, of which he himself
was scarcely in need. It recommended, for example, that 'If you
have not a business when you are sixty either get one or get a
hobby',[69] and the day-to-day pattern of Hardy's final years was
above all characterized by the close attention he continued to pay to
the specifically professional aspects of his career. His occasional
secretary, May O'Rourke, who admired everything about her
employer except his lack of religious faith, later testified to the
orderliness and self-discipline of these late years, and especially to
Hardy's fidelity to a set pattern of living: 'He went to his study
every morning at ten o'clock, as punctually as a city man to his
office, and worked there for a fixed time.'[70]
     Unless he was actually ill, indeed, Hardy would remain in his
upstairs study throughout the middle part of the day, having his
lunch brought up on a tray and manifesting himself only at teatime
to the day's quota of friends and admirers, his wife having been left
in the meantime to her manifold secretarial and domestic tasks, to
the doubtful mercies of the frequently troublesome Max Gate
servants and the dank pleasures of the then overgrown Max Gate
garden, with its untrimmed trees and its lawns like green patches at
the bottoms of wells. So closeted and protected, Hardy dealt

promptly and efficiently with the voluminous correspondence of a world-famous man of letters, still sending handwritten notes to old friends but drafting longer items to be typed by either his wife or May O'Rourke and directing that still other replies (especially standard letters to anthologists, publishers, literary agents, journalists, enthusiasts, autograph-seekers, advocates of causes) should be sent out not over his own name or initials at all but over his wife's or, sometimes, the secretary's. He did send a personal negative to a request from a member of the government for a poem supportive of the activities of the Empire Marketing Board, but simply scrawled 'Regret can find nothing pertinent' on an enquiry from the Federation of Calico Printers as to passages in his works descriptive of wall papers—passing on to his wife or Miss O'Rourke the problem of conveying that message politely.[71] Demands for autographs, autograph letters, or signatures in books were met with silence, a stock third-person reply, or, on occasion, a request for a one-guinea fee, to be forwarded to the Dorset County Hospital.[72] Somewhat absurdly, perhaps, he went to the trouble of drafting in full the message May O'Rourke was to send to an importunate Australian correspondent: 'Were Mr Hardy to answer the mass of letters he receives from strangers like yourself he would have no time whatever for any work of his own, or even for taking rest.'[73]

As the demands on his time and diminishing energies became ever greater, so he fell back more and more on the available strategies of old age, invoking his years and exaggerating his infirmities as grounds for saying no to invitations and requests that he would at almost any time of his life have found some means of turning down. He had always fought shy of dinners, presentations, and other formal occasions, but it was now much easier to say that 'for physical reasons, I am never sure of being able to keep an engagement in winter time nowadays'.[74] Nor was it just his eighty-six years that in October 1926 prompted the telegram declining, 'owing to age', an invitation to join the committee of the *Daily Express* community singing movement.[75] Poor eyesight became a convenient excuse for sending skimpy or typewritten letters[76] and for postponing (indefinitely, in almost all cases) the reading of the books so inexorably presented by friends, acquaintances, and even total strangers.[77]

There was, of course, some inevitable deterioration of his physical faculties as he drew further into old age: in those famous photographs which show him sitting alongside Edmund Gosse in the Max Gate garden just seven months before his death a degree of deafness is clearly signalled by the hand he has cupped behind his right ear.[78] It is also true that he lamented the passage of time, the onset of old age, and the heavy incidence of bereavements: the Christmas of his eightieth year prompted the observation that 'anniversaries to people of my age cannot be, in the nature of things, very cheerful occasions';[79] in the following May a series of memories evoked by the death of an old friend concluded with the remark, 'However, all that is past, & I am old likewise, & the shadows are stretching out';[80] and in October 1922 the poignant sense of irrecoverability created by such losses was characterized as 'the penalty we pay for not dying early'.[81] But his mental faculties suffered no significant decline, he kept steadily at work until the onset of his last illness, and Gosse, reporting on that June 1927 visit to Max Gate, seems not even to have registered the deafness: '[Hardy] is a wonder if you like!' he exclaimed. 'At 87½ without any deficiency of sight, hearing, mind or conversation. Very tiny and fragile, but full of spirit and a gaiety not quite consistent in the most pessimistic of poets.'[82] And Florence Hardy told Richard Purdy in August 1931 that the poem 'He Resolves to Say No More', printed as the conclusion to the posthumously published *Winter Words*, was not to be taken seriously as a valediction: Hardy had experienced just before his death a great burst of creative energy and felt that he was capable of writing volumes.[83]

It was, indeed, in the hope and expectation of writing or rewriting poems as well as of keeping up with his correspondence that Hardy withdrew with such regularity to his Max Gate study. 'I never let a day go without using a pen', he told a visitor in the summer of 1920. 'Just holding it sets me off; in fact I can't think without it. It's important not to wait for the right mood. If you do, it will come less and less.'[84] Even when confined to bed during the weeks prior to his death he still managed to complete the revision of 'Christmas in the Elgin Room', promised for publication in *The Times* on Christmas Eve 1927, and on the very day he died he remained capable of dictating to his wife his savage grudge-based epitaphs on G. K. Chesterton and George Moore. The Chesterton poem collapses in the middle—perhaps Florence Hardy simply did not get it all down—but the ending at least of the Moore piece, 'On One Who Thought No Other Could Write Such English As

Himself', is complete, terse, and nakedly vindictive, constituting a perhaps distressingly unrelenting literary last word:

> Heap dustbins on him: they'll not meet
> The apex of his self conceit.[85]

If the two epitaphs are striking demonstrations of Hardy's capacity for rigorous unforgiving, they seem scarcely less striking as instances, together with 'Christmas in the Elgin Room', either of remarkable death-bed creativity or of equally remarkable death-bed memory. But 'Christmas in the Elgin Room' appears to have existed in some form by 1905, and a good many other poems in the final volumes were identified by Hardy as having derived from versions of earlier date.[86] 'Retty's Phases', first published in *Human Shows* in 1925, is the most fully documented instance of a poem dating right back to the 1860s,[87] but 'Gallant's Song' and 'The Musing Maiden' of *Winter Words* are similarly dated,[88] and several other poems in the same volume are authorially ascribed to the last two decades of the nineteenth century or the first two decades of the twentieth. There are also grounds for suspecting that more of the late poems than Hardy directly acknowledged were in fact based upon drafts, notes, and story outlines that at that date still existed either as separate documents or as entries in one or other of his notebooks. When asked for poems, he would often speak of looking out items that were already in existence, though not necessarily in finished form. Invited in March 1919 to contribute to the first issue of the *Athenaeum* under Middleton Murry's editorship, Hardy replied: 'I have been searching everywhere for some poem that would meet your views, but so far have not been able to find anything at all up to date, or quite in keeping with the first number of a review.'[89] To Ezra Pound, seeking a contribution to the *Dial* in November 1920, he was even more explicit: 'As to your question, I have been hunting some MS. pieces, written and half-written, but have not found anything yet that would exactly suit. I will have a further search.'[90]

Even allowing for the possibility of a certain temporizing disingenuousness in replies of this sort, it seems reasonable to assume that on many such occasions Hardy did indeed search among his papers—in that apparently inexhaustible 'drawer' of which he sometimes spoke—for existing drafts and fragments which might prove susceptible of refinement, expansion, or simple adaptation. Hardy's dating of 'According to the Mighty Working', the poem subsequently sent to the *Athenaeum*, indicates that it had been written at least two years previously; 'The Two Houses', sent to the *Dial* in December 1920, is of unknown date, but its architectural subject-matter would seem to point towards its having been worked up from a draft of considerably earlier origin.[91] This is not, of course, to argue that Hardy wrote no new poems during the 1920s, nor to question the intensity of the creative engagement represented by his work of revision. Florence Hardy, indeed, seems scarcely to have distinguished between the two kinds of activity; on 27 November 1927, just before the onset of her husband's final illness, she recorded that he had 'been writing almost all the day, revising poems', including one she had not seen before, called 'An Unkindly May'.[92] It is, however, to suggest that Hardy's truly astonishing octogenarian output of the 1920s was dependent not only upon the resources of his memory but also, and perhaps even more heavily, upon the physical records of what he had thought and written as much as sixty years earlier and upon the particular occasions which led, either deliberately or incidentally, to the revisitation of such materials.

When the Mellstock Edition volumes were being prepared and published during the winter preceding his eightieth birthday, Hardy made significant changes to only one of the novels, *A Pair of Blue Eyes*, explaining to Siegfried Sassoon that he had felt free to do so because the 'people shadowed forth in the story being now all, alas, dead, I am able to give lights here & there on the locality, &c., which I had to obscure when the book was written'.[93] Though neither extensive nor especially consequential in themselves, the revisions were significant for their direct references to Hardy's courtship of his first wife in the early 1870s and for their having been prompted not by Emma Hardy's death alone but also by Hardy's subsequent experience of writing 'Poems of 1912–13', that extraordinary sequence of remorseful elegies in which just that time and just that setting were so persistently and centrally invoked.

Hardy, in that letter to Sassoon, seems to take a somewhat melancholy satisfaction in the deaths, the definitive departures, of all those—himself excluded—whom *A Pair of Blue Eyes* had originally, as he puts it, shadowed forth, and it seems appropriate enough that in the 'Poems of 1912–13' themselves he should so

often have addressed his dead wife as if she were a potentially
visible and visitable ghost. 'After a Journey', for example, opens
with the line 'Hereto I come to view a voiceless ghost'; 'The Voice'
begins 'Woman much missed, how you call to me, call to me'; other
poems are called 'The Phantom Horsewoman' and 'The Haunter'.[94]
Not only is the evoked ghost of Emma Hardy as she was in the days
of their courtship the central figure in the sequence, but it is possible
to see—and likely enough that Hardy himself came to recognize—
the process by which that evocation was achieved.

Underlying all of the Emma poems was the same simple, brutal
realization of loss, compounded by regret at the failure of love and
lovingkindness. But they emerged and took shape with some
immediacy and directness from Hardy's profoundly disturbing
experience of reading through his dead wife's papers, including the
private diaries in which she had so bitterly recorded her grievances
against him over the last two decades, and from the scarcely less
disturbing but more deliberately undertaken experience of revisiting
after her death the church and hamlet of St Juliot, that remote
corner of Cornwall where they had first and so romantically met
more than forty years before. Although 'In Time of "the Breaking
of Nations"' was not one of the 'Poems of 1912–13', it had its
acknowledged origin in the Cornish experience of 1870 and was
famously cited by Hardy as an instance of his capacity for
'exhuming' long-buried emotions 'as fresh as when interred'.[95] Its
composition in 1914, however, cannot usefully be separated from
Hardy's entire imaginative recovery of the courtship period,
especially since the specific generative memory was almost certainly
activated by his deliberately seeking out or accidentally stumbling
upon the notes he had made, back in 1870, inside the back cover of
a textbook from which he was attempting to teach himself
German.[96]

Memory was of course crucial to Hardy's persistent invocation
of the past, but whether he possessed, practically speaking, a
remarkable memory—by comparison, say, with the memories of
other writers—is by no means easy to determine. It is amusing to
find that in his correspondence with Hermann Lea, compiler of the
authorized guide to Wessex locations, he sometimes needed to be
reminded of what he had obviously not been very sure about in the
first place. 'Have you a note of which story (in Noble Dames) I said
was fixed at Longleat?' Hardy rather plaintively asks. 'And where

did I say "Batton Castle" was in the D[uche]ss of Hamptonshire?'[97] Perhaps that critic was right after all who said, in a helpful footnote, that the place names in Hardy were *usually* either invented or real. Evidently Hardy himself wasn't always sure, and it may be significant that his first wife compiled a checklist of fictional locations for her husband to refer to;[98] in 1880, indeed, he reportedly confessed to a visitor that 'he had the greatest difficulty in remembering the people and incidents of his own stories so that Mrs. Hardy had to keep on the look-out for him'.[99] Whatever the quality of his memory, in short, he seems in practice not to have trusted it overmuch, and it is obviously relevant that he should have been, like many Victorians, an active, almost an obsessive, keeper of notes. The habit may have derived from his early interest in water-colour painting—the instructional book he used[100] having recommended the practice of capturing in words the precise quality of the passing visual moment—but it soon became an element in his autodidacticism, his determination to make good the deficiencies of his formal education, and was later kept up chiefly as a general record of experiences and events and as a means of assembling basic 'material' for his writings. Even as late as 1890, he somewhat disconcertingly records, he was still gathering what he called 'novel-padding' from London music-halls and police-courts.[101]

On such occasions, and for most day-to-day purposes, he seems to have used, at least from his early twenties onwards, a long series of those now-vanished working pocketbooks, easy to carry about and convenient for jotting down ideas, images, plots, observations, notes from his reading, even occasional pencil sketches of places, paintings, and so forth. Much used in the composition of his novels and stories—as their occasional repetitions of descriptive passages rather strikingly reveal—these notebooks were no less crucial to Hardy's late productivity as a poet. They served as repositories of still unused materials, from complete drafts to single images, that might still constitute the ingredients of publishable poems—the notebook to which Hardy gave the name 'Poetical Matter' appears to have been a compilation of suggestive scraps culled during such re-perusals[102]—and they provided, as such, an assurance of his continuing activity as a poet on into such future as might remain. Above all, they facilitated real or imagined 'recoveries' of the past and directly stimulated the composition or at least the completion of specific poems—to the extent, indeed, that the major resurgences of Hardy's creativity during his last two decades can be more or less directly associated with his deliberate or enforced consultations of documentary reminders of time past.

The rich resources of Hardy's childhood experience, so central to his prose and verse alike, seem to have become available to his working imagination only as they were gradually and variously released by the sheer passage of time and by a series of specific and increasingly deliberate actions on Hardy's part. The productive revival of early memories during the writing of *The Mayor of Casterbridge* appears to have been triggered not just by Hardy's experience of returning to Dorchester and his native countryside but also by the element of imaginative self-projection involved in his systematic research, ostensibly for the novel's sake, into local newspapers dating from the years preceding his own birth. And in so far as his work on his collected editions was inherently retrospective—leading, for example, to the revelation of locations associated with his childhood as the originals of his fictional settings—those editions, prepared and published just before the return to poetry and then at roughly decade-long intervals, must clearly be counted among his significant episodes of release, of enforced or enabled return to his personal past, hence among the sources of his extraordinary range and productivity as a poet, even into his ninth decade. They also served, by that same token, as devices for ensuring the textual permanence of a passionately reconstituted childhood world and its ultimate projection into a future beyond his own lifetime.

The composition of the 'Life' was in itself a characteristic autobiographical exercise of old age, an occasion for coming to terms with the personal past, and as he worked on it Hardy also took stock and at least partial control of a lifetime's accumulation of documents and records and miscellaneous paper. Proofs and other pre-publication documents deemed inessential were turned out of cupboards and destroyed, together with stacks of old newspapers and magazines that had accumulated over the years. Reviews of his own books were re-read and then selected either for destruction or for preservation in organized scrapbooks. Incoming letters from all periods were sorted, read, and for the most part burned. Since the writing and revision of the 'Life' took him repeatedly back to those working notebooks—full of observations, ideas, images, plots, descriptions of people, places, and things—it is clear not only that old memories were numerously disinterred but that some of the written materials brought to the surface proved quite readily adaptable to the resurrection of old poems or the generation of new. 'Christmas in the Elgin Room', for example, could well have re-emerged in this fashion, or 'An Unkindly May', poems which if not precisely impersonal seem not to attain or even attempt the deeper levels of intensity and engagement.

But those teeming documentary witnesses to the past also reinforced his sense of continuity with his family, his locality, and his own earlier selves, and spoke powerfully and irrefutably to the sheer bleak facts of time and distance, absence and loss. What made the composition of the 'Life' in Hardy's late seventies so crucial an event within his own lifetime was precisely the stimulus to his still creative imagination provided by the complexity of his response—part acceptance, part avoidance—to his evoked, his conjured past. 'I have not been doing much', Hardy wrote to his friend Sir George Douglas in May 1919, '—mainly destroying papers of the last 30 or 40 years, & they raise ghosts.'[103] Hardy was already, of course, an accomplished raiser of ghosts: in 'The Photograph' (first published in 1917) the speaker, engaged in just such a 'casual clearance of life's arrears', watches in horror as the portrait of a former lover is progressively consumed by the flames, feeling as if he had 'put her to death'.[104] The writing of 'Poems of 1912–13' taught him—not for the first time, to judge by such a poem as 'Wessex Heights'[105]—that one's personal ghosts, like one's deepest memories, did not just manifest themselves by chance but were best summoned by the more or less conscious practice of specific disciplines and techniques. The use of preserved fragments of personal observation as both material and stimulus in the construction of the 'Life' constituted just such a technique, and—despite the loss of those working notebooks—ample evidence remains of Hardy's persistent cultivation during his seventies and eighties of multiple connections with his own past, with the past of his family, and with the past of that locality in which he had been born, from which he had exiled himself in youth and early adulthood, but to which he had deliberately and permanently returned in the days of his literary success.

'Yesterday', Florence Hardy told Sydney Cockerell in September 1916, 'we went to look at the heath from a point which I did not know & stood on the old coach road to London—now overgrown

with bracken and heather—& my husband had visions of coaches
rolling along, bearing George III—& the Princesses, & Pitt &
Nelson, & Captain Hardy—& then his mother, as a child.'[106] The
inclusion of Hardy's mother in this spectral roll-call nicely
illustrates the extent to which his imaginative identification with
his parents and grandparents had become merged with that
specifically historical—and extensively researched—obsession with
the Napoleonic period which emerged most strongly in *The
Dynasts*. But the passage seems above all remarkable for its
description of a visionary experience consciously sought and
expertly achieved. Hardy used the phrase 'Moments of Vision'
as the title of his fifth poetry volume, having earlier rejected
'Moments from the Years' as a title for what became *Satires of
Circumstance*, and it seems appropriate to interpret in similar terms
the kind of temporary remoteness from the immediate present
reported by T. E. Lawrence following a visit to Max Gate in the
early 1920s: 'a film seems to slip over his mind at times now: and
the present is then obscured by events of his childhood'.[107] And on
another occasion: 'Then [Hardy] is so far-away. Napoleon is a real
man to him, and the country of Dorsetshire echoes that name
everywhere in Hardy's ears. He lives in his period, and thinks of it
as the great war.'[108] Such slippages between different levels of
memory may be characteristic of old age, but in Hardy's case they
seem to have had at least as much to do with the intensification of
habits of creative reverie which he had adopted, or fallen into,
much earlier in his career.

Hardy's study at Max Gate constituted in itself a permanent
aide-mémoire of a complex and powerful kind, a repository of
objects rich in associative significance: books dating back to his
earliest years, family photographs, illustrations to *Jude* and other
novels, portraits of admired writers, a painting that had once
belonged to William Barnes, the Dorset dialect poet, the portable
writing desk[109] he had bought in Dorchester as a boy from the
father of Sir Frederick Treves, another famous son of Dorset, best
remembered now as the saviour of the 'Elephant Man'. Florence
Hardy, showing Richard Purdy the study for the first time in the
summer of 1929, spoke of Hardy's resistance to the replacement of
old and familiar objects and pointed to the presence on his desk of
an old pair of scissors, his first wife's paper-knife, the paper-knife
she had herself bought him the day before their marriage, the ink-

well given him by Florence Henniker, and the perpetual calendar set always at Monday, 7 March, the day and date of his first meeting with Emma Gifford.[110] Among the books on the study shelves were the four volumes of John Hutchins's massive *History and Antiquities of the County of Dorset*, much annotated and amplified by Hardy during the 1920s—one inserted cutting from *The Times* dates from as late as August 1927—and stored away in drawers and cupboards were his own early sketches, together perhaps with some of his sister Mary's, and the music books that had been used by his father and grandfather as members of the old Stinsford choir. In one corner hung his father's 'cello and the fiddle that he had himself played as a child.[111] From the upper windows of Max Gate he could see much of that countryside of his childhood on which he had subsequently based so much of the imaginary territory of his fiction and verse. To walk out of its gate was to enter into a regional world that he had not just imaginatively but actually altered for ever. And by crossing the watermeadows to Stinsford churchyard he could place himself in the presence of the beloved dead and attain a sense of renewed communion and communication with them.

Hardy's profound validation of Stinsford emerges clearly from a letter of 1924 in which he told a friend that he frequently revived his 'childish memories' by 'going to "a slope of green access" about a mile from here, finding no pain in so doing'[112]—'a slope of green access' being Shelley's phrase, in *Adonais*, for Keats's grave in the Protestant Cemetery in Rome, a location once visited by Hardy and doubly revered for its having become Shelley's own resting place as well. Such deliberate cultivation of the relatively serene memories of childhood seems increasingly to have displaced, though not altogether to have obliterated, the remorse and bitter regret associated with more recent recollections, especially of the later stages of his first marriage. Not only do the final volumes of verse contain a remarkable number of poems relating to some of the most important of Hardy's early relationships,[113] but from about 1919 onwards his letters to friends make open and easy reference to childhood events and memories—to his mother, his grandmother, and even his great-grandmother, to his confirmation by an early Victorian bishop of Salisbury and his first sight of Salisbury cathedral itself, to his childhood unawareness of sexual innuendo, to his arrival in London in the early 1860s, and so on. There is no indication that Hardy was apprised of the danger that his conscious acts of revisitation would inevitably distort the authenticity of original memories by superimposing upon them the successive layers of elaboration, reinterpretation, and new association introduced by each revisitation's particular moment and mood. Nor, had he been aware of such dangers, would they necessarily have troubled him. Recall may be almost always constructive, but it is also impenetrably subjective, so that even in the relatively well documented instance of 'In Time of "the Breaking of Nations"' the only person in a position to estimate the accuracy with which the original emotion had been revived after forty years was the necessarily fallible forty-years-older Hardy himself.

For Hardy in his later years memories, true or false, were alike the source of emotions, hence of poems; and memories, faithful or fictionalized, were most readily prompted by acts of deliberate self-exposure to memorials of the personal, dynastic, or local past. The mere contemplation of the past as generalized loss could generate a powerful emotional response, whether in the form of a correspondingly generalized regret or of a more sharply focused sense of the inevitability and even the desirability of personal extinction: 'Why do I go on doing these things? | Why not cease?' asks the speaker of 'Why Do I?', the final poem in *Human Shows*, the last volume Hardy published in his lifetime.[114] But Hardy himself did continue to do those things—to work, think, and write—as he moved with frail resilience through his ninth decade, and his sustained activity as a poet during his last years remains in many respects the most astonishing and impressive aspect of his entire career, imposing a sense of direction and proportion upon the successive discontinuities of that career and making it seem so shapely overall. It was not simply that he rose, so remarkably, from a position of rural obscurity to one of scarcely equalled national and international renown, but that he realized his genius in such a variety of literary forms and presented, by the time of his death, a model of a life lived to the limits of its creativity, active and even innovative to the very end and yet leaving no substantial literary tasks undone.

Florence Hardy

THE moment of Thomas Hardy's death can with some precision be fixed at 9.05 p.m. on 11 January 1928, just a month after he had first fallen ill and approximately thirty-five minutes after the onset of a massive heart attack.[1] The family physician, Dr E. W. Mann, had just driven off after making a routine visit but was called back to Max Gate in time to be present, with Hardy's wife Florence and her sister, Eva Dugdale, at the moment of death[2]—he later registered the immediate cause as 'Cardiac Syncope'—and Sydney Cockerell, who was in the house at the time, telephoned through to London in time for an announcement to be made before the conclusion of the BBC's nine o'clock news broadcast. The end came suddenly after a day in which Hardy had been alert enough to talk sensibly and even cheerfully with his doctor and with the only other people allowed into the sickroom—his wife and her sister Eva, his own sister Kate, and one of the servants—and to dictate his hostile epitaphs on George Moore and G. K. Chesterton.[3]

About most of the other details of Hardy's death and its immediate aftermath it is impossible to speak with confidence. Florence Hardy's draft account of these events contains a passage, omitted from the version she published in *The Later Years of Thomas Hardy*, to the effect that just before Hardy's final loss of consciousness 'a few broken sentences, one of them heartrending in its poignancy, showed that his mind had reverted to a sorrow of the past'.[4] She once told a friend that when her husband realized he was dying a look of horror passed over his face,[5] and she was presumably, though not certainly, the source of her solicitor's statement that Hardy had died with 'broken words' about Emma, his first wife, on his lips.[6] The Max Gate housekeeper, however, concurred with Eva Dugdale in recalling Hardy's last words as being 'Eva, what is this?'[7]

The following morning—which happened to be Florence Hardy's birthday—Henry and Kate Hardy, Hardy's surviving siblings, came to view the body. Cockerell, too, now saw it for the first time as he helped Eva Dugdale to dress it in Hardy's Cambridge doctoral robes,[8] but, as Florence Hardy was later to complain,[9] he had not hesitated, in his capacity as co-literary executor, to lay out the will on the dining-room table the very evening of Hardy's death. The choice of someone to share with Florence the responsibilities of literary executorship had exercised Hardy a good deal. Edward Clodd, Edmund Gosse, and the Society of Authors had all been considered at various times, but Clodd was evidently deemed too indiscreet and Gosse too elderly (though he remained in the final will as a potential replacement for Cockerell),[10] and the Society of Authors had responded negatively to a question as to its possible acceptance of executorial roles which Hardy, as its president, had been able to raise as a matter of policy rather than as a personal enquiry.[11] Cockerell was in any case an obvious choice, a man of great intelligence, formidable personality, and wide connections who had consistently made himself useful to Hardy ever since his organization of the manuscript distribution of 1911.

Florence Hardy, melancholy, inexperienced, and lacking in either social or sexual confidence, seems always to have been obscurely troubled by Cockerell's dominating manner and doubtful as to his motives.[12] Over the years, however, her essential loneliness and friendlessness at Max Gate—her constant housebound attendance upon the personal and professional needs of an octogenarian and somewhat hypochondriacal husband who spent the greater part of each day isolated in his study—had made her more appreciative of Cockerell's personal attentiveness to her and her concerns and increasingly reliant upon his ready performance of tasks which might have taxed or even defeated her unaided efforts. He it was, for example, who arranged and supervised on her behalf the production of several privately printed pamphlets of Hardy's verse[13] and who conveyed to the British Museum authorities Hardy's wish that the heading of his entry in the Reading Room catalogue should be changed from 'Thomas Hardy, novelist' to 'Thomas Hardy, novelist and poet'.[14] This convergence of emotional and practical dependence eventually brought Florence Hardy on to terms of some intimacy with Cockerell, to the point of their engaging in an extensive correspondence focused on life at Max Gate but clearly not meant to be seen by Hardy himself, and it was she who summoned him to Dorchester by telegram just two days before Hardy's death.[15]

To Sir James Barrie, the other man she had called upon at this

time of crisis,[16] she was closer still: she seems to have felt confident
of his proposing marriage to her in her widowed state, and he may
even have done so in some form, only to retreat from the offer
shortly afterwards.[17] Even Barrie, however, proved incapable of
giving her the kind of support and advice she needed in her exposed
and difficult position as an isolated woman required to make
decisions in areas of which she had little if any practical experience.
Her relationship with Cockerell, meanwhile, had been in decline
ever since the moment when he opened Hardy's will and began—
almost instinctively, no doubt, and out of a sincere and even
elevated sense of incumbency—to assert his male authority over
what he had earlier described to his wife as a 'housefull of
women'.[18]

Hardy's will, signed and witnessed on 24 August 1922, assigned to
Lloyds Bank Limited all the financial responsibilities of executorship
and trusteeship and appointed Cockerell and Florence Hardy as
joint literary executors.[19] Technically speaking, the responsibilities
of the two literary executors were confined to matters relating to
Hardy's literary estate, but the will, as events were to prove, was
not lacking in ambiguities, and it was specifically to the question of
Hardy's funeral and interment that Cockerell immediately addressed
himself that first evening. The letter he wrote home the next day
spoke of going into Dorchester after Hardy's death to send off some
messages, returning to Max Gate at about 11 p.m., and sleeping
that night in the dining-room in the clothes he was wearing.[20] From
his diary it emerges that the messages were chiefly telephone calls to
The Times and to Barrie, who was now in London, well placed to
conduct the high-level negotiations that he and Cockerell had
already agreed to set in train.[21] During the afternoon of 12 January,
therefore, while Hardy's death was being announced in newspaper
headlines around the world, Barrie armed himself with the
approval of the prime minister, Stanley Baldwin, and went with
Geoffrey Dawson, the influential editor of *The Times*, to call upon
the Dean of Westminster, the Very Revd W. Foxley Norris, and
obtain his approval to Hardy's burial in Poets' Corner. 'All was
immensely cordial,' Barrie wrote to Cockerell. 'The Dean's first
words were that he of course agreed that it was T. H.'s proper
resting place.' The ceremony, he added, had been fixed for the
following Monday, 16 January, at 2 p.m.[22]

Awareness of Hardy's immense fame and of the potential power of public opinion, immediately and impressively represented by the combination of the Government and *The Times*, had doubtless left Norris with little real choice. And yet the decision was, from his own point of view, by no means unproblematic, the difficulty lying not so much in Hardy's being the first man of letters since Tennyson to be granted interment in the Abbey, and the first novelist since Dickens, as in his being rather notoriously not a Christian. In 1909, when Meredith was denied an Abbey burial—though not a memorial service—on just such grounds, Hardy had written only half-jokingly to Gosse: 'Why don't you write to the Times suggesting a heathen annexe to the Abbey, strictly accursed by the Dean & clergy on its opening day, to hold people like Meredith, Swinburne, Spencer, &c.' He added, with a reminiscence of the controversy over the exclusion of George Eliot's remains: 'The Abbey itself is, as [T. H.] Huxley said, a Christian temple after all.'[23] More recently, in July 1924, he had publicly supported a scheme for a tablet to Byron's memory to be installed in the Abbey in the centenary year of his death,[24] and greeted rejection of the proposal with a satirical poem, 'A Refusal' (later published in *Human Shows*), in which Norris's predecessor as Dean of Westminster was represented as declaring:

> And passed is my patience
> That such a creed-scorner
> (Not mentioning horner)
> Should claim Poet's Corner.[25]

Norris's decision to admit Hardy's ashes to Poets' Corner was directly or inferentially supported by a number of letters in the columns of *The Times*, most of them citing Hardy's long-held 'belief' in the social and moral functions of the Church of England as an institution,[26] but the Dean himself, challenged by his superiors within the Church, felt obliged to write to the vicar of Fordington St George, the Dorchester parish in which Max Gate stood, in search of reassurance as to Hardy's faith, religious practice, and moral standards. Though forced to admit that his famous parishioner had never attended any service at Fordington during the previous twenty-one years, the Revd R. Grosvenor Bartelot valiantly invoked Hardy's moral rectitude, upbringing within the church, interest in old church music, contributions to parochial funds, and occasional attendance at services in other local churches as grounds for characterizing him as a Christian and churchman 'at heart'.[27] It is not known how persuasive such evidence may have seemed either to Norris or to his critics, but it is perhaps worth noting—as it was certainly noted at the time—that no members of the royal family were present at a funeral that was in all other respects a national occasion.[28]

The Dean's response to the initiative taken by Barrie and Cockerell had meanwhile had repercussions of quite another kind at Max Gate. In his letter to Cockerell of 12 January Barrie had said that there was 'obviously a great feeling in London that [Abbey burial] is the proper offer to one of her great ones', adding almost as an afterthought: 'Of course cremation is necessary.' In Dorset, however, Hardy was naturally viewed as the peculiar possession not of London nor even of the nation—Barrie's phrasing having betrayingly elided the two—but of the county and region with which he had been so long, so intimately, and so famously identified, and such local chauvinism was undoubtedly intensified by suspicion and even abhorrence of the non-traditional practice of cremation. To Hardy's deeply conservative brother and sister the necessity for cremation was, as the latter wrote in her diary, 'Another staggering blow', and Hardy himself would probably have shared their view.[29] For Florence Hardy, grieving, exhausted, and bewildered, a further difficulty lay in the simple fact that her husband's will distinctly specified, as the first of its many clauses, the 'wish that I may be buried in Stinsford Churchyard Dorset near to the Grave of my parents, and if possible in my wife Emma's Grave or close to the foot thereof according to considerations detailed in my directions to my Executors on a separate paper'.

The apparent non-survival of such directions poses serious problems for the interpretation of this as of certain other sections of the will, and it is not easy to challenge directly Cockerell's much later assertion that Hardy would not have been opposed to the burial of his ashes at Westminster: 'He was far too humble a man to conceive of such a thing as at all likely. But, as one of his executors, I had put the matter before him, and in the directions he gave for his burial at Stinsford, as well as in the provisional inscription that he designed for his tombstone, he was careful to leave a loophole for a possible alternative.'[30] It may reasonably be doubted whether Cockerell, as a prospective *literary* executor merely, would have confronted Hardy with such an issue in quite such terms, but while Hardy may indeed have been 'humble' in certain respects he could scarcely have been unaware, even without such prompting, of the likelihood that some at least of his friends and admirers would wish to see him buried in the Abbey.

Kate Hardy's diary does in any case record that when she and Henry went to Max Gate the morning after Hardy's death they were told of, though not shown, a 'notice' among his papers 'to the effect that "if the nation desires it otherwise" he can be buried at Westminster A.',[31] and the surviving full-scale design which Hardy prepared for a memorial tablet to himself in St Juliot Church, though meticulously finished and specific in every other respect, significantly supplies as the place of burial only the lightly sketched-in words 'STINSFORD DORSET'—just one letter short of those required for the words 'WESTMINSTER ABBEY' which appear on the tablet as erected.[32] Years earlier, when writing to Edward Clodd during the controversy over Meredith's exclusion from the Abbey, Hardy had expressed a regret 'that M. did not leave a special injunction that he was to be buried at Dorking, so that the question might not have arisen',[33] and the possibility has therefore to be entertained that Hardy, in contemplating his own funeral, did in fact recognize, perhaps even hope, that the national desire for an Abbey burial might prove irresistible, at the same time trusting that the clear specification of Stinsford as his preferred resting-place would serve to guard him, even in death, against the stigma of rejection on grounds of either religious or literary insufficiency.

If these were indeed Hardy's thoughts he seems not to have shared them with his wife. For her the indisputable facts remained the unqualified phrasing of the will and her own crowding memories of watching her husband point out, to herself or for the benefit of accompanying friends, the chosen spot in Stinsford churchyard where not only he but she too would in due course lie. 'Hardy', wrote Barrie to Lady Cynthia Asquith in June 1920, 'took me yesterday to the place where he is to be buried, and to-day he took me to see the place where he would like next best to be buried',[34] and the accounts of other privileged visitors to Stinsford amply confirm that the 'slope of green access' which held the closely grouped tombs of his parents, his ancestors, and his first wife was for Hardy complexly sacred ground, invested with the deepest emotional significance. Hardy's widow, in short, had good reason to think that her husband had meant what his will said, and it can only have been with the greatest reluctance that she permitted Cockerell to convey to the press, during the evening of 12 January, her approval of a process that had already been effectively taken out of her hands:

> Mrs. Hardy, after profound consideration, has accepted the Dean's offer. She felt that it was incumbent on her to do so in deference to the very strong body of opinion in favour of the honour which has been offered. She felt sure that although Mr. Hardy had expressed a wish to be buried in Stinsford Churchyard, near his home, the nation's desire in the matter must be obeyed.[35]

The phrase 'profound consideration' scarcely does justice either to the pressure Florence Hardy was under or to the atmosphere of recrimination prevailing at Max Gate and among Hardy's family and Dorset friends. Hardy's sister, it is true, seems to have believed that he 'would never have refused Westminster Abbey',[36] but Henry Hardy was 'very emotional and strongly against' the Abbey[37] and their cousin Teresa Hardy, still living at Higher Bockhampton, was freely sharing with newspaper reporters her view that 'Tom' should be buried 'among his own people, where he so much wanted to be buried'.[38] Cockerell recognized on the morning of the 13th that Florence Hardy remained 'full of doubts' as to the wisdom of what had been decided,[39] but he had left for London in order to make arrangements for the cremation and the engraving of the Abbey casket before the introduction of what was ultimately to prove the most controversial element in the disposition of Hardy's remains, the removal of his heart for separate burial at Stinsford.

The proposal for a heart burial emerged from a conversation between Florence Hardy and the Rector of Stinsford, the Revd H. G. B. Cowley, and his wife, who called at Max Gate during the afternoon of 13 January to extend their condolences to Hardy's widow and voice their unhappiness at the exclusion of Stinsford from the funeral arrangements being proposed.[40] Whether the Cowleys came armed with the idea or whether it arose during the course of the discussion cannot be known, nor whether it was in any sense prompted by a recent (December 1926) lecture by a local antiquary on the practice of heart-burial in Dorset at the time of the Crusades,[41] but to Florence Hardy it seemed to offer the possibility

of compromise, of bowing to what was being represented to her as
the national will while at the same time making at least a symbolic
gesture in the direction of local feeling and of Hardy's own
expressed intentions. Cockerell's consent, sought by telegram, was
given by telephone early that evening and the news passed on to a
press still avidly following the sequence of events. 'Mrs. Hardy
[Cowley was reported as saying] has told me several times that she
wanted her husband to be buried in Dorset, . . . and she repeated
the wish to me again when I saw her this afternoon. Although, of
course, it is a very unusual course, I am quite sure that the latest
decision will give immense satisfaction to Dorset people.'[42] What
neither he nor Florence Hardy seems to have foreseen was that the
intended gesture of reconciliation depended upon an act of
dismemberment that many people would perceive as macabre and
even grotesquely offensive. Gosse called it 'medieval butchery'.[43]
Clodd insisted: 'A man's will as to the disposal of his remains
should be inviolate. . . . I think the compromise as to division of
remains very repellent.'[44] Florence Hardy herself soon learned to
think of the burial arrangements as 'wicked': 'One is not
responsible at such a time', she told Richard Purdy in 1929. 'I never
gave my consent, it never should have been done—it was contrary
to Mr. Hardy's wish.' But she added, 'It can't be helped now.'[45]

The heart was removed during the evening of the 13th by
Dr Mann's partner, Dr F. L. Nash-Wortham, kept overnight in a
sealed tin, and placed in a burial casket the following day. Early
that same morning a hearse left Max Gate for the Brookwood
crematorium, where Barrie oversaw the cremation itself—Cockerell
having been summoned to Cambridge by his wife's illness—and
then carried the ashes to London. On Monday 16 January three
simultaneous services were held: a civic observance in St Peter's,
Dorchester, attended by the mayors of Dorchester and Weymouth;
the heart burial at Stinsford, attended by Henry Hardy; and the
national act of remembrance in Westminster Abbey, organized by
the Macmillans and attended by Florence and Kate Hardy, at which
the prime minister, the leader of the opposition, and six prominent
men of letters—Barrie, Galsworthy, Gosse, Housman, Kipling, and
Shaw—were among the pall-bearers. Ironic in itself, this curious
multiplication-with-division of what Hardy must have envisaged as
a simple act of interment became the occasion of ironies more
'Hardyan' still. At Stinsford, according to *The Times* 'the sky was

cloudless almost to the horizon', but at Westminster, *The Times* reported in an adjoining column, those among the crowding thousands who were fortunate enough to gain admission found themselves 'in a building dimly lit. Slanting rain was falling outside, and little daylight filtered through the windows into the Abbey. Electric lamps dispelled the gloom in the transepts, but the roofs were nearly obscured.'[46] And T. E. Lawrence, receiving in Karachi a copy of the thoroughly conventional Abbey service, readily imagined Hardy as smiling 'tolerantly' at the 'sleek Deans and Canons [who] were acting a lie behind his name'.[47]

Although Hardy, in 1922, must have expected his literary executors to be happily complementary, Cockerell's experience serving to give practical effect to Florence's devotion, the pairing proved in the event to be wholly disastrous, as if imposed by the Spirit Ironic of *The Dynasts*, or even the Spirit Sinister. The tensions between the two were already evident in the immediate wake of Hardy's death, when Cockerell and Barrie had, in effect, conspired to push Hardy's widow into decisions she instinctively felt to be wrong, and the first of their open quarrels had its starting-point in Barrie's Adelphi Terrace flat, to which Florence and Kate Hardy, accompanied by Dr Mann, had retreated following the Westminster Abbey service.[48] It must have been not only an emotional but a somewhat hurried occasion. The service, though not extended by homilies or eulogies, can scarcely have ended much earlier than 3 p.m.; yet Cockerell's diary records that the Dorchester party left Waterloo by the 4.30 p.m. train, and Kate Hardy, already unhappy at getting only 'a crumb to eat & a taste of coffee' on her arrival in London earlier in the day, again complained (to her diary) that all she got at Barrie's was 'another crumb & a taste of tea'.[49] There was apparently time, even so, for Cockerell to raise the question of a public memorial and to obtain some form of assent on Florence Hardy's part to the proposition that Hardy would himself have preferred a tower, such as that erected in Dorset a century earlier in honour of Thomas Masterman Hardy (Nelson's Hardy).

That Florence Hardy, come straight from her husband's funeral, took any of this in seems unlikely in the extreme—even nine months after her husband's death she could still speak of 'living in a sort of evil dream'[50]—but before the Dorchester party left Cockerell had drafted and read out a letter on the subject and obtained permission to send it to *The Times*.[51] Since it appeared in print the following morning, he may well have delivered it in person to Printing-House Square on his way to catch a train back to Cambridge. The letter asserted Hardy's dislike of 'what he called "utilitarian memorials"', such as drinking fountains, lecterns, and village halls, and his preference for those that were 'commemorative, and nothing else'. 'As an example', Cockerell continued, 'he often pointed with approval to the column raised to his famous namesake on a Dorset hilltop within sight of Max Gate. I have heard him admit, when the topic came up in conversation, that if any local memorial were to be raised to him he would like that column to have a fellow. If such an idea were adopted an appropriate site for many reasons would be Rainbarrow, on the heath behind his birthplace at Bockhampton.'[52]

There was prompt objection to the erection of so prominent an object on a spot whose topography was already hallowed by Hardy's description of it in *The Return of the Native*.[53] Other suggestions were forthcoming from other quarters, but a scheme for turning the Dorchester building known as Judge Jeffreys' lodgings into a Hardy museum seems to have been compromised from the start by Hardy's having expressed dismay at the prospect of having his name associated with 'that scoundrel's',[54] and while neither of the two literary executors was wholly unsympathetic to an existing proposal to establish a Thomas Hardy Chair of English Literature at University College, Southampton, Cockerell at least could not regard it as meeting the requirements of a national memorial.[55] Cockerell had meanwhile followed up on his original proposal, and in February 1928 the establishment of a Thomas Hardy Memorial Fund was duly announced: 'The form which this memorial is to take has now been definitely decided, with the entire approval of his representatives. It is to consist of the three following:—(1) The preservation of his birthplace at Bockhampton; (2) an obelisk to be erected on a suitable site in the neighbourhood; and (3) the founding in Dorchester of a Hardy Memorial, housing a collection of his works and relics.'[56]

Barrie, Galsworthy, Gosse, Granville-Barker, Housman, Masefield, Shaw, and the Mayor of Dorchester, Wilfrid Hodges, were among those who publicly supported the appeal for funds,[57] and from time to time over the next few weeks *The Times* published the names of subscribers and the amounts of their subscriptions, the Macmillans promptly putting themselves down for £250, St John Hornby, the printer (named in Hardy's will as a literary executor should Cockerell and Gosse both fail), sending fifty guineas, and someone identified simply as 'B.' (an act of ostentatious shyness almost certainly to be associated with Barrie) fifty pounds. Most subscribers, however, confined themselves to a respectable but not extravagant five pounds (or guineas), and the total of 'just over £1,000' reached by early October 1928, when Hodges declared the fund closed, was distinctly on the modest side.[58] Hodges also announced that the library proposal had been abandoned—presumably because the sum available was far too meagre to initiate, let alone sustain, so ambitious an undertaking—and that Cecil Hanbury, MP, the current owner of the Kingston Maurward estate on which the Hardy birthplace stood, had himself undertaken to keep the cottage in a state of good preservation.[59]

There remained the tower, still prospectively perched atop Rainbarrow, and it was specifically with that object in view that Florence Hardy was asked, shortly after the termination of the public appeal, how much she, Henry Hardy, and Kate Hardy intended to contribute.[60] Kate Hardy showed little enthusiasm at first and Henry made it plain that he was interested in a tower only if he could design and build it himself,[61] but in December 1928 Henry died, and in the spring of 1929 Kate Hardy was gradually, if still grudgingly, brought to modify her initial opposition—though not, it would appear, to commit herself to any specific sum.[62] By then, however, the entire proposal had long been a matter of bitter dispute, Cockerell having again resorted to the correspondence columns of *The Times* to make the more specific claim that in June 1926 he had asked Hardy, 'in Mrs. Hardy's presence, whether his ghost would be pleased to see there a tower that would be a fellow to the well-known and conspicuous memorial to Nelson's Hardy. His reply was a wistful affirmative.'[63]

Whether or not Florence Hardy had been capable of absorbing the implications of Cockerell's original letter to *The Times*, she is unlikely to have given any thought to the question of a memorial up to that point or developed strong feelings either for or against a tower. Local Dorset opinion, however, of which she inevitably heard a great deal, was strongly opposed, favouring instead a statue that would stand, like that of William Barnes, in Dorchester itself:[64] a *Times* report of late March 1929 spoke of increasing

Dorset support for such a solution in light of 'substantial objections to the erection of the obelisk on the heathland at Rainbarrow', especially since the cost would be 'out of all proportion to the comparatively small sum subscribed'.[65] Thus influenced and encouraged, Florence Hardy made it clear that both she and Kate Hardy were withholding any additional infusion of funds until a final decision had been reached: as she told Cockerell, it seemed in any case 'absurd to talk of a *National* Memorial if more than 2/3s of the cost is borne by the widow & sister, & paid for by money left by the one to whom the memorial is to be raised'.[66] She also began to challenge Cockerell's versions of past events, insisting that when asked about the tower her husband had merely given 'a slightly embarrassed smile, & *made no reply*'.[67] In a letter to St John Hornby of 18 May 1929 she went so far as to characterize Cockerell's question as having been put 'in an abrupt & domineering manner',[68] and it was evidently at her request that T. E. Lawrence, four days later, reported to Hornby his own memory of Hardy's making a distinctly negative response to the suggestion that Dorset might one day boast a second Hardy monument. Hardy was a man so reserved and opposed to display, Lawrence insisted, that he ought only to be memorialized on a modest scale.[69]

Hornby was at this point chairing a sub-committee which had been created on 15 May at the first meeting of the Hardy Memorial Committee—of which Florence and Kate Hardy, Cockerell, and Barrie were all members, together with Augustus John, Harley Granville-Barker, and a sizeable representation from the local community—and assigned the task of determining the precise form the memorial should take. Sentiment at the 15 May meeting had been predominantly in favour of a statue located in Dorchester itself, and motions were passed to that effect, but Cockerell, seconded by Hornby, also secured the passage of a final motion to the effect that 'if funds permit, after the provision of the statue, a small obelisk be erected near the birthplace'.[70] Since Hornby had initially spoken in support of an obelisk near the birthplace ('where it could be seen from afar') and Augustus John, also appointed to the sub-committee, had favoured (as 'more symbolical') a statue on the heath,[71] Florence Hardy evidently feared that Cockerell's original tower proposal was not yet dead. She knew that Hornby and Cockerell were close friends and she perhaps suspected—what appears from Cockerell's diary to have been the case—that they had consulted together as to the membership of the Hardy Memorial Committee and its crucial sub-committee.[72] Since she was to speak very positively of Hornby in future years, she presumably neither knew nor suspected that Hornby—concerned, perhaps, at the severity of some of her accusations—was sending copies of her letters on to Cockerell himself,[73] receiving in return a long and angry 'memorandum' in which Cockerell sought to counter, point by point, her explicit and implicit criticisms of his ideas and conduct.

'Mrs Hardy [the memorandum concluded] seems to imply that my inability to regard a statue in Dorchester as the best form of memorial to Thomas Hardy was dictated by some hostility to herself and a desire to "defeat her wishes". This is a complete error. She forgets that my objections (shared by some other friends of his) were expressed to her (and acquiesced in) long before any question of a statue arose. A decision having been arrived at by the subscribers I have now no more to say.'[74] But Cockerell was no more capable than his antagonist of letting such matters rest. He complained to Hornby that Florence Hardy's 'innuendoes', including the 'fantastic' suggestion that he could ever have bullied Hardy in any way, had probably been repeated in other quarters, and wondered whether she might be shown his memorandum by way of discouragement.[75] To have done so, however, would have been to reveal Hornby's breach of confidentiality, well-intentioned though it had perhaps been, and to lay bare the almost instinctive functioning of that intricately interconnected male network which had readily paid court to Hardy himself but could regard his widow only with varying degrees of distanced compassion, amused tolerance, and downright contempt.

When the sub-committee actually met, at Max Gate, on 26 August 1929, Augustus John was absent, and discussion seems to have focused almost exclusively on the selection of a particular Dorchester site and an appropriate sculptor. Once the sub-committee's choices had been endorsed at a 16 September meeting of the full committee (less John, Barrie, Cockerell, and one or two others), the announcement was made that a life-size statue by Eric Kennington would be erected at the upper end of Dorchester High Street (Top o' Town).[76] Kennington appears to have preferred some form of 'symbolic' memorial, but he accommodated himself willingly enough to the committee's unanimous preference for a 'portrait' statue.[77] The unveiling ceremony was performed by Barrie on 2 September 1931 in the presence of Florence and Kate Hardy, Kennington, Gordon and Lilian Gifford (Emma Hardy's nephew and niece), and three of Hardy's Antell cousins[78]—though not of Sydney Cockerell—and celebrated in verse in the local newspaper:

> The Hardy name, in printed page,
> Will live through every cultured age:
> But knowledge of the living man
> Will end with those who in life's span
> Held converse with the Wessex Bard,
> Or looked on him with kind regard.
>
> So 'Casterbridge' holds pride of place
> As guardian for the future race
> Of statue to a Dorset son,
> Whose genius in life hath won
> Immortal fame as writer great
> Of verse and prose which captivate.
>
> James Barrie, genial man of Merit,
> Paid tribute to the Hardy spirit;
> Released the flag which hid from view
> Bronze image of the friend he knew;
> Thus Hardy's face and form we see,
> Perpetuate through the years to be.[79]

But by September 1931 the tablet designed by Hardy himself was already in place at St Juliot,[80] a memorial window had been installed in Stinsford Church,[81] Kate Hardy had bought the same church a new organ in memory of all the Stinsford Hardys,[82] and Richard Little Purdy had organized for the Yale University Library a Memorial Exhibition of books, letters, and manuscripts that effectively marked the beginning of serious Hardy scholarship.[83] What especially stole some of the thunder of the national gesture, however, was the dedication in April 1931 of a modest memorial stone, immediately adjacent to the birthplace, by a group of American Hardyans, stirred to action largely by the enthusiasm of the collector A. Edward Newton, who chose for their spokesperson the Harvard scholar John Livingston Lowes, currently lecturing at Oxford.[84] The precedence thus achieved by the American memorial constituted, as Cockerell put it, 'another of the extraordinary "satires of circumstance"' to have occurred since Hardy's death.[85]

Given Hardy's immense fame at the end of his life, it may seem curious that the Memorial appeal should have attracted so little support. Florence Hardy felt that the appeal had suffered from the lack of any attempt to ensure a wide participation within Dorset itself, but there seems little doubt that the principal negative factor was the coincidence of its launching with the publicity given to the unexpected size of Hardy's estate, especially in relation to what were widely perceived as the ungenerous contents of his will. In *The Times* the details of the appeal and the names of its distinguished and by no means impecunious signatories appeared towards the lower end of a column headlined 'MR. HARDY'S WILL. | AN ESTATE OF OVER £91,000.'[86] In newspapers not quite so staid descriptions of the will were likely to be accompanied by observations to the effect that Hardy 'was a considerably richer man . . . than his simple mode of life in Dorchester suggested',[87] and by self-righteous comments on the clause which specified a halving of Florence Hardy's annuity in the event of her remarriage. The *Daily News* selected as its headline 'THOMAS HARDY'S WIDOW. | PENALTY IF SHE REMARRIES. | £90,000 WILL.'[88] A columnist in the *Sunday Express* even spoke of Hardy's attempting to impose on his widow 'a kind of moral suttee':

Hardy in his works satirised the harshness of our marriage laws. He exhibited their victims as martyrs. Yet he made in his will a harsh law for his own wife. He inflicted on her an unfair humiliation. It is the irony of ironies that the supreme master of irony should himself fill his will with irony. There has been nothing like it in literature since Shakespeare bequeathed his wife his second-best bedstead.[89]

Florence Hardy's discomfort was further increased by the publicity given to the provision, in a will made in Hardy's eighty-second year, that upon her death Max Gate should 'stand seized . . . IN TRUST for the first child of mine who shall attain the age of twenty one years'.[90] There was also a deeper sense in which she was embarrassed by the will as a whole. Although the *Daily News* might implicitly praise as 'characteristic' Hardy's assignment of £50 each to the Society for the Prevention of Cruelty to Animals and the Council for Justice to Animals, it was sufficiently evident that—apart from another £50 to the Pension Fund of the Society of Authors and some prospective payments to his second literary executor—these represented the only bequests of a monetary order to be directed beyond the limits of his own and his first wife's family. Worst of all was the total absence of gifts to Dorset charities, institutions, or causes.

Particularly distressing to Florence Hardy was the pointless extravagance, as she saw it, of the amounts likely to be received as joint residuary legatees by Henry and Kate Hardy—both of them elderly, childless, frugal, and already affluent[91]—and by the comparatively pitiful amounts left to those who might well have expected more generous treatment: Hardy's impecunious first cousin, John Antell, received £200; a somewhat remoter but much liked cousin, Charles Meech Hardy, had died soon after the will was made and there was no provision for his £200 to be passed on to his needy widow; Lilian Gifford, to whom Hardy had long provided financial support, now received a small additional annuity, while her brother Gordon came in for £250. Barrie's assurance that the gifts of valuable manuscripts specified in the will compensated for its apparent lack of generosity in other directions was only partly persuasive: 'He said [Florence Hardy told Cockerell] it would look rather "ugly" if I made any public gifts now, & as if I were ashamed of the will—which indeed I am not, now that he has talked to me about it. He said that I can do all I think ought to be done later on, in a quiet way.'[92] Her immediate concern at this point was to give effect to some instructions for the endowment of hospital beds, one in her own name, the other in Emma's, which she had found among her husband's papers, but since the intended codicil was unwitnessed it was judged legally void. 'It is fatal to put off doing things', she lamented to Gordon Gifford, whom she had always liked and knew to have once had expectations of inheriting Max Gate itself. 'I did not know the contents of the will, & really I thought you would have had ten times that amount. Had another will been made I expect it would have been increased.'[93]

Much of the trouble with the will was indeed the consequence of Hardy's failure to reconsider, in the light of the passage of time and of more expert advice, what he had put his signature to in August 1922. The will was drawn up by the local firm of solicitors Hardy had always used, and with several of whose members he had long been on terms of personal friendship, and some of those features which caused raised eyebrows in London—the provision for a possible child, for instance, or the reduction of the widow's annuity upon remarriage—may in Dorchester have been adopted almost automatically as standard practice, as neither more nor less than what common, traditional prudence would dictate. Reflected in the will's Hardy-centredness was that intense family loyalty of which Florence Hardy had first become fully aware in the wake of Mary Hardy's death in 1915, when the central concern of the surviving siblings—and especially of Kate—had been to find an inheritor both of Max Gate and of Hardy's eventual estate who should be '*a Hardy born*'.[94] But there were no obvious heirs available, especially after the death during the First World War of Frank George, the distant cousin on whom family approval had once been bestowed,[95] and it is conceivable that the idea of holding Max Gate in trust for an as yet unborn child had been Hardy's own, introduced into the will not as an assertion or reflection of sustained sexual capacity but rather as a temporizing device, a means of avoiding any specific acknowledgement of the property's almost inevitable passage out of the family's hands. But the provision of course stood unchanged at Hardy's death, constituting a failure to reach a long-term decision as to the 'real' future of Max Gate which was to leave the way open, less than a decade later, to a similar indecisiveness on the part of his widow.

There were a number of reasons why Florence Hardy in fact redeemed only a few of her husband's testamentary failures of decision, commission, or generosity. She was, after all, deeply schooled through her marriage in the very sources and causes of such failures; she shared, and to an acutely depressive degree, her husband's temperamental lack of optimism; she felt deserted in her widowhood by many who had courted her during her husband's lifetime; she suffered increasingly from the cancer which killed her at the age of fifty-eight; and although she seems to have been effective as a local magistrate and proponent of good causes she had neither the style, the sophistication, nor the personal force to command attention in larger social or literary worlds. She also felt complexly restrained, both personally and financially, by the terms of the will itself. She had her annuity (subject to the 50 per cent reduction in case of remarriage); she had the contents of Max Gate (apart from specific bequests made by her husband); she had a lifetime interest in the initially high but steadily declining royalties on Hardy's works[96] (subject to a possible 10 per cent annual payment to her fellow literary executor); and she could stay rent-free at Max Gate during her lifetime (provided she paid all rates, taxes, and insurance and kept the building 'in tenantable repair and condition').[97]

What she feared she did not have was the assurance of an independent estate which could at her death be passed on to her own family and especially to the needier of her four sisters. Those fears were, as usual, exaggerated,[98] and she died quite a wealthy woman, but during her lifetime they served to inhibit her potential enjoyment of a personal freedom and affluence far greater than any she had previously known. She had a car and a chauffeur much of the time and a flat in London temporarily, and she thought seriously of buying a small house there. But she feared—or was persuaded—that she could not afford both a London establishment and Max Gate, and while she found Max Gate cold, dark, lonely, and depressing, at least during the winter months, she could not bring herself to commit the breach of faith that would be involved in her moving permanently away and dispersing its contents— including a study scarcely disturbed since Hardy's death. To have done so, after all, would have been to strike at the roots of the one sure and universally acknowledged identity, as Mrs Thomas Hardy, that she had established through chance, choice, affection, devotion, and comprehensive service to genius.

Her relationship with her fellow literary executor was, from the first, a further deterrent to action and initiative. It had doubtless been Hardy's intention to ease his widow's burdens by enabling her to depend upon Cockerell's wide experience of the literary and public worlds and, indeed, of the executorial role.[99] But in so far as the arrangement seemed to imply doubt of her capacity to act alone, it both eroded her self-confidence, such as it had ever been, and invited decisive intervention on Cockerell's part. He took the initiative, as of right, not only in determining burials and projecting memorials but in dealing with the specifically literary aspects of Hardy's estate, and Florence Hardy's initial condition of bewildered and hopeless bereavement rendered her ill-equipped to resist or challenge Cockerell's vigorous and even zestful approach.

So far as Hardy's published works were concerned, Clause 14 required his literary executors to 'take such steps as they may be advised to take for carrying on their publication in England and elsewhere . . . with their latest corrections and additions and to

protect their copyrights'; it also expressed a wish for the publication
of an edition of his complete poems at a price 'within the reach of
poorer readers'. In Clause 15 the literary executors were further
authorized 'to deal with such of the Manuscripts of my already
published books as they may find on my premises (if any) according
to the best of their judgment recommending them to present one of
such Manuscripts if not already done to the Library of Magdalene
College, Cambridge'. They were also requested, in Clause 16, to
see to the erection in St Juliot Church of the 'Tablet memorising my
connection with the restoration of the said Church'. Much more
troublesome was Clause 12, which began to set out the duties of his
literary executors in respect of unpublished materials:

I BEQUEATH all my unpublished Manuscripts papers letters and
documents of a literary character to my Literary Executors hereinafter
named and I leave it to their absolute discretion (after considering the
instructions I may leave with my Wife or in writing) to decide which (if
any) of my Manuscripts papers letters and documents may be published
after my death, it being my intention that my Literary Executors with
knowledge of my wishes in the aforesaid writing shall have absolute
control over my unpublished Manuscripts papers letters and documents of
a literary character after my decease.

The most obvious sources of confusion here—apart from the
erroneous implication that Hardy's despatched letters had remained
in some sense his property—lay in the lack of adjudication
procedures should the two literary executors fail to agree and in
that invocation of instructions other than those contained in the
will itself. Not only have such instructions apparently disappeared,
except in so far as they were inscribed on individual documents
which happen to have survived, but they seem even at the time to
have been scattered and disorganized, not brought together in any
comprehensive or fully coherent fashion. Moreover, Hardy's
distinction between instructions made in writing and those left
orally with his wife seems to imply that no lesser status should be
accorded to the latter, though necessarily unverifiable, than to the
former—even though the end of the clause alludes only to 'the
aforesaid writing'.[100]
  Similarly problematic in Clause 12 is the allocation to the literary
executors of joint *property* rights in unpublished manuscripts—

especially in light of the implicit qualification of that allocation in the immediately following Clause 13:[101]

I AUTHORISE my said Literary Executors to remove from my Library such Volumes (if any) as they may deem it desirable to remove on grounds of expediency and to dispose of them as they may think fit, also to retain in their possession such of my unpublished Manuscripts papers letters and documents of a literary character so as to restrain altogether or for a limited period their publication and then to allow my said Wife to keep them if she wishes to do so or if they shall deem it advisable so to do after considering any requests of mine to destroy the said Manuscripts papers letters and documents or any of them or to dispose of such of them as may be so disposed of for the benefit of my estate but without prejudice or injury to any person's character or repute or depreciation of my published writings.

Both literary executors, it would appear, were given the right, in concert, to dispose of books and manuscripts, but only the widow could permanently retain them. But while Clause 12 and Clause 13 certainly ask that 'consideration' should be given to Hardy's separately expressed requests for the destruction of particular documents, neither appears to limit the 'absolute discretion' of the literary executors in making decisions in respect of the publication or non-publication of previously unpublished materials or even of their destruction or preservation.

It is impossible to be certain just what literary documents remained at Max Gate at the time of Hardy's death. Most of the major manuscripts of published works still in his hands had gone to institutional libraries during the systematic dispersal overseen by Cockerell in 1911, but several none the less remained—including those of *Under the Greenwood Tree* and *The Woodlanders* and of the poetry volumes published subsequent to 1913: *Satires of Circumstance, Moments of Vision, Late Lyrics and Earlier, Human Shows*, and *Winter Words*. There was also a mass of unpublished material of every kind, even though Hardy had engaged in an extensive sorting and large-scale destruction of letters and papers some ten years earlier, at the time when he was writing the 'Life', and a further, prospectively final, tidying-up would appear to have been conducted just prior to the making of the will in August 1922.[102] Although instinctively a hoarder, and trained in frugality from childhood, Hardy's obsession with privacy ultimately inclined him towards the destruction of documents, and those which disappeared during his last years included the surviving fragments of *The Hand of Ethelberta*[103] and *The Poor Man and the Lady*—despite Cockerell's provision of a handsome binding[104]—and even, it would appear, a large number of the pocket-sized diary-notebooks: Florence Hardy told Richard Purdy in August 1931 that her husband had personally destroyed some forty notebooks, leaving behind him only those used during his final years[105]—although it is possible that she exaggerated what was done within Hardy's lifetime as a way of minimizing the significance of her participation in similar actions after his death.

Cockerell's diary indicates that he went down to Max Gate on 20 January 1928, four days after Hardy's funeral, and that on the 21st, 22nd, and 23rd, and during other visits through to the end of March, he spent much time in Hardy's study, alone or with Florence Hardy, 'sorting, arranging and tearing up'.[106] In early February they threw out much 'accumulated rubbish' and, as specifically authorized by the will, 'some books that, though not rubbish, did not deserve a place in TH's study'.[107] On 24 March Cockerell—with a view to 'the convenience of any future custodian' —was busy pasting red labels ('FROM THE LIBRARY | OF | THOMAS HARDY, O.M. | MAX GATE') into such books as contained Hardy's own signature or annotations in his hand; the black labels which simply identified a book as coming from Hardy's library were supposed to have been inserted 'by Mrs. Hardy or an assistant', he later explained, but it was possible that 'this plan was not fully carried out'.[108]

Early in their sorting they had turned up 'the little book of sketches that he once showed me—and various very interesting notebooks which we have instructions to destroy',[109] and in later years Cockerell was to speak of having spent 'a whole morning' in Hardy's study burning notebooks of his 'in the presence of F.E.H.'[110] From Cockerell's diary it appears that this complexly emotional moment, described by him in almost lyrical terms, did not occur until 14 December 1928:

Spent the morning with F.H. in TH's study, tearing up & burning the first drafts of the poems in Winter Words & some notebooks on which he had written that they were to be destroyed after his death. The little grate in which he had himself burned the MSS. of The Poor Man & the Lady, The Hand of Ethelberta, the scenes excluded from the Dynasts & I know not what else, was heaped up with charred remains. It had to be done & I was glad when I saw them as his injunctions had been on my mind.[111]

It has already been suggested that Clauses 12 and 13 of Hardy's will do not in fact appear to have mandated any across-the-board destruction of unpublished documentary materials. But Cockerell always claimed authority over and above that contained in the will itself, insisting that the incinerated notebooks were marked by Hardy 'to be destroyed at my death'[112] and that all his actions had been in compliance with 'the explicit instructions I had from Hardy in writing and by word of mouth to prevent the printing of entries and notes intended as private memoranda'.[113]

Lack of information about the supplementary instructions Hardy left behind him is again a problem here. That there were such instructions there seems no reason to doubt—Florence Hardy made reference to them in a letter to Daniel Macmillan of 16 February 1928[114]—and some of the surviving notebooks do still contain Hardy's explicit, if not always unambiguous, directions for their disposal.[115] But Cockerell's phrasing, curiously enough, appears to refer back to a letter of August 1914 in which Hardy, thanking him for his willingness to act as a literary executor, had explained that his task would be 'mainly to see that nothing in the way of entries & notes obviously intended as private memoranda should be printed'.[116] Even here, however, as in the will itself, Hardy seems to have been more concerned with preventing the publication of such documents than with ensuring their actual destruction, and it seems reasonable to assume that the executionary zeal with which Cockerell pursued his executorial tasks derived in large measure from his strongly and sincerely held belief that the raw early stages of the creative process ought never to be exposed to public view— that authors had a right and even a duty, transferable to their executors, not to stand revealed to posterity in the nakedness of their foul papers: 'I cannot help wondering', he wrote to Laurence Housman of A. E. Housman's poetical notebooks, 'whether your brother would have wished to have the processes of composition so much revealed. Poets like us to imagine that their performances are spontaneous.'[117]

Hardy's widow seems to have been altogether less certain as to her husband's intentions—it is perhaps significant that Cockerell speaks of the burning of the notebooks as having been done in her presence rather than with her consent—and the survival of notable documents that must at some point have been under threat can perhaps be attributed to what Cockerell later characterized as the clear disregard of Hardy's wishes demonstrated by 'her preservation of various memoranda that were definitely marked by him "to be destroyed after my death". I did myself burn a good many papers so marked, but some escaped me.'[118] Those sessions of disinterment and destruction in Hardy's study must have been peculiarly stressful for Florence Hardy, and the arguments or stratagems on which she depended for her occasional stayings of Cockerell's hand can only be guessed at. Some of the smaller items—such as the very early 'Studies, Specimens &c.' notebook[119]—she may actually have hidden. Others—typically a good deal larger than the pocketbooks and more stoutly bound—were clearly not the miscellaneous jottings of everyday but compilations of a more systematic sort: the volumes of 'Literary Notes', for example, would have been in this category,[120] and, less surely, the 'Architectural Notebook' (perhaps to be identified with the 'little book of sketches' mentioned in Cockerell's diary).[121] In other instances she was presumably able to invoke her responsibility for completing the official biography of her husband as warrant for retaining, at least temporarily, any documents directly or potentially relevant to it.

During the weeks and months following Hardy's death his widow had seen the completion and publication of the 'Life' as the most urgent but by no means the least complex of her many responsibilities. She knew all too well that Hardy had worked over the typescripts in great detail and left little doubt of what he wanted said. She was no less aware that the later sections, covering roughly the final decade of his life, remained in unfinished condition, and that he had in any case assigned to her an unrestricted right to determine the final form of the published text. In an undated 'Private Memorandum. Information for Mrs Hardy in the preparation of a biography' Hardy had specifically declared that the 'facts' to which his wife had access were 'not enjoined to be included every one in the volume, if any should seem to be indiscreet, belittling, monotonous, trivial, provocative, or in other ways unadvisable; neither are they enjoined to be exclusive of other details that may be deemed necessary'.[122] Florence Hardy was thus empowered to make both deletions from and additions to the text that her husband had left, and while the changes she made on her own responsibility cannot always be confidently distinguished from those she made during her husband's lifetime and in accordance with his directly expressed wishes, there can be no doubt that she exercised her mandate with some freedom.

Before the end of January 1928 the entire typescript as it then stood was sent up to Daniel Macmillan and then passed on to Charles Whibley, one of the firm's most trusted readers, who recommended substantial reductions in the quotations from Hardy's diaries and especially in the long catalogues of London social engagements.[123] Macmillan, returning the typescript to Max Gate on 21 February, seems to have suggested that Whibley might assist in making the book ready for publication, but Florence Hardy replied with some firmness that while she would be glad to receive advice she did not need a collaborator, as she could see for herself 'a great deal that must be altered'. The biography, she added, 'is just as it left my husband's hands after a lengthy revision and correction. I should not like it to be pulled to pieces and rewritten, which is what he warned me would happen if I had a too-eminent literary man to help me.'[124] Hardy's 'Private Memorandum'—of which Daniel Macmillan had perhaps seen a copy—had in fact specified that the book, before it went to the printer, 'should be put into correct literary form, by an experienced writer and scholar. Should Mrs Hardy wish that her name alone should stand on the title page, such a one might possibly be found for her who would do what was required if paid a reasonable fee.'[125]

But Florence Hardy, in her uncertainty and distress, was already seeking advice from some of the men whose friendship Hardy himself had valued during his last years. T. E. Lawrence, who knew something of the 'Life', was now in Karachi with the RAF and unavailable for consultation, and while E. M. Forster evidently read one of the typescripts he does not appear to have offered any criticism of a detailed kind. Cockerell also read through the 'memoir' during the course of his visits to Max Gate immediately following Hardy's death, and in March 1928 he went through it again, cutting out 'some uninteresting passages'—including, no doubt, some of those lists of names whose value Whibley had already questioned.[126] It was on Sir James Barrie, however, that Florence Hardy most depended. She sent him one of the typescripts in late January 1928, at the same time as she was submitting another typescript to Macmillan, and on 3 February he wrote to praise the book as a 'remarkable achievement' but also to regret its tedious namings of London names and its too naked display of Hardy's sensitivity to criticism.[127]

Towards the end of March, just as she was about to resubmit the first volume to Macmillan 'after having made some important additions', Florence Hardy received from Barrie a long list of characteristic Hardyan anecdotes for possible inclusion, among them the stories of the young Hardy's accepting payment for playing his violin for a country dance and using the money to purchase *The Boy's Own Book* and of the somewhat older Hardy's despair when reading the *Spectator* review of *Desperate Remedies*.[128] She held back the manuscript until the necessary insertions had been made—it seemed important, as she told Macmillan, that 'the very early part should be as complete as possible'[129]—but *The Early Life of Thomas Hardy 1840–1891*, as she had decided to call it, was nevertheless in proof by late June, and Cockerell spent a stormy weekend at Max Gate when his hostess discovered that he had already discussed those proofs with Barrie.[130] Since she saw Barrie as her supreme ally, the thought of his colluding with Cockerell against her was complexly threatening, and her resulting emotional state is reflected in the unusual frankness of the letter she wrote to Forster on the day of Cockerell's departure: 'I have had a trying week-end here with Mr Cockerell, my co-literary executor, & I am seriously thinking of resigning my executorship—if it would not be an act of faithlessness to the trust my husband reposed in me.'[131] For Cockerell the weekend served only to confirm him in his low estimate of his yoke-mate's intelligence and stability.[132]

Early Life was respectfully though not, for the most part, enthusiastically received following its publication in November 1928, and Florence Hardy continued with her work on what was, from her point of view, its more demanding sequel, *The Later Years of Thomas Hardy 1892–1928*. Because Hardy had certified the text of the 'Life' as ready for publication only up to the end of 1918, it fell to her to fill out the record of the nine remaining years, following closely the outline her husband had provided for the years 1919 and 1920 and drawing extensively even in the two final chapters on materials he had, so to speak, prefabricated for her use. She did, however, insert several of Hardy's letters, reduce the social chronicling and hostility towards critics, and cut out (as in *Early Life*) a number of references to her predecessor, Hardy's first wife, whose role in the overall narrative she perhaps resented as being so much more prominent than her own. Clearly, then, *Early Life* and *Later Years* cannot in any straightforward sense be regarded as Hardy's covert autobiography. Covert his participation certainly was, but even if the changes independently authorized by Florence Hardy seem insufficient to establish the 'Life' as a fully collaborative work, they surely compromise its categorization as autobiography —as the unmediated expression of the self-image that Hardy wished to pass on to posterity. What she cut out he must be assumed to have deliberately inscribed. What she put in he must in some sense have deliberately omitted. Even now that there is available an edition of the 'Life' which distinguishes between what Hardy wrote and what actually appeared in print, it can perhaps still best be thought of as a biography quite exceptionally 'authorized', as a full-scale working out of Hardy's conception of what an official biography might ideally (that is to say, unintrusively) be like.

The ghost-writing of his own 'official' biography was only the most radical of Hardy's techniques for self-projection into a future beyond the moment of his death, and it was extremely successful, at least in the short run, in forestalling the publication of other, potentially less sympathetic, 'lives' and in facilitating the posthumous reiteration of Hardy's most consistently cherished themes —his disenchanted view of the universe, for example, his grudges against the critics, and his dedication to the cause of animal welfare. Its longer-term consequences—like those flowing from Hallam Tennyson's *Memoir*—have also proved considerable, in that biographers, forced into dependence upon its unique record of many aspects of Hardy's life, have found themselves trapped within the limiting patterns established by its silences, special emphases, inaccuracies, and textual distortions. It is one thing to question its version of crucial episodes in Hardy's story—the circumstances of his birth and childhood, the motivations for his first marriage, the precise reasons for his shifts between poetry and fiction—quite another to assemble the evidence upon which an alternative narrative might convincingly be built. Even the informed reinterpretation of published documents is fundamentally undercut by the suspicion that the documents have themselves been tampered with.

Early in his executorial career Cockerell had taken it upon himself to challenge the firm of Macmillan over the serial rights to *Winter Words*, to push for the publication of a volume of Hardy's miscellaneous non-fiction writings, and to argue on Florence Hardy's behalf for better terms for the first volume of the official biography.[133] Cockerell had already told the secretary of the Society of Authors that he understood it to be his role to deal with the 'business side' of the joint literary executorship,[134] and when Barrie wrote to defend the Macmillans as 'a great firm and I presume very honourable men',[135] Cockerell rather tartly replied that it would of course be 'easier & pleasanter to submit, but I take it that I was appointed to protect Mrs Hardy'.[136] She, for her part, was uneasy at thus confronting the firm on which her husband had always so much relied—her letter to Cockerell of 8 March indicates a readiness to 'let them take what they want'[137]—but when the terms of her contract were in fact improved she was unstinting in her expressions of gratitude: 'Thank you so much for all you have done for me in a business way', she wrote. 'You have been marvellous.'[138]

She was not often to address Cockerell again in such positive terms. The strains already evident in other aspects of their relationship were soon exacerbated by a battle over the nature of the co-executorship from which they can each be said to have emerged with a Pyrrhic victory. The essence of the quarrel over 'Old Mrs Chundle'—a short story which Hardy had apparently withheld because of its association with members of the Moule family—was that Florence Hardy gave permission for the story's publication in the United States without consulting Cockerell, whose subsequent criticism of such unilateral action was intensified by his poor opinion of the story itself and by the understandable scepticism with which he received her increasingly positive assurances that Hardy had intended it for eventual publication.[139] Florence Hardy gained her initial point in so far as 'Old Mrs Chundle' was in fact published in the United States (though not in Britain). Cockerell had his moment of dubious triumph when, in January 1929, she conceded the wisdom of his position and promised not to question his judgement in the future.[140] But the remnants of trust and respect between them had effectively been broken, their differences over the Hardy memorial and other such issues drove them still further apart, and by August 1929 almost all communication between them was at an end.

Since Cockerell technically remained one of the literary executors, their connection could not be formally dissolved, but Florence Hardy became accustomed to acting as though she were the sole literary executor—it was to her, for example, that the BBC regularly turned in search of permissions to broadcast Hardy poems or prose extracts[141]—and when she got wind, in 1934, of a forthcoming American edition of Hardy's uncollected novella 'An Indiscretion in the Life of an Heiress' she did not hesitate to arrange for a limited edition to be privately printed in Britain, in the hope, as she later explained to Daniel Macmillan, that it would achieve the status of a first edition.[142] The one hundred privately printed copies were not offered for sale, and Cockerell evidently knew nothing of the edition until early March of 1935, when Desmond Flower, who had seen it through the press, pointed out in a letter to *The Times* that it did indeed have precedence over the American edition just announced.[143] Writing to Florence Hardy that same day, Cockerell reminded her that he too had been appointed one of her husband's literary executors and that she had promised after the 'Old Mrs Chundle' affair never again to act in such a matter without seeking his advice.[144] Her reply, if any, seems not to have survived, but ten days later Cockerell attacked her publicly in the correspondence columns of *The Times Literary Supplement*:

As one of the literary executors of Thomas Hardy, the other being Mrs. Hardy, I desire to state that I was not consulted about the printing of a limited edition of 'An Indiscretion in the Life of an Heiress,' concerning which an announcement appeared in *The Times* of March 4. Nor have I seen a copy, but I read it some years ago in an American magazine of 1878, and came to the conclusion that Hardy had some reason for not reprinting it and that it would be a mistake to do so.

He added that Mrs Hardy had shared his judgement when a previous proposal for an American edition of 'An Indiscretion' had been brought forward in 1929 and that when consulted about 'Old Mrs Chundle' he had expressed his 'very strong objection to the publication'.[145]

Though undoubtedly distressed by this public criticism, Florence Hardy was able to point to it as evidence of Cockerell's combativeness and intransigence. She told Daniel Macmillan on 10 May 1935 that while she was quite ready to resign her literary executorship in favour of Sir Sydney Cockerell (as he had become in 1934) she refused to work with him. And since she had received a legal opinion that her own resignation was out of the question, it was her hope that Cockerell might himself be persuaded to resign in favour of St John Hornby, in whose judgement she entirely trusted.[146] Partly at issue was the 10 per cent of the annual royalties on Hardy's works which Cockerell had expected to receive under the terms of the will, beginning with the third year after the date of death.[147] But when Florence Hardy consulted a distinguished estate lawyer, Charles Douglas Medley, she was in effect told—so Medley repeated in a letter to Cockerell—that while neither of the literary executors could legally resign there was in fact so little for them to do that Cockerell could hardly expect to qualify for a payment which, according to the will, should be made to 'the one acting with my wife' only in years 'in which my Literary affairs may in the opinion of the Chairman and two of the Council of the Society of Authors require his attention'.[148] In any case, Medley pointed out, the will—'a document which is in some respects inconsistent and somewhat difficult to construe'—seemed to allocate almost all powers and responsibilities to the general executors (Lloyds Bank) and give the literary executors rights over the unpublished materials only. Implying, though not quite stating, that the literary executors had from the beginning exceeded their proper powers, he concluded that a possible future edition of Hardy's letters remained almost the only significant matter in which they were 'entitled to interfere'. And since Mrs Hardy's acknowledgement that such an edition would need the approval of both literary executors appeared to leave no current grounds for disagreement—since, too, the squabble over 'An Indiscretion' had no real basis—he hoped that 'this discussion may now be allowed to drop'.[149]

Drop it did, at least in so far as there seem to have been no more exchanges between the two literary executors at either a public or a private level. The dispute, however, continued to rankle with each of them individually, providing matter of complaint and hostile anecdote within their own circles.[150] It was a melancholy conclusion to an artificial partnership of which Hardy, its confident begetter, had obviously expected so much. Florence Hardy had come to think of Cockerell not only as her own implacable enemy but as someone who had probably hated even Hardy himself. She, in Cockerell's eyes, was in an admittedly difficult position but 'dull beyond description—an inferior woman with a suburban mind, but

very ambitious to be well off'.[151] Wilfrid Blunt's biography of
Cockerell, published in 1964, accepted wholeheartedly its subject's
view of the quarrel and of Florence Hardy and concluded that the
breach was entirely her fault. Richard Purdy, however, who had
known Cockerell and dedicated his Hardy bibliography 'To F.E.H.
in affectionate remembrance', wrote to Blunt[152] to question such
emphases in a book that was otherwise remarkably direct in its
references to Cockerell's quarrelsomeness and sometimes abrasive
inflexibility: 'Since he was always right [Blunt had written], it
followed that those who disagreed with him were always wrong. If
a quarrel arose, it was *they* who started it, and he could never
understand why.'[153] Blunt seems to have been sympathetic to
Purdy's concerns—he had already confessed that he should ideally
have consulted more people expert in the Hardy field[154]—and
when the American edition of the book was published he did at
least make the gesture of changing the final sentence of the 'Thomas
and Florence Hardy' chapter: in place of the British edition's 'That
the fault was wholly hers is, however, not to be doubted', the
(otherwise identical) American text now read, 'No doubt there
were faults on both sides.'[155] Indeed.

Richard Purdy, when challenging Wilfrid Blunt's presentation of
the relationship between Cockerell and Florence Hardy, had
observed that their differences had been further exacerbated by
Cockerell's desire to be named the executor of her will.[156] She had
in fact consulted Cockerell about her will several years earlier[157]—
to the point of asking him to draw one up for her to sign—but the
subsequent collapse of friendship and trust between them made it
impossible for Cockerell to be consulted, let alone named as
executor, at the time when she had, as Hardy's effective heir, more
substantial and significant dispositions to make—when, in fact,
Cockerell's expertise and decisiveness (however overbearing) could
conceivably have been of genuine service. As it was, she remained
in a state of perpetual indecision, uncertain as to the most
appropriate ways of disposing of Max Gate and of discharging her
responsibility—at once 'a burden and a satisfaction', as her
solicitor shrewdly noted[158]—for her husband's books and papers.
She kept the study for some years almost exactly as Hardy had left
it, dealt as best she could with the (mostly trivial) publishing
arrangements that called for her attention, and veered between

suspiciousness, co-operativeness, and downright indiscretion in her dealings with such visiting scholars as William R. Rutland, Frederick B. Adams, Richard Purdy, and Henry Reed.[159]

Constitutionally melancholy, often weak and in pain as a result of her worsening cancer, she delayed in acting upon the well-intentioned but sometimes contradictory advice available to her, until in the last distressing months before her death (on 17 October 1937) she found herself forced to leave her indecisions unresolved and trust to the judgement of Irene Cooper Willis, whom she had appointed (jointly with Lloyds Bank) as the executor of her will. Professionally a solicitor, with chambers in the Temple, Cooper Willis had also done research for Bertrand Russell, written books on the Brontës and Elizabeth Barrett Browning, and been the friend and, as of 1935, the executor of Violet Paget, the formidable woman of letters who wrote under the name of Vernon Lee. But if Cooper Willis's qualifications were thus considerable, it is possible to suspect that her handling of the Vernon Lee estate would scarcely have commended itself to Florence Hardy, had she ever become aware of it.

'I absolutely prohibit any biography of me', Vernon Lee had declared in her will. 'My life is my own and I leave that to nobody.' She placed, moreover, a fifty-year limitation on the use of some papers she gave to Somerville College, Oxford, and attached a directive, 'Not to be read except privately until 1980' on a packet of letters to her family that was discovered after her death.[160] Cooper Willis, however, brought out a privately printed selection of those letters in fifty copies in 1937, arguing in a Preface that Vernon Lee had evidently contemplated their eventual publication: 'But 1980 is a long time ahead, and as the letters are not likely to interest posterity half as much as they will interest those who knew Vernon Lee personally, I decided to have a small number of copies of them printed privately, and the response to a circular which was sent out to friends of Vernon Lee has enabled this to be done.'[161] Inclusion in the preface of some details of Vernon Lee's family, upbringing, and subsequent career received a similarly questionable justification: 'I do not think I shall be offending against Vernon Lee's prohibition of a biography in giving some details of the Paget family.'[162] Cooper Willis none the less regarded it as her responsibility to restrict the use of unpublished Vernon Lee materials at least until 1980, although she in fact abandoned this position prior to the publication of Peter Gunn's biography in 1964—evidently in response to the genuinely difficult though in context somewhat embarrassing question Gunn poses in his own preface: 'for what period of time should testamentary instructions bind the hands of posterity?'[163]

Florence Hardy's will, drawn up by Cooper Willis and dated 18 May 1937, was, by comparison with her husband's, a fairly straightforward affair, though subsequently expanded by four last-minute codicils. She was perfectly specific about the destination of her remains—'I wish to be cremated and that my ashes be placed in the grave at Stinsford Churchyard in which my husband's heart is buried and I desire that the inscription which my husband composed with my name and the necessary particulars be placed on the south side of the tomb'[164]—and gave £100 to Stinsford Church to provide an annual income for its future maintenance. She made substantial financial bequests to members of her family and to one or two local charities—including the Dorset County Hospital, accidentally overlooked in her husband's will—created a trust fund for the education of one of her nieces, and named her sister Eva Dugdale as the recipient of her personal possessions and the sole residuary legatee. Gordon Gifford, acknowledged to have been shabbily treated in Hardy's will, none the less received only 'the grandfather clock in the drawing-room' and an inscribed silver salver. Burdened with the responsibility of determining the future of Max Gate but unable in the end to decide upon any particular use or destination for it, she directed that the house be sold and the proceeds become part of her estate—little imagining, surely, that it would be purchased at auction by Kate Hardy, the lonely but now wealthy family survivor, and given by her to the National Trust on the condition that it be maintained 'in its present condition so far as possible'—that is to say, as a private dwelling rather than as a Hardy 'shrine'.[165] Less happily, the furnishings of the house—everything eloquent of the Hardys' long occupation—were sold at a separate auction, and although some items have since found their way to the Dorset County Museum the great majority were irrecoverably dispersed in individual lots. Included in that sale, rather surprisingly, were a few of Hardy's books: some of those excluded by Cockerell in 1928 had perhaps not been thrown out but stored away in a remote cupboard.

So far as the Hardy copyrights were concerned, Florence Hardy simply stipulated that they be dealt with by her trustees, Lloyds Bank and Irene Cooper Willis, for the general benefit of her estate: she did not exclude the possibility of their sale, and the copyrights of the published works were indeed sold to Macmillan & Co. in 1944.[166] But the remaining manuscripts and unpublished materials obviously needed to be treated on a more individual basis, and her solution was to assign to Cooper Willis—who thus in effect became sole literary executor—'absolute discretion' in selecting 'articles manuscripts books and letters' for deposit and exhibition 'in a separate room to be provided in the Dorset County Museum at Dorchester aforesaid or in such other museum or institution as the said Irene Cooper Willis shall think best so as to form a permanent memorial of my husband Thomas Hardy the selected articles to be forever kept and exhibited together and no articles not connected with my husband to be exhibited in the same room which shall be described and labelled "The Thomas Hardy Memorial Collection".' She expressed her wish that 'the things so selected should include the more important manuscripts and those articles which were most closely associated with my husband or may be regarded as most characteristic of him and his work',[167] and in another clause directed that part of the proceeds of the sale of Max Gate should be used to create an endowment for the establishment of such a memorial collection and its subsequent maintenance and preservation.

It was as a consequence of these directions that the Dorset County Museum constructed the replica of Hardy's Max Gate study which was officially opened by John Masefield, the Poet Laureate, on 10 May 1939, with Kate Hardy somewhat shakily assisting in the cutting of the ribbon. The reconstructed study, into which the visitor gazed as if through its external window, featured Hardy's own desk, chair, table, and bookcases, together with the original fireplace, the original carpet, complete—so Cooper Willis said in her presentation speech—with some of the original dust,[168] and various memorabilia, including several of Hardy's pens and, according to *The Times*, 'the blotting paper unchanged since he last used it'.[169] It also contained, on deposit from Florence Hardy's trustees, a rich representation of Hardy's books and manuscripts, the latter including *Under the Greenwood Tree*, *The Woodlanders*, *Satires of Circumstance*, *Late Lyrics and Earlier*, and *The Queen of Cornwall*.[170] Other items—including most of the surviving notebooks—were subsequently handed over to the Museum, but Cooper Willis, like Florence Hardy before her, seems to have found trusteeship a satisfaction as well as a burden, and these additional deposits were made only gradually over the next three decades, significant groups arriving in 1957, 1958, and 1962, and even subsequently to Cooper Willis's death in 1970.[171]

The selection of books from Hardy's library, however, remained less impressive than it ought to have been. Although Cooper Willis possessed genuine literary credentials, she had few qualifications for the delicate and detailed decisions about Hardy's literary remains that confronted her in the course of settling Florence's estate. She had never met Hardy and possessed at this point no special knowledge of his life and work, and in choosing the books for the Dorset County Museum she not surprisingly overlooked several significant volumes which Hardy had owned and marked while he was still young (including translations of Euripides, Sophocles, and Aeschylus[172] and the two volumes of Mantell's *The Wonders of Geology*, obtained from Horace Moule in 1858)[173] as well as some works on which he had heavily relied for his background in philosophical thought (among them Herbert Spencer's *First Principles*[174] and George Henry Lewes's *The History of Philosophy*).[175] Important copies of some of his own books were also passed over,[176] and after the residue of the library had been sold at public auction Cooper Willis was obliged to make good some prospective gaps on the 'study' shelves by purchasing copies of a number of Hardy first editions from booksellers who happened to have them in stock.[177] Cockerell, consulted again in the wake of Florence Hardy's death, urged Cooper Willis to give the Dorset County Museum more books than she had originally planned and to make a special point of including those used in the writing of *The Dynasts*.[178] In acting on this suggestion, however, she made the mistake of choosing the French text of, for example, Thiers' *Histoire du consulat et de l'empire de Napoléon* rather than the English translation which Hardy seems almost exclusively to have used.[179]

These unfortunate, if in the circumstances forgivable, errors were less forgivably compounded by the London auction house of Hodgson & Co., entrusted with the cataloguing and sale of the remaining books.[180] No attempt seems to have been made to list the contents of the library in their entirety,[181] and the printed catalogue of the actual sale on 26 May 1938 was ill-informed and insufficiently detailed: in lots of as many as forty volumes only two or three titles were generally cited, and at a subsequent sale on 10 June 1939 some left-over items were sold in unanalysed 'parcels'—one of which, subsequently presented to the British Library, contained in fact nearly fifty maps and guidebooks, some of them of considerable interest.[182] Cockerell, who was of course familiar with the Max Gate library, further pointed out in a letter to *The Times Literary Supplement* that Hodgson & Co. had not only included in the sale, undiscriminated, a considerable number of Florence Hardy's books but had further confused matters by distributing among 'about half a dozen purchasers at the sale' some Max Gate library labels left over from the time when he and Florence had gone through Hardy's books together in 1928. He added that some other booksellers, not so privileged, had simply had imitation labels printed for their own use.[183] One of the Hodgson directors wrote to Cockerell to provide details of the number of labels handed out,[184] but the provenance of books bearing the Max Gate label had already been put permanently and complexly in doubt and the possibility of confidently reconstructing the contents of Hardy's study shelves, already profoundly undercut by the inadequacies of the Hodgson catalogue, had been pushed still further out of reach.

Though this may seem a purely scholarly complaint, it is impossible to believe that Hardy would have wished his library to have been so casually dispersed—any more than he would have wished his widow to have been so burdened by her responsibilities, his chosen literary executors to have become so fiercely at odds, or the control of his literary remains to have fallen so rapidly into the hands of someone at once so little connected with his family or with Dorset and so tenuously familiar with his work. It seems reasonable to assume, on the other hand, that he would have been gratified by the reconstruction of his study, by the preservation of Max Gate, and by the fact that even the distressing coincidence of his one hundredth birthday with the fall of France and the British retreat from Dunkirk did not prevent its being celebrated in Dorchester by a civic march to the Kennington statue and the laying of a wreath by Earl Baldwin—who, as the prime minister of the day, had been a pall-bearer at his funeral. If it is harder to imagine his ghost being so benignly present at the Stinsford memorial service later that same day, when the then Bishop of Salisbury sought to claim him as a Christian, or even at the more intellectually hospitable services held both in Stinsford Church and in Westminster Abbey on the occasion of his sesquicentennial in June 1990, such celebrations, spaced over the decades, have at least provided assurance that his reputation, almost uniquely among modern writers, has remained high ever since his death, never suffering more than the shallowest of declines and, indeed, becoming enhanced in recent years by greater recognition of his distinction and importance as a poet.

Testamentary Acts

ONE of Florence Hardy's bitterest experiences in the years immediately following Hardy's death was the defection of friends whom she had thought of as hers as well as her husband's, and her combination of acute loneliness with a burdensome sense of responsibility left her cruelly exposed to the publication of Somerset Maugham's *Cakes and Ale, or The Skeleton in the Cupboard* in the autumn of 1930. No one who knew her could in fact have recognized Florence Hardy in the ruthlessly managerial second wife of Edward Driffield, the famous novelist at the centre of *Cakes and Ale*, but she herself believed, with some justice, that she was being widely and derisively identified with the novel's unflattering portrait of a relatively young woman who had obsessively dedicated herself to the service of a much older husband in the roles of wife, nurse, gate-keeper, and 'amanuensis and secretary' and now, in her widowhood, felt neglected and bereft of all occupation save that of guarding the shrine at which she still dutifully worshipped.[1]

Suggestive parallels between Driffield and Hardy were hinted throughout the novel—the former's collected edition, for example, being assigned the same number of volumes as Hardy's Mellstock[2]—and no reader of the novel at the time of its first appearance in 1930 could have failed to see the pattern of Hardy's final decades as lying behind the narrative of Driffield's:

When he was a young fellow in [his] sixties (the cultured having had their way with him and passed him by) his position in the world of letters was only respectable; the best judges praised him, but with moderation; the younger men were inclined to be frivolous at his expense. It was agreed that he had talent, but it never occurred to anyone that he was one of the glories of English literature. He celebrated his seventieth birthday; an uneasiness passed over the world of letters, like a ruffling of the waters when on an Eastern sea a typhoon lurks in the distance, and it grew evident that there had lived among us all these years a great novelist and none of us had suspected it. There was a rush for Driffield's books in the various libraries and a hundred busy pens, in Bloomsbury, in Chelsea and in other places where men of letters congregate, wrote appreciations, studies, essays and works, short and chatty or long and intense, on his novels. These were reprinted, in complete editions, in select editions, at a shilling and three and six and five shillings and a guinea. His style was analysed, his philosophy was examined, his technique was dissected. At seventy-five everyone agreed that Edward Driffield had genius. At eighty he was the Grand Old Man of English Letters. This position he held till his death.[3]

It is the narrator's conclusion, in *Cakes and Ale*, that Driffield's claims to greatness lay not in any literary quality attributable to his work but solely in his having lived so long within a society which regarded old age with such reverence ('Who but the English would fill Covent Garden to listen to an aged prima donna without a voice?')—that, in short, 'longevity is genius'.[4]

The point is shrewdly taken, and there can be no doubt that simple survival can, in certain circumstances, create a public interest in those who might otherwise be found uninteresting—that obscure or forgotten figures, once 'discovered' to be still alive, can receive in old age an attention unprecedented during their earlier years. But if longevity can bring with it a new availability to fame, it can also—as Hardy himself remarked—provide some writers with an opportunity to 'finish their job'. Kenneth Clark, in his 1970 Rede Lecture, spoke of the contribution to 'the sum of human experience' made by certain artists even in extreme old age: 'There is undoubtedly what I may call, translating from the German, an old-age style, a special character common to nearly all their work.'[5] In Clark's view, however, it was a style found much more often among composers, painters, and sculptors than among literary figures: 'I fear that after the age of seventy, or at most seventy-five, not only is the spring of lyric poetry sealed up in depths which cannot be tapped, but the ordering, or architectonic faculty, which depends on a vigorous use of memory, with its resulting confluence of ideas, is usually in decline.'[6] Clark did acknowledge exceptions to these generalizations—chiefly Yeats, Ibsen, and two non-septuagenarians, Milton and Rilke—and was willing to allow of Hardy that he 'wrote movingly in old age', but when citing 'An Ancient to Ancients' he endorsed only the 'classic instance' of Sophocles from among Hardy's confidence-sustaining muster of those writers and thinkers of antiquity who 'Burnt brightlier towards their setting-day'.[7]

It is a view of authorship somewhat reminiscent of the

superficially attractive though ultimately alarming argument, once advanced by John Galsworthy, that professional writers should be regarded as businesses for income-tax purposes and allowed to make claims in respect of the 'depreciation' of their 'intellectual and imaginative faculties'.[8] Clark appears to exaggerate the necessary dependence of elderly authors upon the remembered emotions of the past, and his references to literary figures are in general limited by the inadequacy of 'style' as a categorizing tool and by the assumption, central to his overall argument, that late works of genius are, or should be, characterized by anger and despair—by a profound pessimism about human life and about a creativity that has itself become a 'torture'.[9] There are indeed writers of whom this might in some degree be said, but the essential arbitrariness of Clark's position is revealed by his rejection of Goethe as an exemplar of the old-age style on the grounds of his excessive optimism.

T. S. Eliot, some thirty years earlier, in an essay occasioned by Yeats's death, had similarly if less portentously sought to identify that 'special character of the artist as artist'—'a kind of moral, as well as intellectual, excellence'—which he saw as enabling certain writers to move deliberately in middle age beyond the scope of their early work to the production of late masterpieces of a wholly different kind:

Now, in theory, there is no reason why a poet's inspiration or material should fail, in middle age or at any time before senility. For a man who is capable of experience finds himself in a different world in every decade of his life; as sees it with different eyes, the material of his art is continually renewed. But in fact, very few poets have shown this capacity of adaptation to the years. It requires, indeed, an exceptional honesty and courage to face the change.[10]

If Eliot's clutch of instances—the Yeats of the late poems and plays and the Dickens of *Bleak House*—was even smaller than Clark's, that was perhaps because he was more concerned to identify the qualities he recognized in Yeats than to offer world-historical generalizations. Had he pressed his point further, he might at least have extended it to Milton, among writers in English, and the weight of subsequent critical opinion would seem to provide support for further additions, among them the Henry James of the New York Edition and the Hardy of the poems.[11]

James and Hardy were certainly conscious of having adapted themselves and their work to the new pressures and perceptions generated by increasing age and changing times—of having attempted and achieved new styles, structures, themes, and genres. They saw middle and even old age in terms not just of moral, intellectual, and physical challenge but of an earned freedom to pursue kinds and levels of expression for which both the opportunity and the maturity had previously been lacking. Like most writers, they thought of themselves as having developed and progressed as artists in and through time, and they saw, respectively, the New York Edition and the successive volumes of verse as embodying the best work of which they were or ever had been capable. Like Tennyson and Browning—like Wordsworth, indeed, and Scott and many other writers who have retained not just their faculties but their creativity into later life—they made conscious and clear-headed (if not always clear-sighted) preparations for their own deaths and for the subsequent survival and prosperity of their own works and reputations. By revising and collecting their texts, publishing their memoirs, choosing their biographers and literary heirs, destroying or preserving their personal papers and literary remains, and, ultimately, making their wills, they sought not only to promulgate their last wishes and 'intentions' in respect of their works and lives but also to place their posthumous representatives under the strongest obligations, at once legal and moral, to observe those wishes and intentions and seek their fullest realization.

Not even the verbal resourcefulness of authors, however, has exempted them from the defeat or distortion of their testamentary intentions or from the consequences of those irresolvable tensions between respect for the wishes of the dead and recognition of the needs of the living which Hardy so richly epitomized in *The Mayor of Casterbridge*. When Susan Henchard dies Mother Cuxsom's poignant lament seems assured of universal audience assent: 'Well, poor soul; she's helpless to hinder that or anything now. . . . And all her shining keys will be took from her, and her cupboards opened; and little things a' didn't wish seen, anybody will see; and her wishes and ways will all be as nothing!' Within the same passage, however, a degree of subversive sympathy is also extorted for precisely that deed which Mrs Henchard has become 'helpless to hinder', the spending of the four full-weight pennies she had carefully set aside, 'a-tied up in bits of linen', for keeping closed her eyelids after death. 'Faith,' says the perpetrator, slaking his thirst at a local inn, 'why should death rob life o' fourpence? Death's not of such good report that we should respect 'en to that extent.'[12]

What is particularly regretted on Susan Henchard's behalf is just that loss of privacy against which so many writers have sought to protect themselves in life and death alike. In July 1955 William Faulkner, then in his middle fifties, became sufficiently angered by journalistic intrusions into his personal and family affairs to publish an essay, 'On Privacy. The American Dream: What Happened to It?', devoted to deploring the erosion of American traditions of individual freedom and the threatened destruction of that 'last vestige of privacy without which man cannot be an individual'. The belief he had once cherished, and still sought to reinstate and defend, was that

only a writer's works were in the public domain, to be discussed and investigated and written about, the writer himself having put them there by submitting them for publication and accepting money for them; and therefore he not only would but must accept whatever the public wished to do or say about them from praise to burning. But that, until the writer committed a crime or ran for public office, his private life was his own; and not only had he the right to defend his privacy, but the public had the duty to do so since one man's liberty must stop at exactly the point where the next one's begins.[13]

Faulkner's own situation, initially exacerbated by the perceived remoteness of his Mississippi background, was perhaps a little compromised by the extent to which he himself had become an increasingly public, though not of course elected, figure during the years following the award of the Nobel Prize in 1950: it was, in effect, from a platform afforded by the prize that his protest was being delivered. At the same time, it had been no light thing for him, as a professional author, to forgo, purely for privacy's sake, the opportunity of a cover-story in *Time* to coincide with the publication of *A Fable* just a year previously.

The basic plea for privacy has in any case been repeatedly articulated over the years, and it is presumably one with which most contemporary authors, despite their almost unavoidable collusion with the promotional apparatus of modern publishing, would continue to agree. Nor would there necessarily be much disagreement among their readers and the public at large. The personal desire and professional need for privacy on the part of writers may not be universally respected, but it does appear to be quite generally understood: literary gossip abounds, and yet the determined reclusiveness of a J. D. Salinger is accepted (and legally endorsed), if not especially admired, and only the most extreme partisan of Sylvia Plath fails to sympathize with at least the initial protectiveness of Ted Hughes towards the children of their marriage.

. Any expectation of privacy after death, on the other hand, is much less securely grounded. Voltaire's dictum—'We owe consideration to the living; to the dead we owe only truth'—is not only austere in itself but somewhat compromised, at least in British and North American jurisdictions, by the impossibility of bringing an action for libel or slander on behalf of a person deceased. Scandal rather than sympathy characteristically rewards the attempts of public figures to close off their private concerns at death and take their secrets to the grave, and 'official' or authorized biographies are especially likely to be criticized for their acts, real or imagined, of concealment and restraint. The jostling nonentities heavily commemorated along the walls of Poets' Corner are evidence enough that reputation may not be permanent, but in the shorter run, at least, the illustrious literary dead tend to be viewed as national cultural property, subtly secured as such by the honours bestowed upon them in life and by the subsequent proliferation of obsequies, eulogies, and memorials. 'You see', wrote George Bernard Shaw to Florence Hardy after her husband's funeral, 'a man like T.H. does not belong entirely to himself; and he cannot leave his widow more than he owned.'[14]

Within such a scenario the biographer, ideally considered, might become a narrator of heroic and exemplary lives, an almost bardic interpreter and transmitter of cultural values, and at least one contemporary American biographer seems able to think of his work in just such terms.[15] But in the twentieth century the dominant mode of biography has been, and remains, critical and investigative rather than didactic and celebratory, and writers continue to respond to its perceived threat with a fundamental hostility far in excess of the objections commonly voiced by other public figures, and even by other artists. Such biographobia also seems out of proportion to what little, in any conventional terms, seems likely to warrant concealment, even authors of unstained and apparently unstainable reputation seeming possessed by the fear of closure as the ironic harbinger of disclosure and searching almost obsessively for the maximum attainable privacy both in life and after death. Tennyson would seem to have been less fearful of death itself than of the sensationalizing journalistic 'ghouls' whom he expected to descend upon his corpse. Henry Adams described his *Autobiography* as 'a mere shield of protection in the grave' and advised his friend Henry James 'to take your own life in the same way, in order to prevent biographers from taking it in theirs',[16] little imagining, perhaps, how extravagantly James would in due course take that advice, arrogating to himself in his own autobiographical volumes an absolute authority not only over his own life and works but over the lives and works of others.

Julian Barnes, whose *Flaubert's Parrot* at once probes and potentially expands the formal and methodological boundaries of modern biography, has suggested that authors respond negatively to biography and biographers because they find it intolerable to think of their work-filled and otherwise uneventful lives as being given precedence over their writings: 'What novelist, given the choice', he asks, 'wouldn't prefer you to reread one of his novels rather than read his biography?'[17] But in confronting a revulsion so pervasive and profound it does not seem enough to insist—with Lawrence, Faulkner, and many others—on the primacy of the tale over the teller, nor even to recognize that to think of oneself as a potential biographical subject is necessarily to contemplate one's death. The intense self-scrutiny characteristic of authors is evidently an important factor, and for those with a fragile sense of selfhood and worth what may be most dreaded is nakedness itself. Authors may also be sensitive to the essential exploitativeness of their own past careers as narrators, truth-enhancers, and myth-creators, and especially to their intrusive use of the 'real-life' materials unknowingly supplied by families, lovers, and friends. If famous, they have grounds for fearing, not just (with Tennyson) their treatment at the hands of journalists and biographers, but also (with the central figure of Michael Frayn's novel *The Trick of It*)[18] the exploitation of their lives and personalities by fellow writers—the likelihood that they themselves will soon be helplessly providing infinitely manipulable material for the novels, plays, and film and TV scripts of the next literary generation.

Not all writers have feared to submit themselves to biographical scrutiny. Simone de Beauvoir is said to have long entertained the fantasy that her entire life could be recorded on a giant tape-recorder; Anne Sexton, described by her daughter and executor as having had 'no sense of privacy', might have made few objections to the biographical use of the actual tapes of her psychotherapy sessions; and David Marr's biography of Patrick White concludes with a memorable image of its subject's distressed but unprotesting acceptance of its by no means flattering portrait: 'He confessed he found the book so painful that he often found himself reading through tears. He did not ask me to cut or change a line.'[19] Although Edith Wharton had followed James's lead in writing an autobiography, *A Backward Glance*, she none the less made careful arrangements for the preservation of her papers at her death—a packet 'For My Biographer' among them—and it is somewhat ironic that the thirty-year embargo placed on those papers by a cautious executor should have served to create the biographical vacuum within which Percy Lubbock's elegant but ungenerous *Portrait of Edith Wharton* could establish at least a temporary authority.[20] Many, however, have sought specifically to erect baffles and barriers against posthumous exposure, often by way of ensuring an anticipatory occupation of the biographical ground by a narrative or documentary record to which they have in some degree given their co-operation and approval. Browning worked directly with Alexandra Sutherland Orr, Tennyson with his son. Graham Greene collaborated with Norman Sherry, if in character-istically labyrinthine ways. Walt Whitman frankly instigated and oversaw the biography of himself written by his disciple, Richard M. Bucke,[21] and Hardy, as we have seen, went to what has widely been regarded as an extreme in his ghost-writing of his own posthumous official biography—although his selective manipula-tions and omissions may in fact appear relatively mild when set alongside the more downright misrepresentations lodged in the acknowledged autobiographical writings of others, Henry James not least among them.

James and Hardy also engaged in the burning of personal and literary documents, as has many another author determined upon posthumous privacy. Edmund Gosse, visiting Whitman seven years before his death, found his bedroom strewn with 'heaps, mountains of papers in a wild confusion, swept up here and there into stacks and peaks';[22] Whitman, however, subsequently disposed of many, though by no means all, of these materials, often taking the additional precaution of 'editing', by alteration or disguise, those which still remained.[23] Dr Johnson similarly destroyed his diary, his mother's letters, and other intimate records in the days immediately preceding his death, to Boswell's evident chagrin: 'as they were in great confusion, it is much to be lamented that [Johnson] had not entrusted some faithful and discreet person with the care and selection of them; instead of which, he, in a precipitate manner, burnt large masses of them, with little regard, as I apprehend, to discrimination.'[24] Ivy Compton-Burnett, on the other hand, perhaps simply did not preserve such items: Hilary Spurling, embarking on a biography found only 'a shoebox half full of engagement diaries, and a small, apparently random selection of fanmail'.[25]

Somerset Maugham sought to prevent the appearance of any biography by directing his executor neither to authorize any such work nor to provide any assistance to would-be biographers, and T. S. Eliot seems to have left (though not in his will) instructions to much the same effect.[26] The element of the chimerical in all such gestures, however, emerges strongly from the decision of Maugham's chosen representative to depart from that instruction within only a few years of his death, and from the powerlessness of Valerie Eliot to prevent the publication of biographies of her husband of an unauthorized but by no means insubstantial kind. An obvious impediment to the absolute control or comprehensive destruction of personal documents, before or after death, consists in the simple fact that letters once despatched cannot readily be recovered. Though the publication rights to letters remain with the sender and the sender's representatives, the rights of ownership, hence of disposal, belong to the recipient, and many a man of letters, it has been truly said, would be glad to have them back. James may have destroyed most of his incoming correspondence, but his own letters have been preserved in vast numbers, coming to the Houghton Library at Harvard, in particular, by both gift and purchase. Eliot's many letters to Emily Hale are under seal at Princeton University until the year 2020,[27] and although W. H. Auden begged his friends to destroy his letters without showing them to anyone else,[28] it seems reasonable to suspect that the level of compliance has been extremely low. But while the deliberate or casual preservation of letters and manuscripts in other hands may be perceived as a threat by the elderly famous, it can have very different implications for those without recognition in their own lifetimes. Robert Bridges' fortunate accumulation of Hopkins material is a striking case in point, and Keats, who might indeed have expected his name to be 'writ in water', was largely secured in his reputation by the devoted and deliberate efforts, textual as well as biographical, of friends such as Richard Woodhouse and Charles Brown.

Willa Cather, in her will, addressed the entire question more deliberately and thoughtfully than most, directing that 'neither my Executors nor my Trustee shall consent to, or permit, the publication in any form whatsoever, of the whole, or any part of any letter or letters written by me in my lifetime, nor the use, exploitation or disposal of any other right therein'. Realizing, as she said, that rights in her letters would eventually pass into remoter hands, she 'earnestly' requested that the same restrictions should continue to be imposed, at the same time making it clear that she was not mandating automatic legal action in defence of such rights but leaving it 'to the sole and uncontrolled discretion' of her executors and trustee to act as they thought fit in each particular instance.[29] These terms have indeed been effective, thus far, in preventing either collective or piecemeal publication of her correspondence, but they have been interpreted as permitting inspection of that correspondence by biographers,[30] and the resulting accounts of her life suggest by their increasing amplitude and specificity the likely long-term ineffectiveness of any general restrictions on documentary evidence. As Cather's publisher, Alfred A. Knopf, remarked in 1973, on the centenary of her birth, 'anyone who abhors contact with members of the public is best advised not to produce work which has public interest'.[31]

It is a truth—it is at any rate a commonplace—that contemporary society seeks to avoid confronting or even contemplating matters so unpleasant as dying and death, preferring to hide them in hospitals and blur them with drugs. Browning, Tennyson, James, and Hardy, however, all died in domestic surroundings and in the presence of their nearest relatives, and even for the contemporary writer the threat of death remains not only inescapably present, especially with advancing age, but peculiarly challenging, as marking the end of creativity as well as of bodily existence. 'The bitterness of an interrupted life', wrote Vladimir Nabokov, 'is nothing compared to the bitterness of an interrupted work: the probability of a continuation of the first beyond the grave seems infinite by comparison with the hopeless incompleteness of the second.'[32] William Faulkner, who spoke in his obituary of Albert Camus of that 'foreknowledge and hatred of death' which every artist carries through life, also described how he had deliberately postponed until his fiftieth birthday any stock-taking of his own work: 'Then one day I was fifty and I looked back at it, and I decided that it was all pretty good—and then in the same instant I realised that was the worst of all since that meant only that a little nearer now was the moment, instant, night: dark: sleep: when I would put it all away forever that I anguished and sweated over, and it would never trouble me anymore.'[33]

Faulkner declared on several occasions the unimportance of the artist as individual and his personal desire to disappear, traceless, at the moment of his death, leaving only his work behind as the sign of his passing, his scratch on the face of the universe.[34] For Whitman, on the other hand, as he explained shortly before his death in a note to one of his 'Good-Bye my Fancy' poems, 'Behind a Good-bye there lurks much of the salutation of another beginning—to me, Development, Continuity, Immortality, Transformation, are the chiefest life-meanings of Nature and Humanity, and are the *sine qua non* of all facts, and each fact.'[35] Neither of them, however, neglected to make a will, and few writers have in fact eschewed that final opportunity of extending some measure of posthumous control over the future of their work and the aftermath of their lives.

In the matter of wills the law which otherwise excludes the dead is presumptively, if not unchallengeably, on their side, as is also that ancient, atavistic reverence for those last wishes, death-bed confessions, and other ultimate retrospections of which Walter Benjamin once wrote: 'Just as a sequence of images is set in motion inside a man as his life comes to an end—unfolding the views of himself under which he has encountered himself without being aware of it—suddenly in his expressions and looks the unforgettable emerges and imparts to everything that concerned him that authority which even the poorest wretch in dying possesses for the living around him.'[36] If the portentousness of wills chiefly derives from their intimacy with the solemnity and paraphernalia of death itself, it is further enhanced by their association with secrecy, concealment, and the labyrinths of the law, by their ritualization of the successive stages of making, witnessing, proving, and reading— the withheld moment of formalized revelation—and by their concern, so momentous to the living, with the transmission of property. In the standard phrase 'last will and testament', the term 'testament'—originally applicable to personal property as distinct from the immovable or real property (chiefly houses and land, as in 'real estate') covered by the term 'will'—has popularly taken on something of the aura of its now archaic meaning of 'covenant', especially as found in scriptural accounts of the Last Supper (according to the Authorized Version)[37] and in the naming of the Old and New Testaments. Its use in legal contexts may also have tenuously attracted to it the sense of testifying or bearing witness, the word 'testator', indeed, having historically been used as meaning both 'one who makes a will' and 'one who or that which testifies; a witness'.[38]

As testators authors have property other than real to dispose of—'All my estate real and personal', wrote Keats in his unwitnessed 'will', 'consists in the hopes of the sale of books publish'd or unpublish'd'[39]—and a particular sensitivity to the generic distinctiveness of wills as such. Gary Saul Morson has described Tolstoy's fascination with the death-bed as affording the opportunity for quasi-posthumous speech, transcending as such the contexts and limitations of every day: writing to the Tsar during a serious illness, he claimed to be speaking 'as it were from the other world'. Tolstoy, Morson adds, wrote a succession of wills on this basis, well aware that 'a last testament is a privileged one, its privilege marked by the ceremony of its reading and derived in part from its closure to response or qualification'.[40] This deafness of wills to expostulation is well suggested by Irene Cooper Willis's recollection of the 'explosions and exits and slammed doors'[41] that accompanied her reading of Florence Hardy's will to the assembled members of the Dugdale family, and it might perhaps be argued that Hardy's secret composition of his 'Life' for posthumous publication can best be understood as a projective 'testament' *d'outre-tombe*, a final uninterruptible and unanswerable contribution to that long dialogue between himself and his critics in which strategic and tactical advantage had seemed always to belong to the latter. Some such element of aggressive self-defensiveness may ultimately have entered into Wordsworth's postponement of publication of *The Prelude* until after his death, even though the poem was not written with such a destiny in view. Hector Berlioz, on the other hand, wrote his memoirs specifically for posthumous publication,[42] and an 'odd thought' struck Dr Johnson when he knew that he was dying: 'we shall receive no letters in the grave'.[43]

When Johnson made his will he included a prefatory declaration of his Christian faith which Boswell regarded as being 'of real consequence from this great man'.[44] It was in no sense an ostentatious statement, however, and literary wills, like wills in general, seem to be less often the vehicles of instruction or exhortation than of gestures towards the belated attainment of unachieved lifetime ambitions: Sydney Cockerell's will, it is true, included a long paragraph in praise of friendship, but George Bernard Shaw's directed funds towards the reform of English spelling; his wife's aimed at nothing less than a vitalization of Irish culture; Arthur Koestler's promoted his interest in parapsychology; and Ivy Compton-Burnett's sought to ensure publication of the collected edition to which she had long but vainly aspired.[45] Wills may equally, of course, seek to discharge personal responsibilities and initiate long-contemplated acts of personal retribution or reward: Dr Johnson's will was exemplary in its care for those (especially his black servant, Francis Barber) who had served him or become dependent upon him, although Boswell among others was distressed at not being mentioned at all; Wilkie Collins made an earnest though ultimately frustrated attempt to ensure adequate and equitable provision for the members of both his unofficial families;[46] while Ivy Compton-Burnett made what seems to have been an essentially mischievous distribution of specific mirrors to ten different friends, further directing these and other beneficiaries to collect their bequests from her flat, immediately following the cremation, in what some of them felt to be 'a final strange scene' that she herself had devised.[47]

But while the act of making a will and anticipating its consequences may yield various satisfactions, a testator is in fact possessed of strictly limited power. Wills are assertions of authority but also implicit acknowledgements of impending surrender—

attempts, at best, to make terms with death—and if they cannot be directly answered, they can be openly challenged in court or silently disregarded in private. Conversely, if very rarely, a court may recognize a will that is in fact non-existent: Frieda Lawrence, in November 1932, succeeded in persuading a British judge that her husband, D. H. Lawrence, had simply mislaid during the couple's many travels the will he had made in her favour in November 1914.[48] The absence of any valid will by Pen Browning led to his being declared intestate, and thence to the dispersal of the Browning papers, while Sylvia Plath's failure to make a will, resulting in the legal assignment of all rights and responsibilities to her husband, Ted Hughes, has been a major source of the turbulence that has since surrounded her literary remains. The issues are painful and complex—Jacqueline Rose's book on Plath devotes forty-eight pages to a chapter on 'The Archive'[49]—and have often been extravagantly argued, but while any publication of personal documents within a few years of an author's death almost inevitably involves deletions designed to ensure the (often legally enforceable) privacy of the living,[50] it does seem clear, in lengthening retrospect, that Hughes, instead of personally participating in the editing of Plath's *Journals* and other posthumously published works, might have been well advised to make at least a formal delegation of those tasks to someone from outside the Hughes and Plath families.[51]

Even when wills are made, found, and proved, their objectives may be defeated by fundamental miscalculations in the document itself, by the development of unanticipated circumstances—such as those which led to the swift diversion of W. H. Auden's literary rights into wholly unintended hands[52]—or by simple mismanagement on the part of the living. That last consideration was much invoked by Henry James when begging to be excused from accepting appointment as an executor of Robert Louis Stevenson's will: he was, he insisted, 'utterly and absolutely the creature in the world most abjectly and most humiliatedly unfit for the discharge of any such duties or any duties remotely approaching or dimly resembling them'.[53] The precision and (what may not always be the same thing) the sensitivity with which testamentary provisions are observed necessarily depends upon the loyalty, reliability, and practical efficiency of those appointed to positions of executorial responsibility—perhaps also, to some extent, upon their attitude to those final truth-tellings and expressions of intentionality said to be extorted by the prospect of immediate extinction. Unfortunately, the transmission and protection of literary property remains, on both sides of the Atlantic, a peculiarly difficult, ill-defined, and even ambiguous task, demanding discretion, judgement, and, ideally, a degree of familiarity with the world of contemporary letters. For a testator to trust to the devotion and competence of a single individual may perhaps make for greater efficiency and confidentiality, but the possibility of such an imposition's becoming a kind of doom is suggested not only by the example of Hallam Tennyson but by a recent comment—in a review of a memoir of the American painter Philip Guston—on the extent to which the children of the abstract expressionists

have become the beneficiaries and administrators of complicated trusts. They deal with avuncular lawyers, tax advisers and (regular figures in the trusteeship business) their parents' oldest and most irresponsible friends; negotiate with galleries, museums and collectors, doctoral students and less disinterested parties. They maintain archives, catalogue systems: their daily work is with photographs, slides, the disputed measurements of lost or forgotten paintings.[54]

Joint appointments have often been seen as constituting a less burdensome imposition and as offering an opportunity to bring different kinds of obligation and expertise to bear. The sharing of duties among just two people, however, has the disadvantage, quickly obvious to Florence Hardy and Sydney Cockerell, of lacking any mechanism for the resolution of disputes, and Philip Larkin, perhaps with Hardy's mismatched team in mind, named in his will a total of three literary executors. Inexplicably, he then proceeded to render their task both exceptionally difficult and embarrassingly controversial by instructing his trustees (who included one of the literary executors but not the other two) to destroy 'unread' precisely those unpublished manuscripts whose publication (after consultation with his literary executors) was contemplated and indeed sanctioned by two other clauses in the same will.[55] Larkin's diaries were in fact shredded immediately following his death, but in choosing to publish rather than destroy the remaining manuscripts the literary executors evidently felt secure both on legal grounds and because of their sense that Larkin knowingly appointed them as persons who would wish at least his specifically literary manuscripts to be preserved.[56] It seems in any case conceivable that Larkin intended his destruction order to apply exclusively to personal documents—the limiting word or phrase being omitted by the typist and its absence not noticed at the time when Larkin, already seriously ill, actually put his signature to the will.

Such controversies and confusions are often of long continuance —witness the ambiguity of the prohibition against 'collation' imposed by Kipling, his wife, and his daughter as a condition of acceptance of their gifts of manuscripts to various institutions[57]— and it is obvious enough that literary executors, however responsible, can easily be hampered and even frustrated in the performance of their duties by poorly drawn testamentary documents. Florence Hardy, it may be remembered, was advised, several years after Hardy's death, that she and Cockerell had long been exercising powers which the will, when closely examined, appeared to have assigned elsewhere.

Burial arrangements, so often made under pressure of time and in conditions of distress, are generally the first, and often the worst, test faced both by the wills themselves and by those responsible for their interpretation and implementation, and the passionate differences of opinion over Hardy's burial have been paralleled often enough. When Thomas Carlyle died in 1881 the Dean of Westminster was prompt to offer an Abbey burial, but Carlyle's known objections both to the Anglican rites and to the Abbey itself—'There will be a general gaol delivery in that place one of these days'[58]—determined his executors to bury him at Ecclefechan, as his will directed. The result, according to Froude, was a scanted ceremony, performed 'on a cold dreary February morning' in the presence of 'an *un*ordered if not *dis*ordered assemblage', that made Froude himself, as one of the executors, wonder if the Abbey might not after all have been the more appropriate choice.[59] Shaw, in the middle of the twentieth century, similarly made a very specific request for the disposal of his body, but he also allowed for—while ostensibly discouraging—alternative possibilities: 'I desire that my dead body shall be cremated and its ashes inseparably mixed with those of my late wife now in the custody of the Golders Green Crematorium and in this condition inurned or scattered in the garden of the house in Ayot Saint Lawrence where we lived together for thirty five years unless some

other disposal of them should be in the opinion of my Trustee more
eligible. Personally I prefer the garden to the cloister.'[60] The garden
it was.

Shortly before Walt Whitman died in Camden, New Jersey, in
1892, he had built for himself and his family in nearby Harleigh
Cemetery a large and prospectively time-defying granite tomb, and
it remained only for his executors, who were also his friends,
disciples, and future editors, to carry him thither for an entomb-
ment that another disciple, a former Harvard divinity student, was
moved—perhaps by the sheer massiveness of the mausoleum—to
compare to that of Christ.[61] The executors had also to negotiate a
settlement of the construction costs that Whitman—stimulated by
the gift of the site itself—had recklessly incurred.[62] In Sauk Centre,
Minnesota, in 1951, on the other hand, Sinclair Lewis's obsequies
seem to have been almost farcically lacking in dignity—Mark
Schorer imagines some 'cosmic laughter' as forthcoming from
Lewis himself[63]—while Theodore Dreiser's widow, faced in Los
Angeles in early 1946 with the problem of arranging a funeral
acceptable to both the Communists and the Congregationalists
among her husband's friends, settled upon an expensive ceremony
and interment at Forest Lawn that can scarcely have satisfied either,
even though Charlie Chaplin came to read one of Dreiser's poems
and Dreiser's body, prior to its burial near the grave of Tom Mix,
was visible in an open coffin, 'in his black lecture suit and black
bow tie that accentuated the downy white hair'.[64]

If relatively few authors have been so strikingly present at their
own funerals, fewer still can have matched Hardy's grotesque fate
of being simultaneously, if minimally, present at two: Shelley's
heart was, indeed, buried (in Bournemouth) far from his ashes (in
Rome), but only after a long lapse of years.[65] Duplicated obsequies,
on the other hand, have been by no means uncommon. Browning's
and James's remains, for example, came finally (and by no means
inappropriately) to rest at points far distant from the places where
they died and were first formally mourned. The questions recently
raised about Yeats's burial in wartime France and his post-war
transfer to Sligo have apparently been answered to the satisfaction
of Yeats scholars and of his own family,[66] and if similar doubts
about the fate of D. H. Lawrence's remains—buried in Vence, his
place of death, in 1930, exhumed and cremated five years later, and
then transported, in a journey full of accidents and delays, to their

final resting place within a garishly painted cement altar above
Taos—were less readily allayed, that is perhaps because they were
from the first inextricably involved in the inventive rumour-mongering
by which the rivalry between different groups of Lawrence's disciples
and admirers was at that time so largely sustained.[67]

Some duplication of memorials often results in these and other
instances: Lawrence's original stone at Vence is apparently still in
place and he has had, since 1985, another in Westminster Abbey;
James is remembered in Chelsea and in Cambridge, Massachusetts,
as well as in the Abbey; and if Robert Louis Stevenson's body has
not been reclaimed for Scotland from its romantic (if muddy)
location at the summit of Mount Vaea, that is perhaps because
Edinburgh already possesses the magnificent bronze relief by
St Gaudens in St Giles Cathedral.[68] As Hardy's case would again
suggest, memorials are apt to be as troublesome as funerals: every
aspect of the Scott Memorial in Edinburgh, the most famous and
grandiose of British exemplars, became a subject of years-long
controversy, and even the siting of Watts's statue of Tennyson in
the precincts of Lincoln Cathedral was not accomplished without
opposition, some voices insisting that it was 'too modern, too
impressionistic, for its mediaeval background'.[69] Nor is any
representation of an admired figure, whether ambitious of por-
traiture or symbolism, likely to receive universal approval. Onslow
Ford's Shelley at University College, Oxford, and Epstein's design
for Oscar Wilde's tomb in Père Lachaise have alike been deeply
deplored as well as highly praised, and the foliage with which Eric
Kennington encumbered Hardy's knickerbockered legs is said to
have prompted Augustus John to describe the Dorchester statue as
that of a frustrated market-gardener.[70]

The confusions, complexities, ironies, and absurdities consequent
upon deaths and arising from wills are indeed numerous and
obvious enough, the errors of the deceased becoming further
compounded and contorted by the misinterpretations, inefficiencies,
and occasional defalcations of those appointed to act in their
names. In an extreme instance, Rufus Griswold, the literary
executor of Edgar Allan Poe, used his resulting opportunities as
authorized editor and biographer to ruin the already fragile
reputation of the man who had once been his friend, resorting even
to forgery in his eagerness to present his own actions in a better
light, Poe's in a worse.[71] In general, however, the misinterpreta-

tions of literary wills seem well-meaning, the inefficiencies retrospectively predictable, and it is a point insufficiently appreciated by
some testators that in choosing executors and literary executors in
whose judgement they trust they must expect that judgement to be
exercised from time to time in ways contrary to the ways in which
they would themselves have acted if still alive, and even to their
known wishes as recorded in their wills and other explicitly or
implicitly testamentary documents.

Irene Cooper Willis, in departing from the instructions set out
in Vernon Lee's will, doubtless feared that the latter's reputation might not outlast the limitation she had placed upon
publication for her letters, and that those who had cared for her
personally would certainly not do so, while Spencer Curtis Brown,
Somerset Maugham's literary executor, justified his contravention
of Maugham's prohibition against giving assistance to biographers
on the grounds that he believed Maugham's memory would be
better served by the publication of a responsible biography than by
the continuing proliferation of malicious gossip.[72] Max Brod, faced
(far less equivocally than Philip Larkin's executors) with Franz
Kafka's dying request for the destruction of all his personal papers
and unpublished manuscripts, including *The Trial* and *The Castle*,
acted in fact quite otherwise, insisting that Kafka had appointed
him in the knowledge that he would ignore such instructions and
should have chosen another executor had he been absolutely
determined upon their being carried out.[73] Not everyone has agreed
or will agree with such decisions, however conscientiously arrived
at, nor are those who make them likely to rest entirely satisfied with
themselves. But since literary executors are distinct individuals
existing within time and changing circumstance—and with their
own sense of obligation to other sets of values—it can scarcely be
inappropriate for them to act in whatever way they genuinely
believe to be in the best interests of the deceased and of what might
riskily be called the cultural good. And it must at least be said of
Cooper Willis, Curtis Brown, and Max Brod that they discharged
their implicit responsibility to offer public explanations of the
positions they had taken.

The element of ambiguity, even contradiction, in the executorial
role itself emerges with particular sharpness from that well-
considered will of Willa Cather's, made in 1943, some four years
before her death. Cather was admirably clear about the assignment

of her authorial rights and the disposition of her copyrights, royalties, and unpublished manuscripts, appointing as sole trustee her friend and companion Edith Lewis, authorizing her to publish any hitherto unpublished works deemed 'to be worthy of publication without adverse effect upon my literary reputation',[74] and vesting in her 'the same power and authority to deal with said literary properties as I would have if living'. But Cather's 'same . . . as' is less precise than it initially seems. In making a permanent assignment of her authority, she could not similarly make over the individual experience, judgement, and sensibility with which she had herself exercised that authority. Edith Lewis might command after Cather's death the 'same power and authority . . . as [Cather] would have if living', but, as ineluctably other, she could not in fact 'deal with said literary properties as [Cather] would have if living'. Rudyard Kipling perhaps achieved more precisely appropriate phrasing when instructing his executor (his wife or, should she predecease him, the Public Trustee) 'so to deal with my copyright property . . . as in her or his absolute discretion she or he may think best as fully and effectually as I myself if living could do'.[75]

All executors and literary executors must in practice exercise just such a delegated, hence compromised, authority, either independently or in response to the initiatives of others. Pen Browning's printing of his parents' courtship correspondence and Florence Hardy's decisions in respect of 'Old Mrs Chundle' and 'An Indiscretion in the Life of an Heiress' were actions distinctively their own. Henry James, though capable of taking extravagant quasi-executorial liberties on behalf of deceased relatives, could never have countenanced his sister-in-law's posthumous publication —however well meant—of *The Middle Years, The Sense of the Past*, or *The Ivory Tower* in their unfinished condition. The role of the literary executor may, indeed, be especially delicate, and especially consequential, when textual issues are at stake. Tennyson, though gratified by the realization of his ambition for an authoritatively annotated collected edition of his works, might nevertheless have been disturbed to discover how much of the authority actually exercised was in fact his son's, and recent disputes over Yeats's text have largely centred upon the weight which ought properly be given to his delegation of limited textual authority to his wife and editor even before his death.[76]

Although the resulting profusion of alternative editions of Yeats's collected poems has perhaps caused at least some short-term confusion, the ambition of writers for a collective edition of their works seems in itself as understandable as it has certainly been common—even though that ambition has sometimes had to await a posthumous realization at the hands, for example, of Mary Shelley, Annie Thackeray, or Robert Bridges. Such an edition, especially if handsomely presented and actively promoted, was for writers of the nineteenth and early twentieth centuries simultaneously a reassuring mark of public recognition and a seizable—generally speaking, a seized—opportunity for textual selection and revision, and even (if prefaces were to be written) for the promulgation of newly preferred interpretations and myths of origin. Browning, Tennyson, James, and Hardy, different one from another in so many respects, were alike in their meticulous attention to all aspects of their collective editions and in their hope and expectation that their finally revised texts would represent them to posterity. Bernard Shaw sought in his will to prevent the publication or quotation 'of any edition or extracts from my works in which any earlier text shall be substituted either wholly or partly for the text as contained in the printed volumes finally passed by me for press',[77] and Stephen Gill has recently described the exhaustive process of revision to which Wordsworth, in his 'obsessive pursuit of poetic finish', was accustomed to subject each of his successive editions—not only incorporating additional poems as they accumulated but silently altering those with which his readers were already familiar. Gill particularly draws attention to a letter to Edward Moxon in which Wordsworth affirmed, rather as Henry James was later to do, that the importance of his edition of 1836–7 lay 'in the pains which has [*sic*] been taken in the revisal of so many of the old Poems, to the re-modelling, and often re-writing whole Paragraphs, which you know have cost me great labour and I do not repent of it'.[78] To the comprehensive *Leaves of Grass* of 1891–2 that he knew to be the last he would ever oversee, Whitman prefixed a characteristically trenchant directive to the effect that its matured and completed form should be followed exactly—'a copy and fac-simile, indeed, of the text of these 438 pages'—in any future edition.[79]

In the late twentieth century collected editions of poets have continued to appear with some regularity—although the term has in practice been very variously understood—but the years since the Second World War have seen few, if any, editions of living novelists comparable in either scope or format to James's New York Edition, Hardy's Wessex Edition, Stevenson's Edinburgh Edition, or Kipling's Sussex Edition, left unfinished at his death in 1936. Even when multi-volume editions incorporating authorial revisions and prefaces have appeared—Joyce Cary's Carfax Edition, for example, or Graham Greene's Collected Edition—they have tended to be unpretentiously produced for a general readership. Somewhat ironically, perhaps, this virtual disappearance of the old-style collected edition has been paralleled, from the 1960s onward, by a marked increase in the publication of comprehensive scholarly editions of deceased authors, and as more and more scholars have found themselves accepting responsibility for the preparation of such newly edited texts and their transmission to a further posterity, they have sometimes become subject to the legal restrictions of copyright, particularly the extended copyright in unpublished materials, and thus to the authority of the literary executors concerned.

Those same scholars, however, in adopting an editorial role, may also be said to have self-appointed themselves to positions of supplementary literary executorship, and to have assumed in so doing some portion of the moral burdens more directly shouldered by those specifically named to such positions under the terms of the author's will. When writers have deliberately concerned themselves, in an old age not merely competent but demonstrably creative, with both the construction and the detailed refinement of their final canons, their explicit or implicit (*de facto*) approval of such last-revised versions must be regarded as constituting a final and, effectively, dying directive to both an immediate and a longer-term posterity. An editor, therefore, who chooses to set aside such instructions—to edit, for example, what is sometimes called an 'ideal first edition' text or to intervene beyond the correction of obvious errors in the final version itself—must in some sense be contravening whatever moral obligation may permanently reside in such testamentary acts and committing an offence comparable, in kind if not in degree, to that of an executor who fails to carry out the terms of a will. It seems particularly appropriate, in this context, that the text to which Whitman gave his immediately pre-posthumous approval should have become known as the 'Death-bed edition'.

Though rarely recognized as such, part of the attraction and strength of the modern editorial methodology associated with the names of W. W. Greg and Fredson Bowers has undoubtedly been the element of moral complacency permitted by its standard combination of the author's final decisions as to the words ('substantives') of a text with whatever manuscripts and corrected proofs may reveal of authorial preferences in such matters as spelling and punctuation ('accidentals').[80] The methodology's concern with the realization of an author's textual intentions has many justifications—as James McLaverty has suggested, the textual judgements of a work's originator are likely to be better and in any case more interesting than the editor's own[81]—but its incorporation of a powerful and essentially personal moral ingredient, happily consonant with an experienced editor's sense of ever-growing intimacy with the author's working methods and modes of thought, has undoubtedly contributed to the editorial field's remaining so little touched by the perceived irrelevance of contemporary death-of-the-author debates and only mildly ravaged by arguments over what is generally called the socialization of texts, the extent to which the author should be viewed as merely one element within a multi-stage production process whose end-product possesses its own distinct historico-cultural validity.[82] The taken-for-granted author-centredness, in short, of what was designed by Greg as a logical, chronologically based procedure for choosing responsibility among textual variants and versions has arguably constituted a significant, though largely unrecognized, source of its continuing strength and appeal.

But if sensitivity to an author's departing wishes is incumbent upon, and natural to, an editor, in his or her quasi-executorial capacity, that sensitivity clearly need not be more acute than that expected of an actual executor. 'Why do folks dwell so fondly on the last words, advice, appearance, of the departing?' Whitman once asked. 'Those last words are not samples of the best, which involve vitality at its full, and balance, and perfect control and scope.' And there do indeed seem to be few grounds for assuming that the final textual actions of authors are inherently likely to demonstrate aesthetic superiority. But Whitman's countervailing insistence, in the very next sentence, that last words are none the less 'valuable beyond measure to confirm and endorse the varied train, facts, theories and faith of the whole preceding life',[83] promptly reinstates the testamentary—and, in this instance, editorial—dilemma in all its ultimate irresolvability. The editor, like the executor proper, seems called to act with responsible independence, allowing awareness of the author's final intentions, however sanctified by an aura of dying wishes and last wills and testaments, to fall into place among a complex of felt obligations: to an envisaged readership, to theoretical positions conscientiously held, to the author's reputation as it has developed through time, even to an aesthetically or historically grounded choice between— though not a selection from among—distinctive authorial versions (e.g., the initial and final forms of James's *The American*). Death, after all, may prove too unpredictable in its arrest to render other than arbitrary any concept of finality so defined: Tennyson, had he lived longer, would doubtless have made yet other revisions for his next edition, and even an eventual Jamesian repudiation of the New York Edition is by no means unimaginable. And since works tend to be permanently associated with the date of their first publication, some special significance clearly attaches to the 'substantives' as well as the 'accidentals' of that originary form: a fully argued editorial preference for the first edition readings of, say, *Under the Greenwood Tree* over those of its 'Wessexized' final version might thus be difficult to challenge even on 'executorial' grounds,[84] and the forthcoming Edinburgh Edition of the Waverley Novels is zealous in its ambition to revivify them for a modern audience by stripping away the introductions and annotations Scott supplied to his final *magnum opus* edition.

G. Thomas Tanselle, in his magisterial essay on 'The Editorial Problem of Final Authorial Intention', takes the position that an editor may, without abdication of scholarly responsibility, choose an early form of the text if it is found to be 'a more faithful representation of the author's vision'.[85] Although that sounds rather like being invited to choose the most faithful representation of a person's appearance from among a series of photographs taken at widely different ages, it also constitutes a necessary recognition that the successive states of a single work must in some sense represent a succession of intentions at least prospectively 'final'. As Tanselle also observes, in the case of authors whose beliefs and creative preferences have altered greatly over time, early and late versions of what is nominally the same work may differ so sharply as to justify the preparation and publication of multiple editions, whether simultaneously (as in the parallel texts of Browning's *Pauline*) or separately (as in Edward Mendelson's editions of Auden). The proper business of editors, clearly, is to combine that attentiveness to the last wishes of authors implicit in the quasi-executorial character of editorship itself with the making of informed, responsible, and, if need be, radical discriminations among the textual forms available—their ultimate editorial obligation to authors, readers, and scholarship alike being simultaneously discharged not by any automatic restriction of alternatives but in terms of the thoroughness and accuracy of their work and its respect for the decipherable inscriptions and decodeable intentions of the version chosen.

Some executors have themselves become editors, and a special fascination attaches in this and other contexts to the mutually exploitative nature of Walt Whitman's relationship with his disciples, who attended and supported him in his old age, wrote hero-worshipping biographies of him virtually at his dictation, and then found occupation and justification for the remainder of their lives not only in the collection and editing of his works but in the preservation and publication of even the most trivial of his old-age utterances and the further propagation of his ideas. But if Whitman 'became his admirers' to a degree not quite imagined by Auden when writing of the death of Yeats,[86] some such statement could none the less be made (differences in gender allowed for) of the passing of almost any writer. Obituaries, eulogies, funerals, memorials, biographies, new editions, and executorial actions of every kind, though referred to the dead and to the past, signify only within the present and the future, and keeping 'alive' the memory of departed genius may serve equally, or even primarily, to give meaning to the lives of the living. The point is well illustrated by both the title and the contents of *In the Shadow of the Giant*, a selection of the letters exchanged over the years between Edward Aswell, Thomas Wolfe's last editor, and Elizabeth Nowell, his literary agent and first biographer. As the editors—by an interesting generational shift, the daughters of Aswell and Nowell—freely acknowledge: 'Their letters to each other reflect a commitment—call it an obsession—to keep the memory of Wolfe's greatness alive. But through their work together they recaptured some of the vitality of a past shared with Wolfe.'[87] It is not necessary to question the loyalty of Hallam Tennyson and Florence Hardy—or even the more lightly worn filiality of Pen Browning—in order to suggest that the burdens they shouldered also lent their lives a purposefulness that might otherwise have been lacking. Such elements may also, at a further remove, enter into the experience of biographers, editors, and collectors who have devoted their lives— like Kathleen Coburn, Kathleen Tillotson, Ralph Isham, Wilmarth S. Lewis, Richard L. Purdy, Leon Edel, and many others—to the scholarly pursuit of a particular author.[88]

Scholars, including editors and even biographers, are in the normal course of events less likely to encounter the actual subjects of their research than those who by direction of the deceased, by natural processes of descent and inheritance, or by curious accidents of marriage, find themselves in positions of residual literary responsibility—even at the distance of several generations, as Kathleen Coburn discovered when searching for Coleridge papers, and Colonel Isham, even more dramatically, during his long Boswellian campaign.[89] Such encounters are not without their risks. Although an author may in life wilfully deceive biographers helpless in the grip of informational desire, the dangers of posthumous misrepresentation—perhaps accompanied by some transfer of reverential obligation—are obviously greater still. As Henry Reed so brilliantly suggested in his radio play, *A Very Great Man Indeed*,[90] the friends and enemies of the departed author may not always be readily distinguishable, and a biographer gathering material from such sources clearly needs to be alert to the possibility that the information offered or extracted may already have undergone modification, interpretation, and, above all, selection by persons of unknown reliability and discretion who even if ideally loyal to the deceased are none the less ineluctably other.

The ideally loyal can, indeed, present the greatest obstacles. Prompted by personal or family feeling—or by a simple disinclination to be troubled—they may interpret their roles in terms even more restrictive than the testators themselves would have wished, destroying papers or prohibiting access to them, denying permission to quote or paraphrase, refusing interviews, and declining to enter into correspondence. Kipling's daughter, Elsie Bambridge, maintained until her death in 1976 a defensive attitude towards her parents' privacy, controlling their papers with notorious tightness

and effectively supervising, even while actively assisting, the
biographies written by Lord Birkenhead and Charles Carrington:
the latter, indeed, says in his preface that her name ought properly
to have appeared alongside his on the title-page.[91] When such
responsibilities are experienced as oppressive or morally or
emotionally troubling, those who bear them may sometimes seek
release by the route of either absolute or selective destruction:
Sophia Hawthorne's excision, expurgation, and gentrification of
her husband's notebooks[92] was doubtless undertaken—like Hallam
Tennyson's radical weeding of the family archive—from the most
pious of motives, and Elsie Bambridge evidently felt she had good
reason to destroy her mother's extensive diaries, which now survive
only in the fragmentary notes made by Carrington and Lord
Birkenhead.[93] Pen Browning, on the other hand, might be said to
have struck an excellent balance between what was due to his
parents' memory and what to the claims of literary history, and
even selective destroyers may eventually emerge—like the military
occupiers of certain stretches of the English countryside—as
unexpectedly fortunate preservers: Elsie Bambridge, indeed, was
one such, Hallam Tennyson another, and although Florence
Hardy's failure to destroy the typescripts of the 'Life' may have
reflected a desire to affirm her own authorship it provided in fact
the fullest confirmation of her husband's.

Even when documents are not under family control, their
accessibility may still be in doubt. Institutions sometimes accept
gifts under highly restrictive conditions, or see it as their duty to
limit or even prohibit access to unique and especially fragile
materials, and while the generosity and knowledge of most book
and manuscript collectors can scarcely be overstated, private
owners who are not collectors may sometimes impose their own
rites of passage.[94] Those scholars—biographers, historians, biblio-
graphers, editors—who depend upon original documents, especially
from the nineteenth and twentieth centuries, can scarcely avoid
encountering the problems and rewards of working with (and
occasionally against) curators, librarians, custodians, collectors,
dealers, auctioneers, lawyers, private householders, literary agents,
and the sometimes improbably surviving literary heirs—who may
have to be persuaded that they do in fact possess either the
documents or the rights of which the scholar stands, in his or her
own judgement, so urgently in need. In such situations argument,

blandishment, bribery, and abject supplication may all sometimes fail. Even letters written on Athenaeum Club stationery and slavishly observing the correct form of address to the nobility have been known to remain unanswered. Old ladies, in life as in *The Aspern Papers*, may be understandably reluctant to yield up the faded love-letters of their youth, and the rejected late-coming scholarly suitor—acknowledging the applicability of at least the first part of Miss Bordereau's condemnatory 'publishing scoundrel!'[95]—may in practice have little choice but to respect the right of others not only to their privacy but to their personal concepts of responsibility, especially towards those who, though dead, none the less survive in memory.

The question might, however, arise as to how far it is appropriate that concepts of responsibility towards cultural and historically significant artefacts should be entirely personal. If Hardy in death so 'belonged' to 'the nation' that his physical remains could be disposed of in a fashion quite contrary to his expressed wishes, might it not be feasible to invoke some similar concept of the national interest, of 'public policy', in order to preserve, as cultural property, the literary remains of major artists—even, or perhaps especially, when the destruction of such materials has been mandated by their wills or is being contemplated by their executors and heirs? Arguments of this sort are routinely used to oppose the demolition of historic buildings and the exportation of manuscripts and works of art, and it was Philip Larkin himself—very much a case in point—who, in a paper entitled 'A Neglected Responsibility', testified with particular eloquence to both 'the magical value and the meaningful value' of manuscripts and argued that since 'a country's writers are one of its most precious assets' it was of great importance that British literary manuscripts should be more actively collected by British libraries.[96] Conceivably some form of public entail could be introduced, respecting (through copyright or taxation provisions or direct subsidization) the pecuniary interests of the living in return for a guaranteed preservation of at least certain categories of manuscript material.

The purity of the ethical issues here is of course blurred by such financial considerations, and the tax laws of certain countries already encourage the deposit of cultural property in public collections. Some authors deliver their manuscripts to particular libraries on a regular basis in return either for such tax credits or for direct payments, the large Graham Greene collection at the University of Texas being an impressive case in point, and Humphrey Carpenter has recently offered a humorous definition of the term 'literary executor' as 'Person appointed by subject of biography . . . to "execute" (i.e. destroy) all personal papers', especially those providing evidence of sexual indiscretions—though in practice carefully preserving such papers for eventual sale to American university libraries.[97] Why *should* death rob life of several thousand dollars, it might reasonably be asked—or literary scholarship and biographical curiosity of unique materials? On the other hand, the already troublesome issues associated with the preservation and custodianship of literary documents may be further complicated, even corrupted, by their owner's awareness of the potential market value of the physical artefacts themselves, and the interests of scholarship can be hampered, at least in the short run, by the suggestion—usually originating with dealers and auctioneers—that the prices realizable could be adversely affected by prior publication.

It is in the confusion and distress of death's immediate aftermath that such documents are typically at greatest risk, whether from a deeply felt desire to protect the privacy of the dead and perhaps of the living as well, from an equally understandable zeal for order, or from some fundamental failure of imagination, knowledge, responsibility, or affection. When Richard Hillary, author of *The Last Enemy*, crashed and was killed during the Second World War, it was presumably a combination of orderliness, discretion, and convenient simplification which prompted the RAF 'effects' officer to dispose, briskly and irrevocably, of items seen as either compromising—as referring to another man's wife—or unimportant.[98] When Gerard Manley Hopkins died in his middle forties his poetic achievement, because unpublished, was little recognized, but it is hard to determine to what extent it was a genuine misunderstanding of Hopkins's will—rather than indolence, philistinism, or institutional rivalry—which allowed the responsible Jesuit authorities in Dublin not only to ignore the comprehensive bequest of his possessions to the English Province of the Society of Jesus but actually to destroy some papers, forward others to his family or to Robert Bridges, and leave still others lying in his room.[99] Growing appreciation of the scholarly and monetary value of documentary materials may tend in future to reduce the merely unconsidered destruction of literary remains—though perhaps at a time when such remains will consist increasingly of computer disks and largely repetitive print-outs and proofs. By the same token, however, authors eager to ensure permanent and undeviating compliance with their testamentary instructions would perhaps do well to entrust all responsibilities under their wills to rigidly impersonal institutions—or, better, to achieve as many as possible of their objectives while still alive.

The biographies of writers who have lived into old age rarely devote more than a minimum of space or attention to their subject's ultimately declining years and months. Much is doubtless due to the uncongeniality of the material itself—'We have finished the biography of S. Butler, [wrote Florence Hardy from Max Gate in December 1919] which is depressing at the end as all biographies must be—decay, disillusion, death'[100]—and to the impending sense, and not only for non-religious biographers, of a nonsense ending. Froude, for example, devotes only a minute proportion of his biography of Carlyle to the events of Carlyle's last decade, arguing that 'In a life now falling stagnant it is unnecessary to follow closely henceforth the occupation of times and seasons. The chief points only need be now noted. The rocket was burnt out and the stick falling.'[101]

But in modern biography it is the post-romantic and especially post-Freudian fascination with origins and early development which has most encouraged the tendency to move rapidly over the later and apparently uncreative stages of a literary career. Eager for information about their subject's childhood and youth, biographers typically push aside the sometimes overwhelming mass of material relating to the years of fame—letters, interviews, journalistic articles on habits and houses, opinions and pets, the too respectful memoirs of friends, the joyously retaliatory reminiscences of cooks, chauffeurs, hairdressers, and gardeners incapable of forgiving a great man's small tips. Even Justin Kaplan's striking ploy of starting out with an evocation of Whitman's dying and death turns out to be essentially a technique for treating the final years almost as if they constituted a single tableau-like moment. But access to the earlier stages of an ultimately famous life is often difficult and indirect at best, and scholars and biographers perhaps need to consider more narrowly the extent to which their presented narratives and images of childhood and youth have in fact derived from the 'official' lives, laudatory memoirs, and cautiously selective editions of letters for which the bereaved families and activated literary executors have been directly or indirectly responsible, and from the interviews, autobiographies, retrospective prefaces, and other self-projections of their subject's posterity-conscious final years—such familiar, indispensable sources as Hallam Tennyson's *Memoir* of his father, Alexandra Sutherland Orr's *Life and Letters of Robert Browning*, Eckermann's conversations with Goethe, Isobel Fenwick's notes of Wordsworth's late reflections, Horace Traubel's day-to-day and almost minute-by-minute record of Whitman's last years, and the proferred reminiscences of James, Hemingway, Graham Greene, Patrick White, Vladimir Nabokov, and so many others. Joseph Conrad as he grew older indulged in what one of his biographers has called 'flights of retrospective imagination', the German-born Canadian novelist Frederick Philip Grove retrospectively reinvented himself and his life in a series of pseudo-autobiographical writings,[102] and much of what is known, or believed to be known, about Hardy's childhood will always derive from what Hardy himself chose to relate in that self-ghosted 'Life' to which he devoted so much attention during his last years.

For editors, too, the respect naturally and indeed appropriately accorded to final textual decisions should not obscure the frequent dependence of those decisions—buttressed, perhaps, by authorial prefaces and annotations and the complex apparatus of collective editions—upon the elderly judgement of authors who wrote their most important work at a time when they were not only much younger but also a good deal less affluent and conservative. There seems little doubt, in fact, that the immediately pre-posthumous years of writers, so often dismissed as periods of passive fame, physical decay, and unelected creative silence, may in fact deserve rigorous scrutiny as the locations of deliberate, comprehensive, and effectual rewritings of both texts and lives—as well as of testamentary acts with profound and often unanticipated consequences both for future scholarship and for the long-term prosperity of the author's own work and reputation. But if anything emerges strongly from this study it is simply that of the four authors considered—mindful of posterity as they all were and anxious as to the showing they would eventually make before its duly constituted court—none proved to possess any special gift for foreseeing the subsequent pattern of events, or any privileged immunity to the always tragi-comic ironies of human mischancing.

Abbreviations

Balliol	Balliol College, Oxford University
Beinecke	Beinecke Rare Book and Manuscript Library, Yale University
Berg	Albert A. and Henry W. Berg Collection, New York Public Library
BL	British Library
Colby	Colby College, Maine
DCM	Dorset County Museum, Dorchester, Dorset
Houghton	Houghton Library, Harvard University
Huntington	Huntington Library, San Marino, California
Leeds	Brotherton Library, Leeds University
Lock	Lock Collection, Dorset County Library, Dorchester, Dorset
Millgate	Collection of the author
Murray	John Murray, Albemarle Street, London
NLS	National Library of Scotland
Pierpont Morgan	Pierpont Morgan Library, New York
Princeton	Princeton University Library
Texas	Harry Ransom Humanities Research Center, University of Texas
TRC	Tennyson Research Centre, Lincoln

Notes

ROBERT AND PEN BROWNING

1. Ritchie, *Records of Tennyson, Ruskin and Browning* (London: Macmillan, 1892), 191.
2. RB to Sarianna Browning, 30 June 1861, in *Letters of Robert Browning Collected by Thomas J. Wise*, ed. Thurman L. Hood (New Haven: Yale Univ. Press, 1933), 62.
3. See 'Robert Browning at Home', *Pall Mall Gazette*, 16 Dec. 1889, 3.
4. Anon., 'Poets in Private Life', *The World* (London), 7 Dec. 1881, 7.
5. Harrison, *Autobiographic Memoirs*, 2 vols. (London: Macmillan, 1911), II. 106.
6. Arthur Warren, *London Days: A Book of Reminiscences* (London: T. Fisher Unwin, 1921), 44.
7. Hardy's widow told Richard Purdy in 1933 that Hardy, having once spoken intimately with Browning at Anne Procter's, was snubbed by him on a subsequent occasion when more notable guests were present (Purdy, conversations notebooks, Beinecke).
8. Hardy to Gosse, 6 Mar. 1899, in *The Collected Letters of Thomas Hardy*, ed. Richard Little Purdy and Michael Millgate (Oxford: Clarendon Press, 1978–88), II. 217, 216.
9. Paul F. Mattheisen, 'Gosse's Candid "Snapshots"', *Victorian Studies*, 8 (June 1965), 345.
10. First published in the *Atlantic Monthly* in April 1892 and in book form in 1893; RB was identified as the subject in the preface to vol. XVII of the New York Edition, in which the story was collected.
11. This topic is extensively explored in Ross Posnock's *Henry James and the Problem of Robert Browning* (Athens, GA: Univ. of Georgia Press, 1985).
12. James, *The Middle Years* (London: W. Collins Sons, 1917), 106, 104.
13. See the entry for her in the *DNB*. A sister of Lord Leighton, Mrs Orr (1828–1903) was widowed in 1858; that she was a beautiful woman is apparent from surviving photographs (for example, in the Browning collection at Balliol) and from the Leighton portrait reproduced in Mrs Russell Barrington, *The Life, Letters and Work of Frederic Leighton*, 2 vols. (London: George Allen, 1906), opp. II. 57. RB's letters to her are not known to survive: see *The Brownings'*

Correspondence. Volume I: September 1809–1826, ed. Philip Kelley and Ronald Hudson (Winfield, KS: Wedgestone Press, 1984), xl, and the intimacy between them was, in any case, based largely on frequent meetings.

14. Meredith, 'Speaking Out in Venice and London', in Sergio Perosa, ed., *Browning e Venezia* (Florence: Leo S. Olschki Editore, 1991), 85–94.

15. Bronson, 'Browning in Asolo', *Century Magazine*, 59 (April 1900), 931.

16. Long estranged from her husband, Katharine Bronson became a widow in 1885. Her relationship with Browning is fully documented and explored in *More Than Friend: The Letters of Robert Browning to Katharine de Kay Bronson*, ed. Michael Meredith (Waco, TX, and Winfield, KS: Armstrong Browning Library of Baylor Univ. and Wedgestone Press, 1985), esp. lxxii–lxxiii.

17. In 1883, however, Anne Procter and George Smith agreed in conversation with Thomas Hardy that there was 'something tender' between Browning and Mrs Orr, and Anne Procter expressed the wish that they would 'settle it': Thomas Hardy, *The Life and Work of Thomas Hardy*, ed. Michael Millgate (London: Macmillan, 1984), 166.

18. Quoted as part of the excellent note on the poem in *Robert Browning: The Poems*, ed. John Pettigrew and Thomas J. Collins, 2 vols. (New Haven: Yale Univ. Press, 1981), II. 1155–6. For a brief but relevant comment on Browning's verbal violence see the introduction to *Letters of the Brownings to George Barrett*, ed. Paul Landis with Ronald E. Freeman (Urbana: Univ. of Illinois Press, 1958), 14–16.

19. *Poems* (Pettigrew and Collins), II. 972.

20. Robert Weidemann Barrett Browning (subsequently, in notes, RWBB) to W. Hall Griffin, 30 Oct. 1903 (BL); Chesterton, *Robert Browning* (London: Macmillan, 1903).

21. As Michael Meredith sums it up in 'Browning and the Prince of Publishers', *Browning Institute Studies*, 7 (1979), 8, Browning had found Chapman & Hall altogether 'casual' in the conduct of their affairs and the promotion of his work: 'poor advertising, low payment, inefficient bookkeeping, slow and inaccurate printing, all were legitimate complaints'. The firm's historian speaks rather of Browning's having 'never really conquered the literary taste of his native land': Alec Waugh, *A Hundred Years of Publishing: Being the Story of Chapman & Hall, Ltd.* (London: Chapman & Hall, 1930), 78. See also *New Letters of Robert Browning*, ed. William Clyde DeVane and Kenneth Leslie Knickerbocker (New Haven: Yale Univ. Press, 1950), 393–400; on Smith and Smith, Elder, see Meredith,

'Publishers', and Lachlan Phil Kelley, 'Robert Browning and George Smith: Selections from an Unpublished Correspondence', *Quarterly Review*, 299 (July 1961), 323–35.

22. Huxley, *The House of Smith Elder* (London: printed for private circulation, 1923), 156; George M. Smith, 'The Recollections of a Long and Busy Life', bound typescript, 2 vols., I. fol. 244 (NLS).

23. Meredith, 'Publishers', 6–8.

24. RB to G. Smith (subsequently, in notes, GS), 20 Nov. 1884 (Murray).

25. RB to GS, 10 Dec. 1867, quoted in Meredith, 'Publishers', 9.

26. Both Murray.

27. RB to F. J. Furnivall, 17 Feb. 1884, quoted in *Browning's Trumpeter: The Correspondence of Robert Browning and Frederick J. Furnivall 1872–1889*, ed. William S. Peterson (Washington: Decatur House Press, 1979), 93. Browning claims in the same letter to have imposed this condition upon his publishers for the past 'fifty years'.

28. RB to GS, 20 Apr. 1885 (Murray).

29. RB to GS, 25 Jan. 1888 (Murray).

30. RB to GS, 10 Oct. 1884 (Murray), and RWBB to Reginald Smith, 11 Dec. 1909 (Murray); see also Peterson, *Browning's Trumpeter*, 87, n. 1, and Kelley, 'RB and GS', 330–3.

31. RB to GS, 24 Nov. 1887, quoted in Philip Kelley and William S. Peterson, 'Browning's Final Revisions', *Browning Institute Studies*, 1 (1973), 91. See also *The Poetical Works of Robert Browning*, IV, ed. Ian Jack, Rowena Fowler, and Margaret Smith (Oxford: Clarendon Press, 1991), xiii–xvi.

32. RB to GS, 24 Jan. 1888, quoted in Kelley and Peterson, 'Browning's Final Revisions', 92; *Pall Mall Gazette*, 31 Dec. 1889, 3.

33. For Browning's characteristic habits of revision, see Michael Meredith, 'Learning's Crabbed Text: A Reconsideration of the 1868 Edition of Browning's *Poetical Works*', *Studies in Browning and His Circle*, 13 (1985), 97–107.

34. RB to GS, 7 Feb. 1888, quoted in Alexandra Sutherland Orr, *Life and Letters of Robert Browning* (London: Smith, Elder, 1891), 403–4. Orr herself observed (328): 'But to the end of his life he could at any moment recast a line or passage for the sake of greater correctness, and leave all that was essential in it untouched.'

35. The editors of the Clarendon Press Browning, for example, print them as continuously parallel texts, without attempting a conflation: *The Poetical Works of Robert Browning*, I, ed. Ian Jack and Margaret Smith (Oxford: Clarendon Press, 1983).

36. For Furnivall see John Munro *et al.*, *Frederick James Furnivall: A Volume of Personal Record* (London: Henry Frowde, 1911). For Hickey see Enid Dinnis, *Emily Hickey: Poet, Essayist–Pilgrim*.

A Memoir (London: Harding & More, 1927). The story of the Society and of Furnivall's overall role in Browning's affairs has been admirably told and documented by William S. Peterson in *Interrogating the Oracle: A History of the London Browning Society* (Athens, OH: Ohio Univ. Press, 1969) and in *Browning's Trumpeter*.

37. Anon., 'The Browning Society', *Saturday Review*, 6 Dec. 1884, 721.
38. James, 'Browning in Westminster Abbey', *The Speaker*, 4 Jan. 1890, 11.
39. Symons, 'Browning's Last Poems', *Academy*, 11 Jan. 1890, 20.
40. Clyde de L. Ryals, *Browning's Later Poetry, 1871–1889* (Ithaca, NY: Cornell Univ. Press, 1975), 190.
41. RB to Furnivall, 22 Aug. 1882, in *Browning's Trumpeter*, 56.
42. RB to Sarah FitzGerald, [22 July 1882?], in *Learned Lady: Letters from Robert Browning to Mrs. Thomas FitzGerald 1876–1889*, ed. Edward C. McAleer (Cambridge, MA: Harvard Univ. Press, 1966), 144.
43. RB to T. J. Nettleship, 10 Mar. 1889, in Hood, *Letters of RB*, 304.
44. For the American Browning Societies, see Louise Greer, *Browning in America* (Chapel Hill: Univ. of North Carolina Press, 1952).
45. Rosaline Masson, 'Robert Browning in Edinburgh', *Cornhill Magazine*, NS 26 (February 1909), 235.
46. See, e.g., *Browning's Trumpeter*, 195, etc.; *Interrogating the Oracle*, 182–7; and DeVane and Knickerbocker, *New Letters*, 284, 291, 294, and 297. The Pierpont Morgan Library has RB's annotations to Constance Smedley's essay, 'Notes on "Prospice" '.
47. Orr, *A Handbook to the Works of Robert Browning* (London: George Bell & Sons, 1885), v.
48. Orr, *Handbook*, 2nd edn. (London: George Bell & Sons, 1886), 331–8. The set of the proofs is at Balliol; RB's comments, as there inscribed, are included among the notes to *Ferishtah's Fancies* in *Poems* (Pettigrew and Collins), II. 1096–102.
49. Gosse, *Robert Browning: Personalia* (Boston: Houghton, Mifflin, 1890), 6.
50. See Ian Jack, ' "Commented It Must Be": Browning Annotating Browning', *Browning Institute Studies*, 9 (1981), 59–77.
51. See Park Honan, 'Browning's Testimony on his Essay on Shelley in "Shepherd v. Francis" ', *English Language Notes*, 2, i (September 1964), 27–31, and 'Law Intelligence', *Daily Telegraph*, 16 June 1879, 2.
52. RB's note seems to have been first tipped into later copies of the one-volume EBB *Poems* of 1887 and then included in 1889 in the first volume of Smith, Elder's six-volume edition of EBB's *Poetical Works*; he refers back to the memoir included in Ingram's recently reissued

edition of *The Poetical Works of Elizabeth Barrett Browning from 1826 to 1844* (first published in 1877) but was perhaps chiefly concerned to anticipate Ingram's more expansive *Elizabeth Barrett Browning* of 1888.

53. See RB to G. Moulton-Barrett, 5 Nov. 1887, in Landis, *Letters to Barrett*, 308–9.

54. Michael Meredith has noted that RB would sometimes send the proofs of new volumes to selected reviewers well ahead of publication date: Meredith, 'Speaking Out', 90.

55. *Handbook*, 2nd edn, 331.

56. *Handbook*, 2nd edn, 339.

57. In 1863 he had described two potential biographers of EBB as having 'their paws in my very bowels': *Dearest Isa: Robert Browning's Letters to Isabella Blagden*, ed. Edward C. McAleer (Austin: Univ. of Texas Press, 1951), 149.

58. See, e.g., W. Hall Griffin and H. C. Minchin, *The Life of Robert Browning* (London: Methuen, 1910), 9–11, 16–17, 19–20, 277, and William Clyde DeVane, Jr, *Browning's Parleyings: The Autobiography of a Mind* (New Haven: Yale Univ. Press, 1927), *passim*.

59. See Thomas J. Wise, comp., *A Browning Library* (London: privately printed, 1929), xxvi.

60. See John Maynard, *Browning's Youth* (Cambridge, MA: Harvard Univ. Press, 1977), 3–4, 179, and Barbara Rosenbaum and Pamela White, *Index of English Literary Manuscripts, IV. 1800–1900, Part 1* (London: Mansell, 1982), 220.

61. Landis, *Letters to Barrett*, 320.

62. Landis, *Letters to Barrett*, 308.

63. *The Letters of Robert Browning and Elizabeth Barrett Barrett 1845–1846* (London: Smith, Elder, 1899), I. 484; see also I. 485.

64. EBB to G. Barrett, 2 Feb. 1852, in Landis, *Letters to Barrett*, 163; Mitford had included an account of EBB's agonized response to the drowning of one of her brothers.

65. *Letters of Elizabeth Barrett Browning Addressed to Richard Hengist Horne . . . With Comments on Contemporaries*, ed. S. R. Townshend Mayer, 2 vols. (London: Richard Bentley & Son, 1877), I. vii.

66. John H. Ingram, *Elizabeth Barrett Browning* (London: W. H. Allen, 1888), vi.

67. Landis, *Letters to Barrett*, 309.

68. Landis, *Letters to Barrett*, 320.

69. James, *Italian Hours* (London: William Heinemann, 1909), 77; first published as the Prefatory Note to Bronson's 'Browning in Venice', *Cornhill Magazine*, February 1902. Katharine Bronson appears under her own initials in Henry James's notebooks as the central

figure in 'the K. B. case', an idea for a novel that he later drew upon in writing *The Ivory Tower: The Complete Notebooks of Henry James*, ed. Leon Edel and Lyall H. Powers (New York: Oxford Univ. Press, 1987), 256–70. Meredith (*More Than Friend*, xxiii) identifies her as the original of Mrs Prest in *The Aspern Papers*.

70. *Life and Work of Thomas Hardy*, 201–2; Constance Fenimore Woolson heard Bronson 'abuse' one of Hardy's novels in 1883: see Woolson's letter to James, 24 May 1883, in *Henry James Letters*, ed. Leon Edel, 4 vols. (Cambridge, MA: Harvard Univ. Press, 1974–84), III. 561.

71. This late decline in RB's health, always denied by Pen, seems sufficiently attested by Orr, by Gosse (*Personalia*, 77–8, quoted *Portraits from Life*, ed. Ann Thwaite [Aldershot: Scolar Press, 1991], 44), and by RB himself (e.g. his letter to RWBB, 4 June 1889 [Balliol]).

72. Henry James in 1890 found the Rezzonico to be 'royal and imperial' but Pen and his style of living rather pathetically the reverse: *Henry James Letters*, III. 287.

73. Quoted in *More Than Friend*, 112.

74. Evelyn Barclay, 'Diary of Miss Evelyn Barclay (Mrs. G. D. Giles)', *Baylor Bulletin*, 35, iv (December 1932), 9.

75. Barclay, 'Diary', 9.

76. *Pall Mall Gazette*, 17 Dec. 1889, 2.

77. *The Times*, 17 Dec. 1889, 7.

78. Most notably by B. R. Jerman's 'The Death of Robert Browning', *University of Toronto Quarterly*, 35 (October 1965), 47–74.

79. Orr, *Life and Letters* (revised edn. of 1908; see n. 135 below), 403; the quoted passage was supplied by Pen to supplement and partially replace Orr's original account of RB's death and funeral. The *uscieri* were minor functionaries of the Venetian judiciary.

80. *The Times*, 1 Jan. 1890, 4. See also the contemporary materials reproduced in 'The Burial of Mr Browning', *Browning Institute Studies*, 3 (1975), 119–30.

81. Tennyson's friend James Knowles, editor of *The Nineteenth Century*, was one of the proponents of this scheme: see his letter to *The Times*, 17 Dec. 1889, 7. Though blamed on Italian red tape, the decision not to move EBB from her tomb (designed by Leighton) in the old Protestant cemetery of Florence seems finally to have been Pen's; G. Smith, 'Recollections', I. fol. 248 (NLS), identifies 'regard for the feelings of the Florentines' as the deciding factor.

82. *Funeral of the Late Robert Browning . . . Order of Service* (BL).

83. *The Times*, 1 Jan. 1890, 4. A. S. Byatt, in *Possession: A Romance* (London: Chatto & Windus, 1990), 443, has plausibly conscripted Leighton and Hallam Tennyson, together with 'the painter, Robert

Brunant', to be pall-bearers at the funeral of the fictional poet Randolph Ash.

84. Gosse, MS account of RB's funeral (BL).
85. Vol. 3, i, 37–8; the inaccuracies derived from a text printed earlier in the *Pall Mall Gazette*.
86. Will (Somerset House).
87. Barclay, 'Diary', 7.
88. *Poems* (Pettigrew and Collins), II. 931. Reading the poem aloud to his daughter-in-law shortly before his death, Browning is said to have expressed himself as embarrassed by its apparent vanity but to have insisted that it was none the less true: Fannie Barrett Browning, *Some Memories of Robert Browning* (Boston: Marshall Jones Company, 1928), 23–4.
89. James to Francis Boott, 21 Oct. 1893, *Henry James Letters*, III. 437.
90. As photographs in the Browning album at Balliol make clear.
91. Thomas Westwood, *A Literary Friendship: Letters to Lady Alwyne Compton 1869–1881* (London: John Murray, 1914), 195.
92. Phelps, 'Robert Browning as Seen by His Son', *Century Magazine*, 85 (1913), 417.
93. That Pen engaged in illicit sexual liaisons with servants and other local women, perhaps with artists' models, seems probable enough, but no entertainable evidence, documentary or otherwise, has been adduced to support the story of Pen's early seductions of Breton peasant girls, first promulgated in the English edition (only) of Frances Winwar's *The Immortal Lovers: Elizabeth Barrett and Robert Browning. A Biography* (London: Hamish Hamilton, 1950), 306, and recently enlarged upon in Margaret Forster's *Elizabeth Barrett Browning: A Biography* (London: Chatto & Windus, 1988), 373. Forster says that Ginevra, Pen's model and housekeeper at Asolo, was the daughter of one of the Breton women, but contemporary accounts of her seem at least to agree that she was Italian: Sarianna Browning, writing to 'Michael Field' (the joint pseudonym of Katharine Bradley and Edith Cooper) on 31 Jan. 1897, speaks of Ginevra's 'Florentine skill in bargaining' and on 23 June [1895] of her visiting her widowed sister in Florence (BL); see also Mabel Dodge Luhan, *European Experiences* (New York: Harcourt, Brace, 1935), 116.
94. Freya Stark, for example, was able to recall him in *Traveller's Prelude* (London: John Murray, 1950), 31–3, and in her foreword to Flora Stark, *An Italian Diary* (London: John Murray, 1945), v. The standard, documented account of Pen's life remains Gertrude Reese's 'Robert Browning and His Son', *PMLA*, 61 (September 1946), 784–803; a few further details are supplied in McAleer's introduction to

Learned Lady, 24–8, but little of substance is added by Betty Miller, 'The Child of Casa Guidi', *Cornhill Magazine*, 163 (Spring 1949), 415–28, or by M. L. Giartosio De Courten, 'Pen, Il Figlio dei Browning', *English Miscellany*, 8 (1957), 125–42. Maisie Ward did gather memories of Pen from people who had known him, but the information and gossip included in her *Robert Browning and His World: Two Robert Brownings?* (New York: Holt, Rinehart and Winston, 1969), 296–304, and expanded upon in *The Tragi-Comedy of Pen Browning (1849–1912)* (New York: Sheed and Ward and The Browning Institute, 1972) remain almost entirely undocumented.

95. *Brownings' Correspondence*, I. xxxviii.
96. GS, 'Recollections', I. fol. 245 (NLS).
97. RB to RWBB and Fannie Browning, 18 July 1888 (Balliol).
98. Barclay, 'Diary', 5.
99. James to his sister Alice James, 6 June 1890, in *Henry James Letters*, III. 287.
100. James to Francis Boott, 21 Oct. 1893, in *Henry James Letters*, III. 437; for some of the 'luxuries' see Harold Spender, 'The Browning Palace at Venice', *Bookman*, 2 (June 1892), 81.
101. Some of these are convincingly evoked in Michael Field, *Works and Days: From the Journal of Michael Field*, ed. T. and D. C. Sturge Moore (London: John Murray, 1933), 216.
102. Balliol also has a marble bust of RB by RWBB, and a bronze bust of Pompilia (of *The Ring and the Book*) is at Ohio Wesleyan University. Two portraits of RB are in the Armstrong Browning Library of Baylor University, as is the very early painting of an Abbé reading Gautier's *Mademoiselle de Maupin* which was purchased by RB's friend Frederick Lehmann and later recollected, in very negative terms, by the latter's grandson, John Lehmann, in *The Whispering Gallery* (London: Longmans, Green, 1955), 4–5. See Philip Kelley and Betty A. Coley, *The Browning Collections: A Reconstruction with Other Memorabilia* (Winfield, KS: Wedgestone Press, 1984), 536–48; a preliminary version of this listing of RWBB's works, accompanied by photographs of some of the items, appeared in *Studies in Browning and His Circle*, 10, i (1982), 7–35. For other such photographs see Ward, *Tragi-Comedy*, 82–95.
103. Sarianna Browning to 'Michael Field', 16 May [1890] (BL).
104. BL.
105. Luhan, *European Experiences*, 115.
106. Whiting, *The Brownings: Their Life and Art* (Boston: Little, Brown, 1911), 262; for descriptions of the Rezzonico during RWBB's ownership see Whiting, 262–4, Spender, 'Browning Palace', 81–2,

and Henry James, *William Wetmore Story and His Friends*, 2 vols. (Boston: Houghton, Mifflin, 1903), II. 284–6. For Whiting herself, see Ward, *Tragi-Comedy*, 115–17.

107. Like Pen himself, they were both buried in Asolo, although in 1929 Pen's widow had his body removed to Florence; see *Browning Collections*, 551–2 (item L36).

108. RWBB to W. Hall Griffin, 18 Mar. 1894 (BL): 'I had the opportunity last year of buying it, curiously enough[,] and I found the temptation irresistible!' See also *Browning Collections*, xx–xxi.

109. BL.

110. RB to RWBB, 17 July 1889 (BL); although RWBB's own letter does not survive, RB's letter quotes the relevant passage. In a letter to Furnivall of 16 July, however, RB had acknowledged that he might 'preferably have left the thing to its proper contempt' (BL).

111. GS, 'Recollections', I. fol. 244 (NLS), quoted in Huxley, *Smith Elder*, 156.

112. RWBB to Griffin, 6 Jan. 1905 (BL).

113. RWBB to GS, 4 Jan. 1896 (Murray).

114. Huxley, *Smith Elder*, 209 n.

115. Huxley, *Smith Elder*, 218.

116. *The Letters of Elizabeth Barrett Browning*, ed. Frederic G. Kenyon, 2 vols. (London: Smith, Elder, 1897), I. vi.

117. *Letters of RB and EBB*, [v]. Present in RWBB's draft of the 'Note' (NLS), but absent from the published version, is the statement that he had only recently ('a little more than a year ago') read the letters for the first time.

118. C. J. Moulton-Barrett accused RWBB of 'a want of delicacy hardly conceivable': letter to the London *Standard*, quoted in *The Critic* (New York), 34 (June 1899), 499.

119. Elliott Felkin, 'Days with Thomas Hardy', *Encounter*, 18, iv (April 1962), 30. Hardy spoke admiringly of the edition shortly after its publication as constituting 'such an excellent novel, & a true one': *Coll. Letters of Thomas Hardy*, II. 277.

120. Furnivall, 'A Few More Words on Robert Browning', *Pall Mall Gazette*, 18 Dec. 1889, 3.

121. *The Letters of Robert Browning and Elizabeth Barrett Barrett 1845–1846*, ed. Elvan Kintner (Cambridge, MA: Harvard Univ. Press, 1969), xxiii.

122. Smith, Elder ledger 35, double-page 213 (Murray).

123. Ibid.

124. Most of the work seems to have been done by Ginevra up until the time of her marriage to a local lawyer in 1898: Sarianna Browning to 'Michael Field', 23 June [1895] and 8 Sept. 1895 (BL).

125. RWBB to GS, 4 Jan. 1896 (Murray).
126. RWBB to Reginald Smith, 22 Oct. 1909 (Murray).
127. Huxley, *Smith Elder*, 210, 208–9; it also appears from Huxley (210) that in 1906 Smith was largely responsible for the addition of EBB's name and the dates of her birth and death to her husband's monument in Westminster Abbey.
128. See *The Times*, 8 May 1912, 7, and William Knight, ed., *The Robert Browning Centenary Celebration* (London: Smith, Elder, 1912), x, 19–30.
129. So *The Times* recorded in his obituary, 9 July 1912, 11. In *The Times* of 8 May 1912, 7, he was said to have entertained the Asolan 'authorities' at luncheon the previous day.
130. SB to 'Michael Field', 16 May 1890 (BL).
131. A. Orr to W. Hall Griffin, 25 Mar. [1897] (BL); the letter is dictated. See also Orr, *Life and Letters* (1891), vi.
132. The letter (Berg), though presumably sent from Italy, is written on mourning stationery bearing RB's 29 De Vere Gardens address.
133. Phelps, 'Robert Browning', 418. Pen had, however, thought well enough of the book upon its first appearance to send an inscribed copy to Horatio Brown, the biographer of John Addington Symonds: *Browning Collections*, 586 (item M253).
134. See Field, *Works and Days*, 216–17.
135. Orr, *Life and Letters of Robert Browning*, new edition, revised and in part rewritten by Frederic G. Kenyon (London: Smith, Elder, 1908), vii.
136. *Life and Letters* (1908), 400.
137. RWBB to Griffin, 20 Dec. 1905 (BL); Sharp had thanked RWBB in an authorial 'Note' to his *Life of Robert Browning* (London: Walter Scott, 1890), 9.
138. Whiting, *The Brownings*, 268.
139. See Gosse to W. Hall Griffin, 8 May 1902 (BL).
140. RWBB to Griffin, 7 Feb. 1898, 2 July 1902, 30 Oct. 1903, and 1 Feb. 1905 (BL).
141. Griffin, *Life of RB*, 299; the phrase occurs in RWBB to Griffin of 30 Oct. 1903 (BL), where it is followed by one of Pen's frequent exclamation marks.
142. See Julia Markus, 'Pen Browning's *History of Half a Portal*: A Translation', *Studies in Browning and His Circle*, 3 (Spring 1975), 32–48.
143. James to Mrs Daniel Curtis, 10 May [1899] (Dartmouth College); Maisie Ward, quoting this letter in *Tragi-Comedy*, 132–3, but without supplying a date or source, includes a passage, not now present with the original at Dartmouth, in which James plausibly speculates that the secret basis of Pen's life in Asolo was his extensive

ownership of local property and the sense of importance, the 'vanity and pride of possession and proprietorship' that flowed from it, 'the being, there, the great swell'.

144. Stark, *Traveller's Prelude*, opp. 34.

145. A possible, though by no means certain, exception was the vanished 'Browning box' of Thomas Lovell Beddoes manuscripts, for which his father had become rather inconveniently responsible: see *Browning Collections*, xxv, and *The Works of Thomas Lovell Beddoes*, ed. H. W. Donner (London: Humphrey Milford, 1935), liii–liv.

146. Fannie Barrett Browning, *Some Memories*, 35.

147. RWBB to F. Kenyon, 31 Oct. 1907 (typed transcript in Balliol College archives). R. A. B. Mynors's *Catalogue of the Manuscripts of Balliol College* (Oxford: at the Clarendon Press, 1963), 363, notes that the poet's son had been permitted to retain the manuscript 'for his own lifetime'. Pen's letter to Kenyon also addresses, and dismisses, the suggestion, originating with Jowett, that RB had intended to leave Balliol all his books.

148. Smith to Edward Hilliard (Balliol senior bursar), 30 Oct. 1912 (Balliol College archives).

149. *Browning Collections*, xxii–xxiv, etc.

150. *Athenaeum*, 13 July 1912, 37; Kelley and Coley, *Browning Collections*, xxii, give the name as Carolina Betti; *The Times*, 17 Dec. 1912, 8, gives the surname as Betto, as does the translated text of the codicil available from Somerset House.

151. *Browning Collections*, xxiii.

152. The English translation of the relevant document in Somerset House shows that the bequest to Carolina Betto was none the less accepted as valid.

153. *Browning Collections*, xxiv and 614–18.

154. Two copies of an unsigned transcript of the agreement are in the NLS: see *Browning Collections*, 558 (item L125), and Huxley, *Smith Elder*, 249.

155. *Brownings' Correspondence*, I. xxxviii and n.

156. For details of the sale and identifications of the major purchasers, see *Browning Collections*, xxviii–xxxvii. A facsimile of the original catalogue is included in A. N. L. Munby, ed., *Sale Catalogues of Libraries of Eminent Persons*, 12 vols. (London: Mansell, 1971–5), VI. 1–192.

157. *Browning Collections*, xxxiv–xxxv; see also Marvin L. Williams, Jr, 'The Fannie Barrett Browning Collection at the University of Texas', *Browning Newsletter* no. 9 (Fall 1972), 3–8.

158. *Browning Collections*, xxxiv and nn; for *A Browning Library* see n. 59 above.

159. *The Times*, 13 Nov. 1961, 12. Michael Meredith informs me that some of the paintings and sculptures were deemed too large to be taken to England for the sale; they remained in Asolo, therefore, but were later destroyed simply because of their size.
160. *Brownings' Correspondence*, I. xxiii.
161. *Browning Collections*, ix.
162. Rosenbaum and White, *Index of English Literary Manuscripts*, 107–273; the assistance of Philip Kelley in preparing the RB and EBB sections is acknowledged on p. xi.
163. Pierpont Morgan. For Tennyson's brief but elegant note of thanks see *The Letters of Alfred Lord Tennyson*, ed. Cecil Y. Lang and Edgar F. Shannon, Jr, 3 vols. (Oxford: Clarendon Press, 1981–90), III. 410.
164. Copy in BL.
165. *The Times*, 23 Dec. 1902, 2.
166. F. Herbert Stead, 'The Robert Browning Settlement', in Knight, *Browning Centenary*, 107–8. See also *The Times*, 10 Apr. 1906, 14, for the engaging letter in which RWBB, protesting that he was 'better able to handle the chisel than my pen', presented the Settlement with one of his busts of his father.
167. *Poems* (Pettigrew and Collins), II. 931. It appears from the essentially fair-copy MS (Pierpont Morgan) that the published 'marched' was a late revision of 'fought', itself revised from 'put'.
168. Sharp, *Life of RB*, 195–6.

ALFRED AND HALLAM TENNYSON

1. A. T. Ritchie to Reginald J. Smith, 21 Feb. 1899, *Letters of Anne Thackeray Ritchie*, ed. Hester Ritchie (London: John Murray, 1924), 250.
2. Hallam Tennyson's MS notes on a conversation with Jowett (Houghton); since HT was quoting Jowett's speech, I have expanded an ampersand.
3. HT MS notes (Houghton).
4. Hallam Tennyson, *Alfred Lord Tennyson: A Memoir*, 2 vols. (London: Macmillan, 1897), II. 467.
5. Emily Tennyson MSS in the Tennyson Research Centre include 'Hail work the bond of love!', identified as a possible 'subject' for AT, and a suggested ending to *Idylls of the King*; these and other materials are broadly described in Catherine Barnes Stevenson, 'Emily Tennyson in Her Own Right: The Unpublished Manuscripts', *Victorians Institute Journal*, 8 (1979), 31–44.
6. *The Letters of Edward FitzGerald*, ed. Alfred McKinley Terhune and

Annabelle Burdick Terhune, 4 vols. (Princeton: Princeton Univ. Press, 1980), II. 538.

7. Carlyle to Jane Carlyle, 3 Oct. 1850, *Thomas Carlyle: Letters to His Wife*, ed. Trudy Bliss (London: Victor Gollancz, 1953), 271–2.

8. Priscilla Metcalf, *James Knowles: Victorian Editor and Architect* (Oxford: Clarendon Press, 1980), 254–61.

9. Paul was one of Hardy's earliest literary friends: see Michael Millgate, *Thomas Hardy: His Career as a Novelist* (London: Bodley Head, 1971), 117–18, 120–3; the original Bailie House in which the school was housed no longer survives, although a later building with the same name stands in the same location.

10. See Robert Bernard Martin, *Tennyson: The Unquiet Heart* (Oxford: Clarendon Press, 1980), 503–7, and Charles Tennyson, *Alfred Tennyson* (London: Macmillan, 1950), 415–23.

11. Charles Tennyson, *Stars and Markets* (London: Chatto & Windus, 1957), 26.

12. See, for example, W. Boyd Carpenter, *Some Pages of My Life* (London: Williams & Norgate, 1911), 256–60.

13. Roden Noel, 'Lord Tennyson. With a Few Personal Reminiscences', *Atalanta*, 6 (January 1893), 269.

14. Brief extracts from his correspondence with these two firms appear in the two final chapters of June Steffensen Hagen, *Tennyson and His Publishers* (London: Macmillan, 1979).

15. HT to [Alexander] Macmillan, 29 Apr. 1885 (BL).

16. HT to [Alexander] Macmillan, 15 Dec. 1886 (BL); 'The Fleet' was first published in *The Times*, 23 Apr. 1885; Mowbray Morris, as editor of *Macmillan's Magazine*, seems to have chosen not to review *Tiresias* at all.

17. TRC; in *The Letters of Emily Lady Tennyson*, ed. James O. Hoge (University Park: Pennsylvania State Univ. Press, 1974), 327, this is printed as if part of the letter to Lear of 27 Aug. 1883.

18. See C. Tennyson, *Alfred Tennyson*, 440–1; HT's MS notes on conversation with Jowett (Houghton); and, for a specific instance, *The Diary of Alfred Domett 1872–1885*, ed. E. A. Horsman (London: Oxford Univ. Press, 1953), 271.

19. Hardy, *The Life and Work of Thomas Hardy*, ed. Michael Millgate (London: Macmillan, 1984), 140.

20. See, for example, Hagen, *T and His Publishers*, 167–8, and *Letters of ET*, 325–6.

21. *Letters of ET*, 330–1, and see Christopher Ricks, 'Hallam's "Youthful Letters" and Tennyson', *English Language Notes*, 3 (December 1965), 120–2.

22. *The Times*, 3 Dec. 1928, 19.

23. See C. Tennyson, *Alfred Tennyson*, 472, and *Audrey Tennyson's Vice-Regal Days: The Australian Letters of Audrey Lady Tennyson to Her Mother Zacyntha Boyle, 1899–1903*, ed. Alexandra Hasluck (Canberra: National Library of Australia, 1978), esp. 1–6.

24. Audrey Tennyson, 'Illness Etc.', disbound notebook (TRC), fol. 14, pub. as 'Death-bed' diary in *Letters to a Tutor: The Tennyson Family Letters to Henry Graham Dakyns (1861–1911)*, ed. Robert Peters and Janine Dakyns (Metuchen, NJ: Scarecrow Press, 1988), 133; Hallam quoted the remark, somewhat decontextualized, in the *Memoir*, II. 426.

25. *Memoir*, II. 354.

26. Charles L. Graves, *Hubert Parry: His Life and Works*, 2 vols. (London: Macmillan, 1926), I. 347. To Blanche Warre-Cornish, Farringford had seemed (charmingly) old-fashioned from a considerably earlier date: see her 'Memories of Tennyson—I', *London Mercury*, 5 (December 1921), 147–8. For Julia Margaret Cameron see below, n. 166.

27. *Memoir*, II. 299.

28. That this isolation from contemporary trends contributed to the rapid decline of AT's posthumous reputation was strongly argued by Paull F. Baum, *Tennyson Sixty Years After* (Chapel Hill: Univ. of North Carolina Press, 1948), 13, 17, 22.

29. *The Poems of Tennyson*, ed. Christopher Ricks, 2nd edn., 3 vols. (Harlow: Longman, 1987), I. 618; subsequently referred to as *Poems* (Ricks).

30. HT to Annie Fields, [?] May 1885 (Huntington).

31. *Memoir*, II. 388.

32. *Memoir*, II. 422.

33. HT postcard to F. Macmillan, 30 Aug. 1892 (BL).

34. *Memoir*, II. 383.

35. A copy of that edition bearing AT corrections is in the Berg collection. A previously uncollected sonnet, 'To W. C. Macready', was fitted into an available space (*The Complete Works of Alfred Lord Tennyson* [London: Macmillan, 1894], 578), but the changes were in general few and minor, no alterations, for example, being reported in *Maud: A Definitive Edition*, ed. Susan Shatto (London: The Athlone Press, 1986).

36. One simple but energizing alteration to the *Demeter* volume at this stage was the substitution of a dash for a comma ('Fell—and flash'd into the Red Sea') in the reference to Lionel Tennyson's burial at sea that occurs in the eleventh stanza of 'To the Marquis of Dufferin and Ava'. The revision appears, in AT's hand, in a BL copy of the first

edition of *Demeter* which bears the date 'Aldworth | 7 July 1890' (not in AT's hand) on the front free end-paper.

37. *Memoir*, II. 423.
38. Browning, 'The Last Ride Together', line 53; the line was quoted by Hardy at the end of the General Preface to the Wessex Edition.
39. See Christopher Ricks, *Tennyson*, 2nd edn. (Basingstoke: Macmillan Press, 1989), 290, 288.
40. HT to Dakyns, 10 Oct. 1894, *Letters to a Tutor*, 150.
41. TRC.
42. *The Death of Oenone, Akbar's Dream, and Other Poems* (London: Macmillan, 1892), 1; *Poems* (Ricks), III. 235.
43. *Death of Oenone*, 111; *Poems* (Ricks), III. 245.
44. *Death of Oenone*, 107; *Poems* (Ricks), III. 251.
45. *Funeral of the Right Honourable Lord Tennyson . . . Order of Service* (BL), where 'Silent Voices' is described as AT's 'latest poem'; words and music appear in *Demeter and Other Poems* (London: Macmillan, 1908 [Eversley VII], 393–5.
46. *Funeral of the Late Robert Browning . . . Order of Service* (BL).
47. Audrey Tennyson, 'Talks & Walks' notebook, fol. 21 (TRC); quoted in James O. Hoge, 'Talks and Walks: Tennyson's Remarks and Observations, 1870–92', *Journal of English and Germanic Philology*, 77 (January 1978), 65.
48. 'Talks & Walks', fol. 20 (TRC; ampersand expanded for quoted speech), quoted in Hoge, 'Talks and Walks', 64.
49. *Memoir*, II. 426.
50. *Memoir*, I. xii.
51. *The Times*, 7 Oct. 1892, 9.
52. *The Times*, 13 Oct. 1892, 4. The comparison with Wellington's funeral was also made by the *Daily Telegraph*, 13 Oct. 1892, 7–8, among others.
53. Gosse, 'Tennyson's Funeral', MS (BL); see also his 'Tennyson—and After', in *Questions at Issue* (London: William Heinemann, 1893), partly reprinted in Gosse, *Portraits from Life*, ed. Ann Thwaite (Aldershot: Scolar Press, 1991), 53–7. The *Star* newspaper for the evening of 12 Oct. ('By the Graveside', p. 3) also commented on the impatience and quarrelsomeness of the crowd.
54. For accounts of the death and funeral, see Martin, *T: Unquiet Heart*, 580–3; Baum, *T Sixty Years After*, 3–7; and Bernard Jerman, 'The Death of Tennyson', *Acta Neophilologica*, 5 (1972), 31–44.
55. An undated letter of his to Macmillan & Co. (BL) sends a list of pall-bearers for release to the press the following day.
56. See Alan Bell, 'Gladstone Looks for a Poet Laureate', *The Times*

Literary Supplement, 21 July 1972, 847, and the supplementary letter from Bevis Hillier, *TLS*, 11 Aug. 1972, 945. Theodore Watts, however, told Gosse that Swinburne had been invited to 'take a prominent place' but 'positively and obstinately refused to come': Gosse, 'Tennyson's Funeral' (BL).

57. Gosse, 'Tennyson's Funeral' (BL).

58. Leon Edel, *Henry James: The Middle Years. 1882–1895* (Philadelphia: J. B. Lippincott, 1962), 309.

59. *The Collected Letters of Thomas Hardy*, ed. Richard L. Purdy and Michael Millgate, 7 vols. (Oxford: Clarendon Press, 1978–88), I. 287; in the same letter Hardy mentions James as one of the people he had encountered at the service.

60. See Richard Ormond, *National Portrait Gallery: Early Victorian Portraits*, 2 vols. (London: HMSO, 1973), I. 450–1. The copyist was Mary Grant.

61. See Elfrida Manning, *Marble & Bronze: The Art and Life of Hamo Thornycroft* (London: Trefoil Books, 1982), frontispiece, 150, 151, and 210.

62. A report of the unveiling is in the *Lincoln Leader*, 22 July 1905, 8; for the statue itself, see Leonée Ormond, 'George Frederic Watts: The Portraits of Tennyson', *Tennyson Research Bulletin*, 4 (November 1983), 47–58, esp. 54–7, and Andrew Wheatcroft, *The Tennyson Album* (London: Routledge & Kegan Paul, 1980), 156.

63. See the photograph in Wheatcroft, *Tennyson Album*, 154–5.

64. *The Times*, 7 Aug. 1897, 5, where HT was reported as believing the memorial to be the one AT 'would have liked the best'.

65. J. H. Woolgar, of Newtown, Isle of Wight, 'Lines on the Tennyson Beacon', 19 Aug. 1897, single printed sheet (Beinecke).

66. *Athenaeum*, 8 Oct. 1892, 483; *The Times*, 7 Oct. 1892, 9, had already stated, 'We understand that Lord Tennyson wished his son, the Hon. Hallam Tennyson, to write his life.'

67. *Lionel Tennyson*, ed., with memoir, by Hallam Tennyson (London: privately printed, 1891); Randolph Caldecott died before completing work on the illustrations to *Jack and the Bean-stalk: English Hexameters* (London: Macmillan, 1886) and HT (as he explains in his Preface) had to make do with the unfinished sketches. HT also edited the sonnets of his uncle, Charles Tennyson Turner, in 1880, and seems to have lectured on 'Shakespeare and His Humour' at Shoreditch Town Hall in March 1876 as part of a series of 'Lectures on Science, Literature, and History' given by members of the University of Cambridge: advertisement and HT notes for lecture (TRC).

68. AT, *Poems II* (London: Macmillan, 1908) [Eversley II], 325; Hallam

quoted the entire poem there, together with an anonymously published companion poem, 'Bluebeard' (both reprinted in *Poems* [Ricks], III. 634–7).

69. HT to [Alexander] Macmillan, [?] Feb. 1885 (BL).
70. *Macmillan's Magazine*, 52 (March 1885), 345. A prose translation of 'The Song of Brunanburh' in the *Contemporary Review* of November 1876 had been signed in full, however, and HT also put his name to a political article in the *Nineteenth Century* of December 1880 and to a later poem, 'English Sapphics', in *Macmillan's Magazine* itself, December 1888.
71. HT to G. L. Craik, 10 Jan. 1893 (BL).
72. HT to Craik, 20 Dec. 1892 (BL).
73. HT to Craik, 22 Dec. 1892; also letters to Craik of 8 and 20 Dec. 1892 (BL).
74. BL.
75. *Memoir*, II. 234.
76. To Anne and Agnes Weld (TRC), quoted in *Letters of ET*, 358.
77. The new MS, in two volumes, is in TRC; see *Lady Tennyson's Journal*, ed. James O. Hoge (Charlottesville: Univ. Press of Virginia, 1981), and the cautionary review of that edition by Philip Collins, *The Times Higher Education Supplement*, 23 Apr. 1982, 15.
78. To Anne Weld (TRC), quoted in *Letters of ET*, 360.
79. ET's letter to Anne Weld, 10 Aug. 1893 (TRC), speaks of HT's working 'every day' and of Audrey's writing 'at his dictation'.
80. TRC. Philip L. Elliott speculates in his valuable *The Making of the Memoir* ([Greenville, SC]: Furman University, 1978), 16, that HT must initially have put together a now-vanished 'ur-MS'.
81. *Memoir*, I. xv–xvi. The friends were Henry Sidgwick and Francis Palgrave.
82. See *The Letters of Alfred Lord Tennyson*, ed. Cecil Y. Lang and Edgar F. Shannon, Jr, 3 vols. (Oxford: Clarendon Press, 1981–90), I. xix; Lang and Shannon also refer (I. xix–xx) to HT's later obliteration of notes in Edward FitzGerald's copy of Tennyson's *Poems* (1842) in Trinity College, Cambridge.
83. For the details of the printing and a partial location list of surviving copies, see Philip L. Elliott, 'Materials for a Life of A. T.', *Notes & Queries*, NS 28 (October 1981), 415–18.
84. See Elliott, *Making of the Memoir*, 8–10.
85. *Memoir*, I. xi, xii.
86. *Memoir*, I. xv.
87. Manuscript *Materials*, I, fol. 9 (TRC); the passage is in Audrey Tennyson's hand.
88. Elliott speaks of 'Hallam's increasing participation' (*Making of the*

Memoir, 8) as an important element in the evolution of the *Memoir*.

89. *Memoir*, I. xvi.

90. According to her *Times* obituary, 11 Aug. 1896, 9, she had been helping HT correct the proofs of the *Memoir* until shortly before her death.

91. Compare *Memoir*, I. 10, with *Letters*, I. 3–5.

92. Compare *Memoir*, I. 178, with *Letters*, I. 188. Elliott, *Making of the Memoir*, 19–32, cites, among other examples, the more radical treatment of AT's letter to Spedding in *Memoir*, I. 127–8, which can now be readily compared with the text in *Letters*, I. 86–7.

93. See, for example, Francis Thompson, 'The Life of Tennyson', *New Review*, 17 (November 1897), 536–48, esp. 536–7, 548.

94. Charles Tennyson, 'Tennyson's Conversation', *Twentieth Century*, 165 (January 1959), 34.

95. James, *The Middle Years* (London: W. Collins & Sons, 1917), 99.

96. *Tennyson at Aldworth: The Diary of James Henry Mangles*, ed. Earl A. Knies (Athens, OH: Ohio Univ. Press, 1984), 121, 125; see the introduction, 19–20, for comments on Tennyson as gossip.

97. HT, 'Stories & conversations taken down by me as a boy in an old Marlborough note book' (TRC); quoted, with differences, in C. Tennyson, 'Tennyson's Conversation', 37.

98. Sydney Waterlow, MS diary (Berg), entry for 16 Nov. 1907. The tomb, inside the church, is currently covered over with matting.

99. Paul F. Mattheisen, 'Gosse's Candid "Snapshots"', *Victorian Studies*, 8 (June 1965), 343, 342; Gosse's 'childishly playful' suggests that he may also have been the indirect source of Sydney Waterlow's reference to AT's 'strong vein of infantile obscenity': Diary, 16 Nov. 1907 (Berg). For Gosse's much later comments on the contrast, seen as damaging to AT's reputation, between the 'real man' and the 'funereal image' created by 'the priesthood circled round their idol', see 'The Agony of the Victorian Age', collected in *Some Diversions of a Man of Letters* (London: William Heinemann, 1919), 320, 321.

100. Edward Clodd, MS diary, entry for 15 Dec. 1892 (Alan Clodd).

101. Mattheisen, 'Gosse's "Snapshots"', 343.

102. As Charles Tennyson once suggested: *Stars and Markets*, 168.

103. His use, for example, of 'For My Sons' (TCR), his mother's account of Tennyson's early life (apparently first written in 1869), was extensive but uncritical. See James O. Hoge, 'Emily Tennyson's Narrative for Her Sons', *Texas Studies in Literature and Language*, 14 (Spring 1972), 93–106.

104. Knowles, 'Aspects of Tennyson. II', *Nineteenth Century*, 33 (January 1893), 164.

105. HT, draft letter to Henry Sidgwick, 23 [Jan?] 1893 (TRC); the

further comments on Knowles, quoted by Martin (*T: Unquiet Heart*, 507), are struck through in the draft and were perhaps omitted from the letter as sent.

106. ET to Anne and Agnes Weld, 15 Feb. 1893 (TRC), quoted in *Letters of ET*, 362; and see Metcalf, *James Knowles*, 339–43.
107. *Memoir*, I. 10.
108. *Memoir*, I. 118.
109. *Memoir*, I. xii, quoted above.
110. *Memoir*, I. 118.
111. HT to [Alexander] Macmillan, 28 June 1885 (BL).
112. *Quarterly Review*, 82 (March 1848), 445; *Poems* (Ricks), II. 214.
113. 'NOTES' (so stamped in gold on spine), 69 (TRC); the volume contains notes to the poems and plays up to and including *The Promise of May*, the latest title included in the enlarged one-volume *Complete Works* of 1889.
114. *The Princess and Maud* (London: Macmillan, 1908) [Eversley IV], 252. In the second annotated edition, *The Works of Tennyson with Notes by the Author* (London: Macmillan, 1913), Hallam kept the same wording but added a footnote.
115. HT to Craik, 30 Aug. 1901 (BL).
116. G. Macmillan to George Brett, 7 Aug. 1907 (New York Public Library, MS Division). See also the statement in the first volume of the Eversley Edition: *Poems I* (London: Macmillan, 1907), 334.
117. C. Tennyson, *Alfred Tennyson*, 472.
118. ET to Anne Weld, 28 July 1893 (TRC): 'Hallam's first vote was about Commons which is rather curious seeing that we have so much to do with them in both houses.'
119. Hardy once addressed him in this capacity: see *Coll. Letters of Thomas Hardy*, III. 349.
120. Obituary, *The Times*, 3 Dec. 1928, 19.
121. For his wife's pleasant, unofficial chronicle of this period see *Audrey Tennyson's Vice-Regal Days*; a large collection of HT's official papers is in the Australian National Library, Canberra.
122. *Isle of Wight County Press*, 9 Feb. 1907, 6.
123. HT to Frederick Macmillan, 9 June 1905 (BL).
124. See, e.g., letters to George A. Macmillan of 24 and 26 May 1908 (BL).
125. Corrected proofs for some of the notes to the 1905 *In Memoriam* and to the fifth volume of the Eversley Edition are at TRC.
126. See *Letters to a Tutor*, esp. Dakyns to HT of 16 Feb. 1908 (251–7).
127. *Poems I* (London: Macmillan, 1907) [Eversley I], 333; *Works* (1913), 895.
128. Interleaved copy of 1884 one-volume *Works*, verso of the front free

end-paper (TRC), quoted in *In Memoriam*, ed. Susan Shatto and Marion Shaw (Oxford: Clarendon Press, 1982), 157. Shatto and Shaw believe that Tennyson undertook the entire annotation project only with 'lugubrious reluctance' (157).

129. 'NOTES', [1] (TRC). Though this quotation and the preceding quotation are in HT's hand, they are clearly of pre-1892 date and AT origin.

130. *Letters to a Tutor*, 254.

131. HT to [George A.?] Macmillan, 13 July 1913 (BL); see also HT to George Macmillan, 20 Nov. 1913 (BL).

132. HT to G. Macmillan, 26 Oct. 1913 (BL).

133. William Knight, 'A Reminiscence of Tennyson', *Blackwood's Edinburgh Magazine*, 162 (August 1897), 265. In Norman Page, ed., *Tennyson: Interviews and Recollections* (London: Macmillan, 1983), 177, this conversation is wrongly assigned to the year 1870.

134. *Memoir*, I. 118.

135. *Memoir*, I. 23.

136. See above, p. 56.

137. *The Early Poems of Alfred Lord Tennyson . . . with a Critical Introduction, Commentaries and Notes, together with the Various Readings, a Transcript of the Poems Temporarily and Finally Suppressed and a Bibliography*, ed. J. Churton Collins (London: Methuen, 1900). Collins in his preface in fact acknowledges the co-operation of Macmillan & Co. in allowing him to make use of still-copyrighted material. For Tennyson and Collins, see Ann Thwaite, *Edmund Gosse: A Literary Landscape, 1849–1928* (London: Secker & Warburg, 1984), 295–7.

138. *Memoir*, I. 118.

139. See *Maud: A Definitive Edition*, ed. Shatto, 51; the shift in Part I, line 76, from 'my books' to 'myself' occurred in 1865.

140. See Christopher Ricks, 'Tennyson's Methods of Composition', *Proceedings of the British Academy*, 52 (1966), 209–30.

141. Shannon and Ricks, ' "The Charge of the Light Brigade": The Creation of a Poem', *Studies in Bibliography*, 38 (1985), 1–44.

142. See, e.g., *In Memoriam*, ed. Shatto and Shaw, 23.

143. Noel, 'Lord Tennyson', 269.

144. Stoker, *Personal Reminiscences of Henry Irving*, 2 vols. (London: William Heinemann, 1906), I. 225; see also *Memoir*, II. 509, and Warre-Cornish, 'Memories of Tennyson—III', *London Mercury*, 5 (January 1922), 275.

145. *Poems* (Ricks), III. 200, and see headnote, III. 198.

146. Knight, 'Reminiscence', 265–6; AT apparently added that he had himself 'suffered in that way'.

147. HT to Craik, 30 Dec. 1892 (BL): 'My Father tore all his up, & I have not got a copy.'
148. See David Sinclair, 'The First Pirated Edition of Tennyson's Poems', *Book Collector*, 22 (Summer 1973), 177–88.
149. See T. J. Wise, *A Bibliography of the Writings of Alfred Lord Tennyson*, 2 vols. (London: privately printed, 1908), II. 16–19.
150. John Pfordresher, ed., *A Variorum Edition of Tennyson's 'Idylls of the King'* (New York: Columbia Univ. Press, 1973), 55; *Poems* (Ricks), III. 562.
151. HT to Craik, 9 Oct. 1894 (BL); see also *Letters to a Tutor*, 150. For *The Death of Oenone* as AT's 'last will & testament' see above, p. 43.
152. This edition is briefly described in Wise's *Bibliography*, II. 44–5.
153. Macmillan archive, MS Division, New York Public Library. This re-use of existing plates was presumably responsible, through wear, for those occasional absences of end-line punctuation from the Eversley volumes to which Ricks, for example, has drawn attention: *Poems* (Ricks), I. xii.
154. HT's letter to G. A. Macmillan of 12 Nov. 1907 (BL) indicates that he wanted his name on the spine of the Eversley volumes precisely in order to draw attention to the annotations within.
155. Will (Somerset House).
156. *Memoir*, I. 118.
157. Catherine Lady Simeon to Montagu Butler, 9 Dec. 1897 (Trinity College, Cambridge).
158. HT to M. Butler, 10 Dec. 1897 (Trinity College, Cambridge).
159. In 1909 they were evidently interpreted as precluding the manuscript's inclusion in the Tennyson Centenary Exhibition of that year, and in lamenting its absence the exhibition catalogue also expressed regret at the departure of other items to the United States, that 'bourne' from which few manuscripts returned: *Tennyson Centenary Exhibition: A Catalogue* (London: Fine Arts Society, 1909), 3.
160. The statement, dated June 1924, is on Farringford stationery but not in HT's own hand (Trinity College, Cambridge). For a brief history of the Trinity MSS see John Charles Yearwood, Jr, 'A Catalogue of the Tennyson Manuscripts at Trinity College, Cambridge' (doctoral dissertation, Univ. of Texas at Austin, 1977), 1–5.
161. HT, ed., *Tennyson and His Friends* (London: Macmillan, 1911), 147.
162. Craik to HT, 3 May 1904 (TRC).
163. HT thought, however, that the United Kingdom terms for the Eversley Edition were 'very fair': HT to G. A. Macmillan, 9 Feb. 1907 (BL).

164. His nephew, Charles Tennyson, was similarly to lose two of three sons in the Second World War.
165. *The Times*, 29 July 1918, 9.
166. See Amanda Hopkinson, *Julia Margaret Cameron* (London: Virago, 1986), 54–5, 58–9, and Brian Hill, *Julia Margaret Cameron: A Victorian Family Portrait* (New York: St Martin's Press, 1973), 95, 122, and esp. 157.
167. C. Tennyson, *Alfred Tennyson*, 511–12; the *Memoir* account (II. 354) does not mention Mrs Hichens's presence.
168. *Letters to a Tutor*, 143.
169. Her obituary in *The Times*, 21 July 1931, 16, spoke of her assistance to her husband in keeping Farringford and its grounds as Tennyson had known them and of her recently announced plan to open parts of the house to visitors, 'together with a specially arranged Tennyson museum containing many manuscripts, personal relics and portraits'. She also helped to maintain the documentary record: among the items in the Beinecke Library which came to Yale through one of Lady Tennyson's Prinsep relatives is a set of the two-volume *Memoir* quite extensively annotated by her and with inserted extracts, copied in her hand, from additional correspondence, unused portions of Emily Tennyson's journal, etc.
170. Lionel Lord Tennyson, *From Verse to Worse* (London: Cassell, 1933), 24.
171. *The Times*, 3 Dec. 1928, 19.
172. Will (Somerset House).
173. L. Tennyson, *From Verse to Worse*, 13.
174. C. Tennyson, *Stars and Markets*, 166.
175. C. Tennyson, *Stars and Markets*, 166.
176. Personal memory.
177. Atherton Powys, letter, *The Times Literary Supplement*, 7 Oct. 1949, 649.
178. Nancie Campbell, comp., *Tennyson in Lincoln: A Catalogue of the Collections in the Research Centre. Volume One* (Lincoln: Tennyson Society, 1971), xv, xvi; these same pages also contain a brief but useful account of attempts to catalogue the Farringford books while AT was still alive.
179. See Edgar F. Shannon, Jr, and W. H. Bond, 'Literary Manuscripts of Alfred Tennyson in the Harvard College Library', *Harvard Library Bulletin*, 10 (Spring 1956), 254–74. The sale, and consequent exportation, was somewhat controversial in Britain, and Sir Charles's autobiography contains a slightly defensive account of his having decided upon it only after taking into account 'the large quantity of Tennyson's material at Cambridge and elsewhere in this country' and

obtaining the approval of a distinguished (though unidentified) man
of letters who 'thought it of great importance to increase by all
possible means American interest in English literature—indeed, if
possible to make Americans think of our literature as their own':
Stars and Markets, 167–8.

180. Campbell, *Catalogue*, xvi.
181. Martin, 'Charles Tennyson: Writer and Scholar', in Hallam Tennyson,
ed., *Studies in Tennyson* (London: Macmillan, 1981), 35–6.
182. For an account of this campaign, see R. A. Carroll, 'The Tennyson
Sales', *Tennyson Research Bulletin*, 3 (November 1980), 141–6.
See also Sotheby's catalogue, 21–2 July 1980, lots 330–457.
183. *Letters*, I. xxi.
184. Charles Tennyson's introduction to his edition of Tennyson's *The
Devil and the Lady* (London: Macmillan, 1930), v, not only makes
this clear but indicates that HT had himself contemplated publication
of the work.
185. Wheatcroft, *Tennyson Album*, 150, where it is described as the very
last such photograph.
186. Charles Tennyson, noting HT's silence about the recordings of
Tennyson that were made in 1890, took it for granted that 'his
passionate devotion to his father . . . made him shrink from
reproducing what he could only regard as a travesty of his voice':
'The Tennyson Phonograph Records', *British Institute of Recorded
Sound Bulletin*, no. 3 (Winter 1956), 3.
187. *Poems* (Ricks), I. 619.
188. *Poems* (Ricks), I. 620.

HENRY JAMES

1. HJ, 'Mr. and Mrs. James T. Fields', *Literary Criticism: Essays on
Literature; American Writers; English Writers* (New York: Library
of America, 1984), 163. Both typescripts of the essay are in the
Houghton Library.
2. *Literary Criticism*, 165.
3. See, for example, Ulric Neisser, 'Nested Structure in Autobiographical
Memory', in David C. Rubin, ed., *Autobiographical Memory*
(Cambridge: Cambridge Univ. Press, 1986), 71–81, esp. 78.
4. *The Complete Notebooks of Henry James*, ed. Leon Edel and Lyall
H. Powers (New York: Oxford Univ. Press, 1987), 438.
5. *Complete Notebooks*, 214.
6. *The Letters of Henry James*, ed. Percy Lubbock, 2 vols. (London:
Macmillan, 1920), I. xiii–xiv.

7. HJ to Urbain Mengin, 1 Jan. 1903, in *Henry James Letters*, ed. Leon Edel (Cambridge, MA: Harvard Univ. Press, 1974–84), IV. 266.

8. HJ to William Blackwood, 28 Oct. 1897 (NLS); a slightly different reading of this sentence is given in *HJ Letters*, IV. 59.

9. See Leon Edel, *Henry James. The Master: 1901–1916* (Philadelphia: J. B. Lippincott, 1972), 127–9. The story there referred to as 'The Beautiful Child' presumably corresponds to the unfinished 'Hugh Merrow', first published (without such identification) in *Complete Notebooks*, 589–96.

10. Weld diary; Leon Edel, *The Master*, 129, gives this date, incorrectly, as 22 September. The late Revd H. P. Kingdon kindly gave me access to his mother's diary and related materials.

11. Compare, for example, the Robert Browning letters in HJ, *William Wetmore Story and His Friends*, 2 vols. (Boston: Houghton, Mifflin, 1903), II. 90–119, with the transcriptions in *Browning to His American Friends*, ed. Gertrude Reese Hudson (London: Bowes & Bowes, 1965), 75–103. Hudson comments in her Preface: 'Henry James, who approached his task as an artist, did not hesitate to alter the letters which he used. The variations between his versions and my transcriptions are too numerous to note' (17–18).

12. See, e.g., HJ to Henry Adams, 19 Nov. 1903, *HJ Letters*, IV. 289.

13. HJ to William Blackwood, 15 Oct. 1897 (NLS).

14. Karen L. Wadman, '*William Wetmore Story and His Friends*: Henry James's Portrait of Robert Browning', *Yearbook of English Studies*, 11 (1981), 210. See also Ross Posnock, *Henry James and the Problem of Robert Browning* (Athens, GA: Univ. of Georgia Press, 1985).

15. *Letters of HJ*, I. 420–1.

16. *The Selected Letters of Henry James*, ed. Leon Edel (New York: Farrar, Straus & Cudahy, 1955), 194.

17. *Letters of Henry Adams*, ed. Worthington Chauncey Ford, 2 vols. (Boston: Houghton, Mifflin, 1938), II. 414.

18. *William Wetmore Story*, II. 166.

19. *William Wetmore Story*, I. 76; the reference is to Rufus Griswold, Poe's literary executor (see below, p. 192).

20. *Letters of HJ*, I. 418.

21. *Letters of HJ*, I. 424.

22. *HJ Letters*, IV. 351–2.

23. *Complete Notebooks*, 237; the editors follow their predecessors, F. O. Matthiessen and Kenneth B. Murdock (*The Notebooks of Henry James* [New York: Oxford Univ. Press, 1947], 318), in supplying 'plunge' to fill the obvious lacuna.

24. 'Henry James', *Fortnightly Review*, NS 101 (June 1917), 1002.
    Bosanquet used slightly different phrasing in the corresponding
    passage of her *Henry James at Work* (London: Hogarth Press, 1924),
    11.

25. Bosanquet notebook diary, entry for 11 Oct. 1907 (Houghton);
    Bosanquet's diary takes different forms (bound notebooks, loose
    typescript sheets, printed pocket diaries), and since these occasionally
    overlap each entry cited will be identified by its location as well as by
    its date. Also in Houghton is a separate, more elaborate, and
    obviously later set of typed notes covering the period of HJ's illness
    and death which Bosanquet prepared specifically for Leon Edel's use
    in writing his biography of HJ.

26. Bosanquet notebook diary, 14 Oct. 1907 (Houghton).

27. *HJ Letters*, II. 410–11.

28. For Pinker—though not for his relationship with HJ—see James
    Hepburn, *The Author's Empty Purse and the Rise of the Literary
    Agent* (London: Oxford Univ. Press, 1968), 57–65.

29. Pinker to Burlingame, 3 Aug. 1904, quoted in *The Tales of Henry
    James. Volume Two 1870–1974*, ed. Maqbool Aziz (Oxford:
    Clarendon Press, 1978), liv–lv.

30. Burlingame to Pinker, 16 Sept. 1904 (Princeton), quoted in Michael
    Anesko, *'Friction with the Market': Henry James and the Profession
    of Authorship* (New York: Oxford Univ. Press, 1986), 144–5.

31. For that history see Anesko, *'Friction'*, 141–62; Hershel Parker,
    'Henry James "In the Wood": Sequence and Significances of
    his Literary Labors, 1905–1907', *Nineteenth-Century Fiction*, 38
    (March 1984), 492–513; and Philip Horne, *Henry James and
    Revision: The New York Edition* (Oxford: Clarendon Press, 1990),
    which combines background information with an extensive, and
    generally celebratory, study of the revision process.

32. See Leon Edel and Dan H. Laurence, *A Bibliography of Henry James*,
    3rd edn. (Oxford: Clarendon Press, 1982), 128; *The Outcry* (1911)
    appeared later and sold even better but was an adaptation of an
    existing play.

33. John 9: 4. Leon Edel has suggested that James intended the title of
    The Middle Years, his third volume of autobiography, to denote 'the
    "middle" span of an individual's life, from the late twenties to the
    late fifties' (*Henry James: The Middle Years. 1882–1895* [Philadelphia:
    J. B. Lippincott, 1962], 18), but if Percy Lubbock, who prepared the
    unfinished *The Middle Years* for the printer, was right in thinking
    that its title referred back to the earlier story, then James must have
    had a larger segment of life in mind: 'Editor's Note', *The Middle
    Years* (London: Collins, 1917).

34. *Terminations* (London: William Heinemann, 1895), 188, 190, 184; the text of the story as it appears in the New York Edition (XVI) shows no alteration at these points.

35. *Terminations*, 181; the New York Edition text is again unrevised.

36. See the facsimile edition, HJ, *'The American': The Version of 1877 Revised in Autograph and Typescript for the New York Edition of 1907* (London: Scolar Press, 1976); the original is in the Houghton Library, together with the less heavily revised working copy of *The Portrait of a Lady*.

37. HJ to Elizabeth Robins, 28 Mar. 1906, in *Theatre and Friendship: Some Henry James Letters*, ed. Elizabeth Robins (New York: G. P. Putnam's Sons, 1932), 256.

38. HJ to Scribner's, 9 May 1906, *HJ Letters*, IV. 403.

39. HJ to Scribner's, 12 June 1906, *HJ Letters*, IV. 409.

40. HJ to E. Gosse, 25 Aug. 1915, in *Selected Letters of Henry James to Edmund Gosse 1882–1915: A Literary Friendship*, ed. Rayburn S. Moore (Baton Rouge: Louisiana State Univ. Press, 1988), 313, 314. See also the extract from HJ to Beatrix Chapman, 8 Jan. 1912, quoted in Horne, *HJ and Revision*, 357.

41. *Selected Letters of HJ to Gosse*, 313.

42. Edel, 'The Architecture of Henry James's "New York Edition"', *New England Quarterly*, 24 (June 1951), 169–78. Edel's suggestion also left out of account the Balzac edition's inclusion of a certain amount of non-fictional material.

43. Anesko, *'Friction'*, 143–54.

44. Anesko, *'Friction'*, 154–61; the expansion of the Edition to 24 volumes was suggested by W. C. Brownell (of Scribner's) in a letter to HJ dated 2 Dec. 1908 (Princeton), quoted in *Tales of HJ*, ed. Aziz, II. lv–lvi.

45. Parker, *Flawed Texts and Verbal Icons: Literary Authority in American Fiction* (Evanston: Northwestern Univ. Press, 1984), esp. 85–114. For more extended references to editorial theory see below, pp. 197–9.

46. *Roderick Hudson* (New York: Charles Scribner's Sons, 1907) [New York Edition I], xii–xiii.

47. *The American* (New York: Charles Scribner's Sons, 1907) [New York Edition II], vi.

48. *The American*, vii; Horne, *HJ and Revision* (60–2), usefully discusses what 'unconscious cerebration' may have meant to James.

49. *The Portrait of a Lady*, I (New York: Charles Scribner's Sons, 1908) [New York Edition III], xvii.

50. *Complete Notebooks*, 13–16. For an instance of the fallibility of James's autobiographical memory see Robert Bernard Martin,

Tennyson: The Unquiet Heart (Oxford: Clarendon Press, 1980), 612–13, n. 17.

51. *The Reverberator* (New York: Charles Scribner's Sons, 1908) [New York Edition XIII], vii–viii. In the New York Edition Preface to 'The Pupil' (XI. xvi) James, speaking not of revision specifically but of epiphanic experiences in general, describes how in a single moment 'an old latent and dormant impression, a buried germ, implanted by experience and then forgotten, flashes to the surface as a fish, with a single "squirm", rises to the baited hook, and there meets instantly the vivifying ray'.

52. As Hershel Parker has well observed in 'HJ "In the Wood"', 494–5, 512–13.

53. Bosanquet, 'HJ', 1002–03, and *HJ at Work*, 12.

54. HJ to Pinker, 25 June 1906 (Beinecke), extracted in Parker, 'HJ "In the Wood"', 499. It appears from this letter and its successor (27 June 1906, Beinecke) that the 'Charleston' and 'Florida' chapters of *The American Scene* were intended for serialization in the *North American Review*, although they never in fact appeared there.

55. See, for example, his letter to Pinker of 7 Sept. 1906 (Beinecke), extracted in Parker, 'HJ "In the Wood"', 501.

56. *HJ Letters*, IV. 422. According to Edmund Gosse, HJ responded to criticisms of his 'wholesale tampering' with the text of *Roderick Hudson* by insisting upon the absolute necessity of correcting its 'disgraceful and disreputable style': 'Henry James', *Aspects and Impressions* (London: Cassell, 1922), 47–8, quoted in Gosse, *Portraits from Life*, ed. Ann Thwaite (Aldershot: Scolar Press, 1991), 137–8.

57. See *HJ Letters*, IV. 370–1.

58. See *HJ Letters*, IV. 408, 409 n. 4.

59. A copy of the prospectus is among the Macmillan papers in the New York Public Library, Manuscripts Division.

60. *HJ Letters*, IV. 366.

61. See, for example, *HJ Letters*, IV. 371, 408.

62. *HJ Letters*, IV. 467.

63. Matthiessen, *Henry James: The Major Phase* (New York: Oxford Univ. Press, 1944), 152–8; Matthiessen's arguments, and HJ's revisions in general, are cogently discussed by James G. Murphy, 'An Analysis of Henry James's Revisions of the First Four Novels of the New York Edition' (doctoral dissertation, Univ. of Delaware, 1987), esp. (for Matthiessen) 22–6.

64. *In Memoriam*, v, 5–8.

65. As Murphy ('Analysis', 96 ff.) has amply demonstrated of the first four novels included in the Edition.

66. On this last point see Horne, *HJ and Revision*, 257–8.
67. HJ to Pinker, 31 Dec. 1907 (Beinecke), quoted in Parker, 'HJ "In the Wood"', 509 (where it is incorrectly located at Harvard).
68. *Literary Criticism*, 1206.
69. *Literary Criticism*, 1212, 1211, 1209, 1210, 1209.
70. *Literary Criticism*, 1214; Horne (*HJ and Revision*, 313) comments briefly on this aspect of the essay.
71. *Literary Criticism*, 1215.
72. For the physical features of the New York Edition see Edel and Laurence, *Bibliography*, 135–9. For HJ's collaboration with Coburn see: Charles Higgins, 'Photographic Aperture: Coburn's Frontispieces to James's New York Edition', *American Literature*, 53 (January 1982), 661–75; Helmut and Alison Gernsheim, eds., *Alvin Langdon Coburn, Photographer: An Autobiography with over 70 Reproductions of His Works* (New York: Dover Publications, 1978); and Ralph F. Bogardus, *Pictures and Texts: Henry James, A. L. Coburn, and New Ways of Seeing in Literary Culture* (Ann Arbor: UMI Research Press, 1984).
73. See Edel's 'Architecture' essay for its brief but effective evocation of the Edition as 'a vast work of art' (170).
74. See *The Letters of Edith Wharton*, ed. R. W. B. Lewis and Nancy Lewis (New York: Charles Scribner's Sons, 1988), 202; in 'The Legend', first collected in *Tales of Men and Ghosts* (London: Macmillan, 1910), 195–240, the James figure is called Pellerin, presumably in allusion to 'The Passionate Pilgrim'. For Wharton's subsidization of Scribner's 1912 advance to HJ for an unwritten novel (*The Ivory Tower*), see Edel, *The Master*, 475–9, 483–4, and *HJ Letters*, IV. 789–91.
75. See, for example, his letter to Pinker of 23 Oct. 1908, *HJ Letters*, IV. 497–9.
76. HJ, *The Golden Bowl*, I (New York: Charles Scribner's Sons, 1909) [New York Edition XXIII], xiii, xiv.
77. They were first collected and published under that title in 1956, in a single volume edited by Frederick W. Dupee (New York: Criterion Books).
78. For the origins of the 'Family Book' see HJ's letter to Henry James, jun., of 15–18 Nov. 1913 (Houghton), extracted in *HJ Letters*, IV. 801–2.
79. *The Letters of William James*, ed. Henry James, jun., 2 vols. (Boston: Atlantic Monthly Press, 1920).
80. *HJ Letters*, IV. 590.
81. HJ to HJ, jun., 23–6 Dec. 1911 (Houghton); see also HJ to Auguste Monod, 7 Sept. 1913, in *Henry James: Letters to A. C. Benson and*

Auguste Monod, ed. E. F. Benson (London: Elkin Mathews & Marrot, 1930), 117.

82. See above, p. 79.

83. Theodora Bosanquet recorded that on 12 April 1912 James 'spent a strenuous morning, wrestling with a rather unmanageable part of his memoirs': typescript diary (Houghton).

84. HJ to HJ, jun., 25–6 Nov. 1912 (Houghton); the relevant passage is not part of the extract in *HJ Letters*, IV. 797–9.

85. HJ to HJ, jun., 23–4 Sept. 1912 (Houghton), extracted in *HJ Letters*, IV. 794–5, which omits the 'a' preceding 'Brother'.

86. See the authorial note prefaced to the previously published pieces gathered into, and revised for, *English Hours* (London: William Heinemann, 1905), vi.

87. WJ to his parents, 'Sunday afternoon' [early Nov. 1861?] (Houghton); the complete letter is in *Letters of WJ*, I. 40–2.

88. *Notes of a Son and Brother* (New York: Charles Scribner's Sons, 1914), 151.

89. WJ to his parents, 12 Aug. [1860] (Houghton); this letter is not in *Letters of WJ*, but see Robert Charles Le Clair, *Young Henry James 1843–1870* (New York: Bookman Associates, 1955), 318–20.

90. *Notes*, 44. For other instances of HJ's interventions, compare WJ's letter to his sister Alice, 13 Sept. 1863, in *Letters of WJ*, I. 49–52, with *Notes*, 152–4; and WJ to Henry James, sen., 'Sunday Afternoon' [19 Aug. 1860?] (Houghton; not in *Letters of WJ*), with *Notes*, 45–6, where it is assigned to early September 1860. See also Horne, *HJ and Revision*, 317.

91. HJ to HJ, jun., 15–18 Nov. 1913 (Houghton); a slightly different version of this passage is in *HJ Letters*, IV. 802.

92. *HJ Letters*, I. xxxv.

93. Compare, for example, the letter from Henry James, sen., 'To the invisible Emerson' in Ralph Barton Perry, *The Thought and Character of William James*, 2 vols. (Boston: Little, Brown, 1935), I. 41–3, with the version, shorn of the first three sentences, in *Notes*, 170–1; the original is in Houghton.

94. See Alfred Habegger, 'Henry James's Rewriting of Minny Temple's Letters', *American Literature*, 58 (May 1986), 159–80.

95. HJ to HJ, jun., 15–18 Nov. 1913 (Houghton), extracted in *HJ Letters*, IV. 803; Horne defends HJ's adaptations on just these grounds, arguing that he saw the act of revision as 'a duty' to the dead rather than 'a disservice or an imposition of self' (*HJ and Revision*, 319).

96. *Letters of WJ*, I. 32.

97. Tintner, 'Autobiography as Fiction: "The Usurping Consciousness" as Hero of James's Memoirs', *Twentieth-Century Literature*, 23

(May 1977), 239; the whole article (239–60) is relevant to this discussion. In *Henry James and the 'Woman Business'* (Cambridge: Cambridge Univ. Press, 1989), Alfred Habegger draws on his reading of *The Portrait of a Lady* as well as on HJ's handling of Minny Temple's letters to argue that she became the 'prey' of HJ's possessiveness, his 'desire to transform her into a text all his own' (164, 165). See also Henry McDonald, 'Henry James as Nietzschean: The Dark Side of the Aesthetic', *Partisan Review*, 56 (Summer 1989), 391–405.

98. Houghton, extracted in *HJ Letters*, IV. 803.

99. HJ, 'The Novel in *The Ring and the Book*', *Transactions of the Royal Society of Literature*, 2nd series, 31 (1912), 269–98; revised text reprinted in HJ, *Literary Criticism*, 791–811. As Susan M. Griffin points out in 'James's Revisions of "The Novel in *The Ring and the Book*"' (*Modern Philology*, 85 [August 1987], 57–64), HJ was less elaborately deferential to Browning in the revised version of the paper published in the *Quarterly Review* (217 [July 1912], 68–87) than he had been at the celebration itself.

100. Bosanquet typescript diary, entry for 3 Apr. 1913 (Houghton).

101. The portrait is now in the National Portrait Gallery, London.

102. HJ to HJ, jun., 7 Apr. 1914 (Houghton); a longer extract from this letter appears, together with other relevant material, in Carol Holly, ' "Absolutely Acclaimed": The Cure for Depression in James's Final Phase', *Henry James Review*, 8 (Winter 1987), 126–38.

103. *Selected Letters of HJ to Gosse*, 313.

104. See Edel, *The Master*, 433–44, and Henry D. Janowitz and Adeline R. Tintner, 'An Anglo-American Consultation: Sir William Osler Refers Henry James to Sir James Mackenzie', *Journal of the History of Medicine and Allied Sciences*, 43 (July 1988), 297–308.

105. John Russell, ed., *A Portrait of Logan Pearsall Smith, Drawn from His Letters and Diaries* (London: Dropmore Press, 1950), 97. Violet Hunt, writing immediately after James's death, extravagantly suggested that he had been killed by the war and that the Kaiser himself was the guilty party: 'The Last Days of Henry James', *Daily Mail*, 1 Mar. 1916, 4.

106. Bosanquet typescript diary, entry for 20 Oct. 1912 (Houghton).

107. Bosanquet, 1914 diary, entry for 19 July 1914 (Houghton).

108. Bosanquet typescript diary, entry for 1 Nov. 1914 (Houghton).

109. Bosanquet typescript diary (Houghton).

110. HJ to HJ, jun., 7 Apr. 1914 (Houghton).

111. *Letters of HJ*, I. xiv.

112. HJ to Prothero, 7 June 1912 (Murray).

113. HJ to Prothero, 9 June 1912 (Murray). HJ's use of a visual metaphor

('the eye of form') is consistent with the practice, apparently standard in his later years, of having his typist prepare continuous copy on which he would himself indicate paragraph indentation with bold strokes of red ink: see, for example, the typescript setting copy of *Notes of a Son and Brother*, formerly in the Gordon N. Ray collection and now in the Pierpont Morgan Library.

114. HJ to Prothero, 10, 12, and 18 June 1912 (Murray).

115. Bosanquet typescript diary, entry for 1 Mar. 1915 (Houghton).

116. HJ to HJ, jun., 4 Nov. 1915 (Houghton). For another late example of his close attention to textual detail, see Horne, *HJ and Revision*, 320–1.

117. Bosanquet to E. Marsh, 5 Dec. 1915 (Berg).

118. Bosanquet typescript diary, entries for 14 and 15 Dec. 1915 (Houghton). In a list of surviving typescripts compiled for James's executors (Houghton), she wrote of the Brooke preface: 'This was the last piece of work finished by Mr. James, towards end of November, 1915. The revised copy is the one from which the preface was printed, but the paragraph containing a criticism of the "Westminster Gazette" for not publishing more of Brooke's work was altered in proof, by Mrs. William James's authority.'

119. Educated at Cheltenham Ladies' College and University College, London, Theodora Bosanquet (1880–1961) was awarded an MBE in 1919 for her work as a wartime civil servant, served as Executive Secretary of the International Federation of University Women from 1920 to 1935, became literary editor and then a director of *Time and Tide*, and published on Harriet Martineau and Paul Valéry as well as on James himself.

120. So HJ's death certificate states.

121. *Letters of HJ*, I. xxxi.

122. For the texts of these dictations, see *HJ Letters*, IV. 808–12. Curiously, HJ's face after death is said to have resembled Napoleon's to a remarkable degree: Edel, *The Master*, 561.

123. Alice James to Gosse, 4 Mar. 1916 (Leeds).

124. Gosse, 'The Funeral of Henry James', *The Times*, 4 Mar. 1916, 7; Bosanquet, typescript diary, entry for 3 Mar. 1916 (Houghton).

125. A booklet available in the church, *Chelsea Old Church: Bombing and Rebuilding* (Chelsea, 1958), narrates the story in modestly heroic fashion.

126. *The Master*, 562.

127. HJ's 'Occupation' is given there as 'Author | O.M.'.

128. See below, p. 181.

129. HJ to Annie Fields, 2 Jan. 1910, *HJ Letters*, IV. 541.

130. Edel, *The Master*, 539.

131. 7 Apr. 1914 (Houghton), extracted in *HJ Letters*, IV. 806.
132. See her typescript diary and notes for Edel (Houghton), also her correspondence with Edith Wharton, pub. in *Henry James and Edith Wharton. Letters: 1900–1915*, ed. Lyall H. Powers (New York: Charles Scribner's Sons, 1990), 361–92.
133. Bosanquet to Pinker, 1 May 1916 (Beinecke); other letters from Bosanquet to Pinker are in the Berg Collection.
134. Edel, however, speaks of HJ's 'greater sense of power' upon his accession to 'what had seemed, for sixty years, an inaccessible throne': *The Master*, 448.
135. Somerset House.
136. Bosanquet, typescript diary, entry for 5 Jan. 1916 (Houghton).
137. See, for example, *Letters of Edith Wharton*, 375–8, 380–1; Wharton to Gosse, 12 June and 6 Aug. 1916 (both Leeds); Bosanquet to Pinker, 1 May 1916 (Beinecke); Alice James to Gosse, 2 Aug. 1916 (Leeds).
138. Lubbock, *Elizabeth Barrett Browning in Her Letters* (London: Smith, Elder, 1906), and (anonymously) 'The Novels of Mr. Henry James', *The Times Literary Supplement*, 8 July 1909, 249–50.
139. Both his sense of responsibility and his lack of comprehension emerge clearly from the absorbing introduction to Edel's first volume of *Henry James Letters*: *HJ Letters*, I. xiii–xxxvi.
140. HJ, jun., to Maxwell Perkins, 10 Mar. 1943 (Princeton).
141. Houghton: HJ had made the suggestion, intended to be propitiatory, that unmodified texts of some of William James's early letters might be published in *Scribner's Magazine*.
142. *HJ Letters*, I. xx–xxi; Powers observes, for example (*HJ and Edith Wharton*, 27), that Lubbock was not necessarily responsible for the edition's omissions from the letters to Wharton.
143. A signed carbon copy of the contract is at Princeton; for the date of publication see Edel and Laurence, *Bibliography*, 260. Alice James also signed the Scribner contracts (Princeton) for *The Middle Years*, *The Sense of the Past*, and *The Ivory Tower*.
144. *HJ Letters*, I. xxiii–xxiv; Edel here quotes from but does not identify the letter from HJ, jun., to Lubbock, 20 May 1919, of which there is a carbon copy (as sent to Gosse) at Leeds.
145. HJ, jun., to Gosse, 21 May 1919 (Leeds).
146. M. Brooke to Gosse, 16 May 1920 (Leeds).
147. *Quarterly Review*, 226 (July 1916), 61.
148. *Letters of HJ*, I. xiii–xiv.
149. *Letters of HJ*, I. xiv.
150. The unfinished and posthumous *The Middle Years*, though edited by Lubbock, was published by Collins.

151. Edel indicates that this plan originated with HJ, jun.: *HJ Letters*, I. xxi.
152. *Letters of HJ*, I. 1.
153. Observing that it was doubtless 'possible to read the "Notes" too literally', he drew upon some reminiscences of Thomas Sergeant Perry's in order to suggest that James had become aware of his literary interests and abilities a good deal earlier than he had chosen to acknowledge (*Letters of HJ*, I. 6–9).
154. *Letters of HJ*, I. xv.
155. For a description of the edition see Edel and Laurence, *Bibliography*, 167–70.
156. See Horne, *HJ and Revision*, 320.
157. Lubbock, *The Craft of Fiction* (London: Jonathan Cape, 1921); for some relevant reflections see Timothy P. Martin, 'Henry James and Percy Lubbock: From Mimesis to Formalism', *Novel*, 14 (Fall 1980), 20–9.
158. For a brief survey of the extant manuscripts see Edel and Laurence, *Bibliography*, 390–3.
159. See 'A Note on the Notes' in *Complete Notebooks*, xix–xxiv, and 'A Note on the Texts' in *The Complete Plays of Henry James*, ed. Leon Edel (Philadelphia: J. B. Lippincott, 1949), 819–23.
160. See Ralph Barton Perry, 'The James Collection', *Harvard University Library Notes*, 4, ii (March 1942), 79.
161. A succinct account of the library's fate is included (1–9) in Leon Edel and Adeline R. Tintner, comps., *The Library of Henry James* (Ann Arbor: UMI Research Press, 1987), a listing of volumes from James's library which have been located in institutional and private collections; not listed are those items known to have been on James's shelves which remain unlocated, and perhaps unlocatable.
162. Edel, *Henry James: A Life* (New York: Harper & Row, 1985), 719.
163. *HJ Letters*, I. viii.
164. See *HJ Letters*, IV. 809.
165. R. W. B. Lewis, noting that with HJ's death 'it seemed to the world at large that the James family itself had passed away', goes on to provide valuable biographical sketches of the next generation—of Henry James, jun., and HJ's other nephews and nieces, his parents' grandchildren: *The Jameses: A Family Narrative* (New York: Farrar, Straus & Giroux, 1991), 595–641.

THOMAS HARDY

1. Thomas Hardy, *The Life and Work of Thomas Hardy*, ed. Michael Millgate (London: Macmillan, 1984), 354.

2. *Life and Work*, 320–1, 414; *The Complete Poetical Works of Thomas Hardy*, ed. Samuel Hynes, 3 vols. to date (Oxford: Clarendon Press, 1982–5), II. 483.

3. *Life and Work*, 435.

4. TH to William Archer, 24 Nov. 1898, *The Collected Letters of Thomas Hardy*, ed. Richard L. Purdy and Michael Millgate, 7 vols. (Oxford: Clarendon Press, 1978–88), II. 206; cf. *Life and Work*, 241.

5. See Richard Little Purdy, *Thomas Hardy: A Bibliographical Study* (1954; Oxford: at the Clarendon Press, 1968), 279–82.

6. TH to F. Macmillan, 17 Jan. 1911, *Coll. Letters*, IV. 137. The map does not appear to have been included in early printings of the *Tess* volume, which were made from the existing plates of the one-volume 'Fifth' edition, published by Osgood, McIlvaine in 1892.

7. See TH's letters to H. Macbeth-Raeburn, *Coll. Letters*, II. 64–5, 69–70, and Simon Gatrell, *Hardy the Creator: A Textual Biography* (Oxford: Clarendon Press, 1988), 134–8.

8. Prospectus for Charles Dickens Edition (BL).

9. Roger Fry and E. A. Lowe, eds., *English Handwriting* (Oxford: S.P.E. Tract XXIII, 1926).

10. See, e.g., Gatrell, *H the Creator*, 99–100, and, for TH's bowdlerizing revisions to *Jude the Obscure* for its first Macmillan printing in 1903, Robert C. Slack, 'The Text of Hardy's *Jude the Obscure*', *Nineteenth-Century Fiction*, 11 (March 1957), 264–8.

11. Gatrell, *H the Creator*, 131–4; TH's revisions to the Osgood, McIlvaine edition were also incorporated into a Colonial Edition published concurrently by Macmillan.

12. The novel had originally appeared, as *The Pursuit of the Well-Beloved*, in the *Illustrated London News*, 1 Oct.–17 Dec. 1892; for details of the revisions, see TH, *The Well-Beloved*, ed. Tom Hetherington (Oxford: Oxford Univ. Press, 1986), 207–56.

13. *Life and Work*, 302.

14. *Life and Work*, 325.

15. TH to G. H. Thring, 4 Mar. 1902, *Coll. Letters*, III. 7.

16. *Coll. Letters*, III. 6.

17. 3 Mar. 1902, *Coll. Letters*, III. 6.

18. TH to F. Macmillan, 22 Mar. 1902, *Coll. Letters*, III. 13.

19. *Wessex Poems* also remained in print as a volume in the Macmillan 'Uniform' series, and in 1907 it was combined with *Poems of the Past and the Present* as a single volume in the Macmillan 'Pocket' format.

20. See, e.g., TH to Arthur Quiller-Couch, 15 Aug. 1906, *Coll. Letters*, III. 221.

21. 18 Jan. 1909, *Coll. Letters*, IV. 7.

22. TH to E. Clodd, 20 Jan. 1892, *Coll. Letters*, I. 254.
23. TH to F. Macmillan, 12 Oct. 1910, *Coll. Letters*, IV. 124.
24. 28 June 1911, *Coll. Letters*, IV. 162, 163.
25. TH to F. Macmillan, 7 Jan. 1912, *Coll. Letters*, IV. 198; F. Macmillan to TH, 9 Jan. 1912 (Macmillan letterbooks, BL).
26. TH to Newman Flower, 8 July 1911, *Coll. Letters*, IV. 164.
27. 22 Aug. 1911, *Coll. Letters*, IV. 168.
28. See TH's footnote to p. 473 of the Wessex Edition text (London: Macmillan, 1912).
29. See Purdy, *Bibliographical Study*, 274–6, and TH to F. Macmillan, 4 Oct. 1913, *Coll. Letters*, IV. 306.
30. Gatrell, *H the Creator*, 127–31, 176.
31. Scott, *Waverley Novels*, 48 vols. (Edinburgh: Cadell & Co., etc., 1829–33), 'Advertisement', I. ii.
32. *Tess of the d'Urbervilles* (London: Macmillan, 1912), xx; although this sentence first appeared in the Osgood, McIlvaine preface of 1895 (x), it then read 'almost word for word' in place of 'as something once said'.
33. *Tess* (1912), xxi.
34. 'General Introduction', *Tess of the d'Urbervilles*, ed. Juliet Grindle and Simon Gatrell (Oxford: Clarendon Press, 1983), *15*.
35. TH, unused foreword to *A Changed Man*, quoted in *The Times Literary Supplement*, 25 Sept. 1913, 402.
36. When *A Changed Man* appeared in 1914, the consecutive numbering of the previously published volumes prevented Hardy from including it, as he would otherwise have done, among the 'Romances and Fantasies'; his solution was to create an entirely new category, 'Mixed Novels', specifically for this one volume: TH to F. Macmillan, 14 Dec. 1913, *Coll. Letters*, IV. 329.
37. 2 Apr. 1912, *Coll. Letters*, IV. 209.
38. See Millgate, *Thomas Hardy: A Biography* (Oxford: Oxford Univ. Press, 1982), 476, and TH to Cockerell, *Coll. Letters*, IV. 178, 180–1, 184, 186–7.
39. TH to S. Cockerell, 11 Oct. 1911, *Coll. Letters*, IV. 181.
40. 8 Oct. 1912, *Coll. Letters*, IV. 229.
41. TH to Herbert Grimsditch, 30 Oct. 1925, *Coll. Letters*, VI. 364.
42. TH's persistent distrust in later years of the way in which Harper & Brothers were handling his books in the United States may have had more than a little to do with their having substituted for the Wessex Edition an unsatisfactory textual hybrid of their own concoction: see Purdy, *Bibliographical Study*, 286.
43. Pound to John Lackay Brown, April 1937, *The Letters of Ezra Pound 1907–1941*, ed. D. D. Paige (New York: Harcourt, Brace,

1950), 294: of TH's *Collected Poems* Pound wrote, 'Now *there* is a clarity. There *is* the harvest of having written 20 novels first.'
44. *Life and Work*, 302.
45. TH to Frederic Harrison, 17 Feb. 1914, *Coll. Letters*, V. 16.
46. The original two volumes were subsequently republished, first in two volumes (1933) and then as a single volume (1962), as *The Life of Thomas Hardy*, the title by which the work is probably best known. The edition of 1984 already identified as *The Life and Work of Thomas Hardy* attempts to reconstruct the text as it stood at TH's death; its introduction (extensively drawn upon in these paragraphs) provides a fuller account of the processes of composition and subsequent revision.
47. Cockerell to TH, 7 Dec. 1915 (DCM), partly quoted in *Life and Work*, xi.
48. TH to S. Cockerell, 29 Nov. 1913, *Coll. Letters*, IV. 325.
49. Beinecke.
50. TH to Edmund Gosse, 18 Feb. 1918, *Coll. Letters*, V. 254.
51. Irene Cooper Willis typescript, 'Copied from pencil notebook' (Boatwright Library, Univ. of Richmond).
52. 'NOTES OF THOMAS HARDY'S LIFE. | by Florence Hardy. | (taken down in conversation, etc.)' (DCM).
53. For a full description of these materials (all in DCM) see *The Personal Notebooks of Thomas Hardy*, ed. Richard H. Taylor (London: Macmillan, 1978), 205–8.
54. Beinecke; partly quoted in *Life and Work*, xiv.
55. See Purdy, *Bibliographical Study*, 265–7, 272–3; the first published announcement, a report on a lecture given by Purdy to the Grolier Club, appeared in the *New York Times Book Review*, 12 May 1940, 25.
56. For examples see *Life and Work*, xiv–xvi.
57. See *Life and Work*, xvi and 56, note for 19 June.
58. *Life and Work*, xv–xvi.
59. *Life and Work*, 489 n.; see also 399–400, 488–9, and *Coll. Letters*, V. 78–9 and notes.
60. *The Life of Thomas Hardy* (New York: Greenberg, 1925).
61. TH to F. Macmillan, 4 Apr. 1925, *Coll. Letters*, VI. 319; TH had received a copy from the American publisher.
62. *The Times*, 11 Apr. 1925, 11; Brennecke's book was never published in Britain.
63. FEH to Maurice Macmillan, 18 Apr. 1926 (BL), partly quoted in *Life and Work*, xviii.
64. FEH to Daniel Macmillan, 19 Jan. 1928 (BL), partly quoted in *Life and Work*, xviii.

65. FEH to S. Cockerell, 7 Feb. 1918 (Beinecke). The 'Life' itself contains a reference to Hardy's 'absolute refusal at all times to write his reminiscences': *Life and Work*, 346; see also 377.

66. Jacobus, 'Hardy's Magian Retrospect', *Essays in Criticism*, 32 (July 1982), 258–79.

67. 'For my part, if there is any way of getting a melancholy satisfaction out of life it lies in dying, so to speak, before one is out of the flesh; by which I mean putting on the manners of ghosts, wandering in their haunts, and taking their views of surrounding things. To think of life as passing away is a sadness; to think of it as past is at least tolerable': *Life and Work*, 218.

68. Hugh Haughton, 'Ghosts', *London Review of Books*, 5 Dec. 1985, 11.

69. A. Lapthorn Smith, *How to be Useful and Happy from Sixty to Ninety* (London: John Lane, 1922), 223; for the gift see TH to Lane, 29 June 1922, *Coll. Letters*, VI. 140–1.

70. O'Rourke, *Thomas Hardy: His Secretary Remembers* (Beaminster: Toucan Press, 1965), 31.

71. TH draft to L. S. Amery, 19 Dec. 1926, *Coll. Letters*, VII. 53; TH note on letter from J. L. Edmonson of 19 Mar. 1924 (DCM).

72. TH to F. Macmillan, 22 Nov. 1922, *Coll. Letters*, VI. 168–9.

73. TH draft to A. M. Parratt, 17 Nov. 1924, *Coll. Letters*, VI. 286–7.

74. TH to Walter Drew, 30 Oct. 1920, *Coll. Letters*, VI. 44.

75. TH draft for telegram, 8 Oct. 1926 (DCM).

76. See, e.g., TH to Lucy Clifford, 15 June 1923, *Coll. Letters*, VI. 199.

77. See, e.g., TH to St John Ervine, 8 July 1925, *Coll. Letters*, VI. 332.

78. See Ann Thwaite, *Edmund Gosse: A Literary Landscape, 1849–1928* (London: Secker & Warburg, 1984), following 440.

79. TH to J. J. Foster, 23 Dec. 1920, *Coll. Letters*, VI. 58.

80. TH to Dorothy Bosanquet, 19 May 1921, *Coll. Letters*, VI. 87.

81. TH to Jane Popham, 6 Oct. 1922, *Coll. Letters*, VI. 160.

82. Gosse to H. J. C. Grierson, 26 Sept. 1927, in Evan Charteris, *The Life and Letters of Sir Edmund Gosse* (London: William Heinemann, 1931), 502; Charteris's reading 'a deficiency' has been corrected to 'any deficiency' from the original letter at Leeds.

83. Purdy, conversations notebooks (Beinecke).

84. Marjorie Lilly, 'The Mr Hardy I Knew', *Thomas Hardy Society Review*, 1, iv (1978), 103.

85. *Poetical Works*, III. 309.

86. Hynes provides a useful listing of such poems: *Poetical Works*, III. 354–64.

87. See Purdy, *Bibliographical Study*, 242, and facing illustration.

88. Purdy, *Bibliographical Study*, 258.

89. TH to J. M. Murry, 2 Mar. 1919, *Coll. Letters*, V. 297.

90. TH to E. Pound, 28 Nov. 1920, *Coll. Letters*, VI. 47.
91. *Poetical Works*, II. 336, 363–5.
92. *Life and Work*, 478; the original version of this note in FEH's '1927' diary (DCM) reads slightly differently. For the poem—dated 1877 in the MS of *Winter Words* (Queen's College, Oxford) though not in the volume itself—see *Poetical Works*, III. 174.
93. TH to Sassoon, 15 Jan. 1920, *Coll. Letters*, VI. 3.
94. *Poetical Works*, II. 59, 56, 65, 55.
95. *Life and Work*, 408.
96. See Dennis Taylor's discussion of the genesis of this poem in *Hardy's Poetry, 1860–1928*, 2nd edn. (Basingstoke: Macmillan Press, 1989), 88–93. For TH's notes, see Millgate, *Biography*, 129; the textbook itself, Charles Lackmann's *Specimens of German Prose* (Beinecke), was still in Hardy's library at the time of his death.
97. 26 Sept. 1911, *Coll. Letters*, IV. 175. Lea did not in fact identify the setting of 'The Duchess of Hamptonshire', the penultimate story in *A Group of Noble Dames*.
98. Her 'Nomenclature' notebook is in DCM.
99. R. R. Bowker's diary, quoted in E. McClung Fleming, *R. R. Bowker: Militant Liberal* (Norman: Univ. of Oklahoma Press, 1952), 146.
100. Aaron Shenley, *A System of Water-Colour Painting*; Hardy's copy (Beinecke), not a first edition, was published in London in 1857.
101. *Life and Work*, 238.
102. See Millgate, *Biography*, 89–90.
103. 7 May 1919, *Coll. Letters*, V. 303–4.
104. *Poetical Works*, II. 208.
105. *Poetical Works*, II. 25–7.
106. FEH to Cockerell, 17 Sept. 1916 (Beinecke). For TH's encounter at Stinsford with a ghost in 18th-century dress, see FEH to Cockerell, 27 Dec. 1919 (Beinecke), extracted in *Friends of a Lifetime: Letters to Sydney Carlyle Cockerell*, ed. Viola Meynell (London: Jonathan Cape, 1940), 305.
107. *The Letters of T. E. Lawrence*, ed. David Garnett (London: Jonathan Cape, 1938), 474.
108. *Letters of T. E. Lawrence*, 429.
109. I am grateful to Mr Stephen Poulter for drawing attention to my erroneous reference in *Biography* (53) to TH's having purchased his *leather* writing case from Treves's mother.
110. Purdy, conversations notebooks (Beinecke).
111. Almost all the objects mentioned in this paragraph are now in DCM.
112. TH to A. C. Benson, 27 Sept. 1924, *Coll. Letters*, VI. 276; see also Elliott Felkin, 'Days with Thomas Hardy', *Encounter*, 18, iv (April 1962), 32–3.

113. See Millgate, *Biography*, 569.
114. *Poetical Works*, III. 157.

FLORENCE HARDY

1. Sydney Carlyle Cockerell (SCC in subsequent notes), diary (BL).
2. Mann himself always spoke of having been still in the house when the crisis occurred, but SCC's diary and the recollections of the servant, Nellie Titterington, who was within earshot in an adjoining room, make it clear that he had left and had to be called back: E. E. T[itterington], *The Domestic Life of Thomas Hardy (1921–1928)* (Beaminster: Toucan Press, 1963), 16.
3. See above, pp. 129–30.
4. MS draft, chap. 38 of 'Life' (DCM).
5. Dorothy Allhusen, interviewed by Harold Hoffman (Hoffman papers, Miami Univ. of Ohio).
6. Irene Cooper Willis, 'Thomas Hardy' typescript (Colby); this passage is absent from the version published in the *Colby Library Quarterly*, 9 (March 1971), 266–79.
7. Titterington, *Domestic Life*, 16; Richard L. Purdy, notes on conversation with Eva Dugdale (Beinecke; all Beinecke references in this chapter are to materials formerly in the collection of Richard L. Purdy).
8. SCC diary, 12 Jan. 1928 (BL).
9. Purdy, conversation with the author.
10. FEH wrote to Gosse, 21 Feb. 1928 (Leeds), to explain that Hardy had expected to live to be over 90 and assumed that by then the role of literary executor would be beyond Gosse's strength; Gosse in fact died less than three months later, on 16 May 1928.
11. *The Times*, 7 May 1920, 9.
12. FEH to Rebekah Owen, 26 Oct. and 3 Nov. 1916 (Colby).
13. Richard Little Purdy, *Thomas Hardy: A Bibliographical Study* (1954; Oxford: at the Clarendon Press, 1968), 349–50.
14. SCC diary, 30 June 1915 (BL).
15. FEH telegram to SCC, 9 Jan. 1928 (Beinecke); FEH's letter to SCC of 8 Jan. 1928 (Beinecke) had already suggested that he should come if he thought it 'well' to do so.
16. Thomas Hardy, *The Life and Work of Thomas Hardy*, ed. Michael Millgate (London: Macmillan, 1984), 480. There is no evidence to support the suggestion that Siegfried Sassoon was also present: see *Thomas Hardy Society Newsletter* no. 14 (April/May 1973), 4–5.

17. Cockerell's account, quoted in Wilfrid Blunt, *Cockerell* (London: Hamish Hamilton, 1964), 223, may perhaps be questioned, but see Robert Gittings and Jo Manton, *The Second Mrs Hardy* (London: Heinemann, 1979), 116–21.

18. SCC to Kate Cockerell, 11 Jan. 1928 (Beinecke).

19. All quotations of TH's will are from a photocopy of the original document, but the texts of TH's, FEH's, and Kate Hardy's wills are accessible in *Thomas Hardy's Will and Other Wills of His Family* (St Peter Port, Guernsey: Toucan Press, 1967).

20. SCC to K. Cockerell, 12 Jan. 1928 (Beinecke).

21. SCC's diary, 12 Jan. 1928 (BL), refers to his conversations with Barrie at Max Gate on the 10th.

22. Barrie to SCC, 12 Jan. 1928 (Pierpont Morgan), quoted in *Friends of a Lifetime: Letters to Sydney Carlyle Cockerell*, ed. Viola Meynell (London: Jonathan Cape, 1940), 315–16.

23. TH to Gosse, 23 May 1909, *The Collected Letters of Thomas Hardy*, ed. Richard L. Purdy and Michael Millgate, 7 vols. (Oxford: Clarendon Press, 1978–88), IV. 23.

24. *The Times*, 14 July 1924, 15.

25. *The Complete Poetical Works of Thomas Hardy*, ed. Samuel Hynes, 3 vols. to date (Oxford: Clarendon Press, 1982–5), III. 123–4.

26. For example, the Dean of Canterbury, 16 Jan. 1928, 13; J. H. Morgan, 19 Jan. 1928, 8.

27. Draft of Bartelot to Norris, 18 Jan. 1928 (Mrs R. M. G. Voremberg); I am indebted to Dr James Gibson for this information.

28. Arnold Bennett wrote angrily on this topic in letters to the editor of the *Daily Express* (17 Jan. 1928, 1–2, and 19 Jan. 1928, 9); messages of condolence from the King and the Prince of Wales did, however, arrive at Max Gate on 12 January (*The Times*, 13 Jan. 1928, 13), and it would in any case appear that the Royal family only very exceptionally attend the funerals of those who are not themselves family members.

29. Katharine Hardy, diary, 13 Jan. 1928 (Lock); Basil Willey, visiting Max Gate in 1930, reported FEH as complaining 'bitterly' about the funeral arrangements and as believing that TH 'would have been horrified at the idea of cremation': *Cambridge and Other Memories 1920–1953* (London: Chatto & Windus, 1966), 55.

30. *The Times Literary Supplement*, 22 Jan. 1954, 57.

31. KH diary, 12 Jan. 1928 (Lock).

32. Berg. TH's designs for his own tombstone and the tombstones of family members are in DCM and the collection of Frederick B. Adams.

33. 28 May 1909, *Coll. Letters*, IV. 26.

34. *Letters of J. M. Barrie*, ed. Viola Meynell (London: Peter Davies, 1942), 175.

35. *Daily Mail*, 13 Jan. 1928, 9.

36. Willey, *Cambridge*, 55; SCC's diary for 12 January (BL) records that KH was 'not averse' to the Abbey.

37. SCC diary, 12 Jan. 1928 (BL).

38. *Daily Telegraph*, 14 Jan. 1928, 14; she herself died a few weeks later.

39. SCC diary (BL).

40. *Dorset County Chronicle*, 19 Jan. 1928, 4.

41. SCC told Purdy (conversations notebooks, Beinecke) that FEH originated the idea but that an unopened copy of G. Dru Drury's pamphlet, *Heart Burials and Some Purbeck Marble Heart-Shrines* (Dorchester, 1927), off-printed from the current volume of the *Proceedings of the Dorset Natural History and Antiquarian Field Club*, was found among the mail received by TH shortly before his death; the report of the original lecture in the *Dorset County Chronicle*, 16 Dec. 1926, 8, does not include a full listing of those present.

42. *Daily Telegraph*, 14 Jan. 1928, 11.

43. Ann Thwaite, *Edmund Gosse: A Literary Landscape, 1849–1928* (London: Secker & Warburg, 1984), 508.

44. Clodd to J. M. Bulloch, 14 Jan. 1928 (Texas).

45. Purdy, conversations notebooks (Beinecke); in a letter of 8 Mar. 1928 (Beinecke) FEH told SCC that TH's cousin, Teresa Hardy, had died angry with her for permitting the Abbey and heart burials.

46. *The Times*, 17 Jan. 1928, 16, 15.

47. *The Letters of T. E. Lawrence*, ed. David Garnett (London: Jonathan Cape, 1938), 582.

48. Blunt, *Cockerell*, 218; SCC diary, 16 Jan. 1928 (BL).

49. KH diary, 16 Jan. 1928 (Lock collection).

50. FEH to Marie Stopes, 16 Sept. 1928 (BL).

51. SCC, draft 'Memorandum on Mrs Hardy's letters to Mr Hornby 18 May & 30 May 1929' (Beinecke).

52. *The Times*, 17 Jan. 1928, 15. SCC's 'Memorandum' (Beinecke) claims that FEH 'particularly asked that Rainbarrows should be mentioned'.

53. A letter to this effect appeared in *The Times*, 19 Jan. 1928, 8, over the signature of H. H. Brindley, a Cambridge friend of Hardy's who had written knowledgeably about the Wessex landscape: see his 'Wessex Books', *Cambridge Review*, 2 and 9 Feb. 1905, 168, 182, and *Coll. Letters*, VII. 146–7.

54. SCC diary, 22 Jan. 1928 (BL).

55. SCC diary, 23 Jan. 1928 (BL.).

56. *The Times*, 27 Feb. 1928, 14.
57. *The Times*, 27 Feb. 1928, 14; the names of Housman and Masefield were added later: *The Times*, 21 Mar. 1928, 19, and 4 Apr. 1928, 17.
58. *The Times*, 8 Mar. 1928, 19; 21 Mar., 19; 4 Apr., 17; 2 May, 16; 26 Sept., 12; 3 Oct., 14. The specific sum of £1,268.19.9 reported to the Thomas Hardy Memorial Committee in May 1929 (Memorial Committee Minute Book, DCM) included £200 subsequently contributed by FEH herself: FEH to SCC, 19 Apr. 1929 (Beinecke).
59. *The Times*, 3 Oct. 1928, 14; see also *The Times*, 30 Mar. 1929, 9. The birthplace is now the property of the National Trust.
60. FEH to SCC, 22 Oct. 1928 (Beinecke).
61. FEH to SCC, 22 Oct. 1928 and 12 Apr. 1929 (Beinecke).
62. FEH to SCC, 19 Apr. 1929 (Beinecke). At a meeting of the Memorial Committee in September 1929, however, KH offered to supply an additional £800 that was then, mistakenly, believed to be needed (Minute Book, DCM).
63. *The Times*, 27 Oct. 1928, 13.
64. FEH to SCC, 12 and 19 Apr. 1929 (Beinecke).
65. *The Times*, 30 Mar. 1929, 9.
66. FEH to SCC, 19 Apr. 1929 (Beinecke).
67. FEH to E. Haigh Roscoe, 4 Apr. 1929 (Beinecke); a spelling error has been corrected.
68. Beinecke.
69. Typed copy, 'T. E. Shaw' to Hornby, 22 May 1929 (Beinecke), partly quoted in Blunt, *Cockerell*, 220.
70. Minute Book (DCM); SCC diary, 15 May 1929 (BL).
71. Minute Book (DCM).
72. SCC diary, 12 Apr. 1929 (BL).
73. Hornby to SCC, 19 July 1929 (Beinecke); SCC draft to Hornby, 21 July 1929 (Beinecke).
74. Draft (or copy) of revised version of SCC's 'Memorandum on Mrs Hardy's letters to Mr Hornby 18 May & 30 May 1929' (Beinecke).
75. Drafts, SCC to Hornby, 21 July and 23 July 1929 (Beinecke).
76. Minute Book (DCM). When a nearby householder objected to the location first chosen, at the SE corner of the crossroads, the site was changed to the NE corner, but it was apparently to another site altogether that, as FEH told SCC on 19 Apr. 1929 (Beinecke), both she and Kate Hardy had objected because it would have necessitated the removal both of a handsome group of trees and an existing underground public convenience: 'the idea of a statue standing where a lavatory used to be is unpleasant to her, & to me, perhaps absurdly, but there it is.'

77. Typed copy, Hornby to Kennington, 17 Sept. 1929 (Beinecke), and Kennington to Hornby, 19 Sept. 1929 (Beinecke).

78. Also present were Walter de la Mare, TH's ancient friend Sir George Douglas, and Marie Stopes, who had recently established a local history museum in 'Avice's Cottage' on the Isle of Portland: *Dorset County Chronicle*, 3 Sept. 1931, 5; photographs of the occasion appeared a week later, 10 Sept. 1931, 4. See also *Order of Proceedings at the Unveiling of the Memorial Statue of Thomas Hardy, O.M.* (Dorchester, 1931).

79. A. C. Cox, 'The Hardy Statue', *Dorset County Chronicle*, 3 Sept. 1931, 5; the allusion in 'man of Merit' is to Barrie's membership of the Order of Merit. Cox had been one of the 'Hardy Players', members of the Dorchester Debating and Dramatic Society who performed dramatizations of Hardy novels between 1908 and 1924.

80. *The Times*, 27 Dec. 1928, 14, FEH and KH having driven down to Cornwall on 12 Sept. 1928 to make the arrangements (KH diary, Lock).

81. KH diary, 21 Nov. 1930 (Lock); G. H. Moule, *Stinsford Church and Parish* (1940; Dorchester, 1949), 2, 25.

82. The formal dedication of the organ, however, did not take place until 9 Sept. 1931: KH diary, 9 Sept. 1931 (Lock); *Dorset County Chronicle*, 17 Sept. 1931, 3.

83. Richard L. Purdy, comp., *Thomas Hardy, O.M. 1840–1928: Catalogue of a Memorial Exhibition of First Editions, Autograph Letters and Manuscripts* (New Haven: Yale Univ. Library, 1928).

84. *Dorset County Chronicle*, 23 Apr. 1931, 3; KH diary, 16 Apr. 1931 (Lock). *A Thomas Hardy Memorial* (Daylesford, PA: privately printed, 1931), a booklet produced by Newton both to record the occasion and help meet its costs, makes it clear that FEH had co-operated with the project from an early stage.

85. Draft, SCC to FEH, 28 Mar. 1931 (Beinecke).

86. *The Times*, 27 Feb. 1928, 14.

87. *Daily News*, 27 Feb. 1928, 7.

88. *Daily News*, 27 Feb. 1928, 7; will, clause 4.

89. *Sunday Express*, 26 Feb. 1928, 12. The column is unsigned.

90. See, e.g., the *Daily News*, 27 Feb. 1928; will, clause 6.

91. On 8 Mar. 1928 FEH wrote to Gordon Gifford, 'What Kate & Henry Hardy will do with their £30,000. [*sic*] I do not know—living as they do' (Mrs L. Skinner).

92. FEH to SCC, 8 Feb. 1928 (Beinecke).

93. FEH to G. Gifford, 8 Mar. 1928 (Mrs L. Skinner).

94. FEH to R. Owen, 30 Dec. 1915 (Colby); and see Michael Millgate,

Thomas Hardy: A Biography (Oxford: Oxford Univ. Press, 1982), 506–7.

95. Millgate, *Biography*, 504–5.
96. Figures quoted to SCC by Daniel Macmillan, 25 Apr. 1935 (Beinecke), show that for the year ending 30 June 1928 the total was just over £5,456, for the year ending 30 June 1934 just over £1,103.
97. Will, clause 6.
98. She seems, for example, to have obtained the consent of Henry and Kate Hardy to an arrangement by which her lifetime interest in Hardy's royalties could be translated into a bequest at the time of her death: FEH to SCC, 22 Oct. 1928 (Beinecke).
99. SCC was already an executor of the wills of William Morris and Wilfrid Scawen Blunt.
100. Another potential conflict between written and oral instructions was created by Hardy's Clause 9 bequest to his 'Executors' (not, here, his 'Literary Executors') of books for presentation to particular friends, either as prescribed in a list he would leave or, in the absence of such a list, as determined by 'such books and friends as my Wife may judge to have been intended by me for such presentations'.
101. In the original will this is in fact the first of two clauses numbered 14.
102. See *The Personal Notebooks of Thomas Hardy*, ed. Richard H. Taylor (London: Macmillan, 1978), 100, nn. 488 and 489, and 102, n. 506, for Taylor's suggestion that the final, tipped-in leaves of the 'Memoranda II' notebook probably date from the early summer of 1922.
103. See below, and Purdy, *Bibliographical Study*, 22.
104. See below, and Meynell, *Friends of a Lifetime*, 295.
105. Purdy, conversations notebooks (Beinecke).
106. SCC diary, 21 Jan. 1928 (BL).
107. SCC diary, 5 Feb. 1928 (BL). The 'accumulated rubbish' perhaps fuelled one of the bonfires described by the Max Gate gardener as occurring shortly after TH's death: Bertie Norman Stephens, *Thomas Hardy in His Garden* (Beaminster: Toucan Press, 1963), 15–16.
108. SCC diary, 24 Mar. 1928 (BL); SCC letter, 'Hardy's Library', *The Times Literary Supplement*, 17 Sept. 1938, 598.
109. SCC diary, 22 Jan. 1928 (BL).
110. SCC to Laurence Housman, 21 Mar. 1937, partly quoted in John Carter, 'A Further Note on A. E. Housman', *The Times Literary Supplement*, 14 Mar. 1968, 278; SCC to Purdy, 2 Nov. 1948 (Millgate).
111. SCC diary, 14 Dec. 1928 (BL).
112. SCC to Purdy, 2 Nov. 1948 (Millgate).
113. SCC to Purdy, 23 Oct. 1943 (Millgate).

114. Though the letter is dated 1927, its contents make it clear that 1928 was intended (BL).
115. See, for example, *Personal Notebooks*, 3.
116. 28 Aug. 1914, *Coll. Letters*, V. 45.
117. Carter, 'Further Note', 278.
118. SCC to Purdy, 23 Oct. 1943 (Millgate).
119. Presented to Richard Purdy, at FEH's wish, after her death and now in Beinecke.
120. *The Literary Notebooks of Thomas Hardy*, ed. Lennart A. Björk, 2 vols. (London: Macmillan, 1985).
121. *The Architectural Notebook of Thomas Hardy*, ed. C. J. P. Beatty (Dorchester: Dorset Natural History and Archaeological Society, 1966).
122. DCM.
123. 'Record of Manuscripts' (Macmillan Papers, BL); copies, D. Macmillan to FEH, 31 Jan. and 7 Feb. 1928 (Macmillan letterbooks, BL). A copy of Whibley's report is among the Macmillan papers in the Manuscripts Division of the New York Public Library.
124. 'Record of Manuscripts' (BL); copy, D. Macmillan to FEH, 21 Feb. 1928 (Macmillan letterbooks, BL); FEH to D. Macmillan, 22 Feb. 1928 (BL).
125. DCM.
126. DCM; in a letter of 17 Apr. 1928 (King's College, Cambridge) FEH thanks Forster for offering to look up the wheelbarrow episode in the *Graphic*'s serialization of *Tess of the d'Urbervilles* and promises to send a copy of 'the biography' within a few days.
127. SCC diary, 21 Mar. 1928 (BL); *Letters of J. M. Barrie*, 152.
128. FEH to D. Macmillan, 28 Mar. 1928 (BL); Barrie's letter to FEH, 26 Mar. 1928 (DCM), makes it possible to identify these and other additions to the 'Life' typescripts as having been made well after TH's death.
129. FEH to D. Macmillan, 28 Mar. 1928 (BL).
130. SCC diary, 29 June 1928 (BL).
131. FEH to Forster, 2 July 1928 (King's College, Cambridge).
132. SCC diary, 1 July 1928 (BL).
133. Relevant here are, e.g., SCC to Daniel Macmillan, 2 Mar. and 11 May 1928 (supplementary Macmillan archive, purchased July 1990, BL), and 22 Mar. 1928 (draft, Beinecke).
134. SCC to G. H. Thring, 26 Jan. 1928 (BL).
135. Barrie to SCC, 4 Mar. 1928 (NLS).
136. Draft (or copy), SCC to Barrie, 5 Mar. 1928 (Beinecke).
137. FEH to SCC, 8 Mar. 1928 (Beinecke).
138. FEH to SCC, 15 Apr. 1928 (Beinecke).

139. A fuller account is given in Pamela Dalziel's forthcoming Clarendon Press edition of Hardy's *Excluded and Collaborative Stories*.
140. FEH to SCC, 16 Jan. 1929 (Beinecke).
141. Several of her letters granting such permissions are in the BBC archives.
142. FEH to D. Macmillan, 6 Mar. 1935 (BL). The story had previously appeared only in magazines, and its American version had never been copyrighted.
143. *The Times*, 4 Mar. 1935, 15, and, for the US edition, 1 Mar. 1935, 14.
144. Draft of SCC to FEH, 4 Mar. 1935 (Beinecke), quoted in Blunt, *Cockerell*, 222.
145. *The Times Literary Supplement*, 14 Mar. 1935, 160.
146. FEH to D. Macmillan, 10 May 1935 (BL). Her refusal to have anything more to do with Cockerell was expressed even more strongly in a letter to Macmillan of 24 Apr. 1935 (BL).
147. Markings by SCC on a statement of royalties sent him by Daniel Macmillan on 25 Apr. 1935 (Beinecke) clearly indicate that he felt entitled to a share of the royalties from 11 Jan. 1931 onwards.
148. Medley to SCC, 27 May 1935 (Beinecke); will, clause 21.
149. Medley to SCC, 27 May 1935 (Beinecke).
150. Richard Purdy heard both sides: see the cited references to his conversations with FEH and to the letters he received from SCC.
151. Blunt (quoting SCC), *Cockerell*, 223.
152. Carbon typescript, Purdy to Blunt, 9 Nov. 1964 (Millgate).
153. Blunt, *Cockerell*, 261.
154. Blunt to Purdy, 31 Oct. 1964 (Millgate).
155. Blunt, *Cockerell*, 223; Blunt, *Cockerell* (New York: Alfred A. Knopf, 1965), 223.
156. Carbon typescript, Purdy to Blunt, 9 Nov. 1964 (Millgate).
157. FEH to SCC, 2 Feb. 1920 (Beinecke).
158. Irene Cooper Willis, typescript, 'Copied from pencil notebook' (Boatwright Library, Univ. of Richmond).
159. Rutland wrote a substantial study of Hardy's books and a short biography; Adams, who became the director of the Pierpont Morgan Library, is best known in the Hardy field as a distinguished and discriminating scholar-collector; Purdy's bibliography remains the keystone of Hardy scholarship; while Henry Reed's researches resulted not in an academic study but in the brilliantly sardonic radio play, *A Very Great Man Indeed*, the starting point for his Hilda Tablet series.
160. Peter Gunn, *Vernon Lee* (London: Oxford Univ. Press, 1964), ix, xi; Willis, ed., *Vernon Lee's Letters* (privately printed, 1937), i.

161. *Vernon Lee's Letters*, i.
162. *Vernon Lee's Letters*, v.
163. Gunn, *Vernon Lee*, x. At her death in 1970 Irene Cooper Willis left all the Vernon Lee copyrights, together with the Vernon Lee papers in her possession, to Colby College.
164. Quotations in this paragraph are from a photocopy of the original will, but see also *Thomas Hardy's Will and Other Wills of His Family*, 5–12.
165. The quotation is from a typed transcription of KH's will supplied by Somerset House, but see also *Thomas Hardy's Will and Other Wills of His Family*, 12–14. KH directed that the income the Trust derived from renting Max Gate should be applied to the maintenance of the property itself and to the 'preservation and protection' of the birthplace (her own as well as TH's) at Higher Bockhampton.
166. Willis to SCC, 24 July 1945 (Victoria and Albert Museum).
167. Will, clauses 8(a) and 8(b).
168. *The Times*, 11 May 1939, 17. As then set up, the study was viewed through a reproduction of the actual study window at Max Gate; the present plate glass window was installed when the study was moved from the south end of the Museum to its present location at the north end.
169. *The Times*, 10 May 1939, 9.
170. TH had presented the MS of *The Mayor of Casterbridge* to the Museum in his lifetime.
171. DCM records.
172. All now in the collection of Frederick B. Adams.
173. Beinecke.
174. Texas.
175. Beinecke.
176. See, for example, the inscribed first editions of *The Hand of Ethelberta* and *The Woodlanders* listed as lots 73 and 74 in the Hodgson auction catalogue, 26 May 1938; the contents of the catalogue are reproduced in J. Stevens Cox, ed., *The Library of Thomas Hardy, O.M.* (St Peter Port, Guernsey: Toucan Press, 1969).
177. Purdy, conversation with the author.
178. Willis to Hodgson & Co., 6 Jan. 1938 (Hodgson papers, BL).
179. Now in DCM and Beinecke, respectively.
180. Hy. Duke & Son to Hodgson & Co., 6 Nov. 1937 (Hodgson papers, BL).
181. The only extended list now among the Hodgson papers in BL was made for probate purposes and is confined to the books assigned to the Dorset County Museum.
182. BL: C.134.bb.1/1–46.

183. *The Times Literary Supplement*, 17 Sept. 1938, 598.
184. J. Q. Hodgson to SCC, 24 Sept. 1938 (Beinecke).

TESTAMENTARY ACTS

1. W. Somerset Maugham, *Cakes and Ale, or The Skeleton in the Cupboard* (London: William Heinemann, 1930), 242.
2. Maugham, *Cakes and Ale*, 28.
3. Maugham, *Cakes and Ale*, 126–7.
4. Maugham, *Cakes and Ale*, 124, 126; text reads 'the sixties'.
5. Kenneth Clark, *The Artist Grows Old* (The Rede Lecture 1970) (Cambridge: at the University Press, 1972), 5.
6. Clark, *Artist*, 5.
7. Clark, *Artist*, 4–5; *The Complete Poetical Works of Thomas Hardy*, ed. Samuel Hynes, 3 vols. to date (Oxford: Clarendon Press, 1982–5), II. 481–4.
8. Quoted in James Gindin, *John Galsworthy's Life and Art: An Alien's Fortress* (Ann Arbor: Univ. of Michigan Press, 1987), 427.
9. Clark, *Artist*, 6, 9. Alternative, if less trenchant, views of artists and writers in old age are offered in Stuart F. Spicker *et al.*, eds., *Aging and the Elderly: Humanistic Perspectives in Gerontology* (Atlantic Highlands: Humanities Press, 1978). See also Kathleen Woodward, *Aging and its Discontents: Freud and Other Fictions* (Bloomington: Indiana Univ. Press, 1991).
10. Eliot, 'Yeats' (1940), in *On Poetry and Poets* (London: Faber & Faber, 1957), 253, 257.
11. For relevant observations on some recent poets, including Eliot himself, see Kathleen Woodward, *At Last, the Real Distinguished Thing: The Late Poems of Eliot, Pound, Stevens, and Williams* (Columbus, OH: Ohio State Univ. Press, 1980).
12. *The Mayor of Casterbridge* (London: Macmillan, 1912), 138, 137. See also TH's poem 'Her Death and After' and his story 'Netty Sargent's Copyhold'.
13. Faulkner, *Essays, Speeches and Public Letters*, ed. James B. Meriwether (New York: Random House, 1965), 72, 66. The essay first appeared in *Harper's Magazine*, July 1955. See Stephen Hahn, 'William Faulkner on Privacy', *Columbia Library Columns*, 38, iii (May 1989), 27–35, and the introduction to *Lion in the Garden: Interviews with William Faulkner 1926–1962*, ed. James B. Meriwether and Michael Millgate (New York: Random House, 1968), ix–xv.
14. Shaw to F. Hardy, 27 Jan. 1928, in Bernard Shaw, *Collected Letters*

1926–1950, ed. Dan H. Laurence (London: Max Reinhardt, 1988), 85.

15. See Stephen B. Oates's 'Prologue' to Oates, ed., *Biography as High Adventure: Life-Writers Speak on Their Art* (Amherst: Univ. of Massachusetts Press, 1986), xi.

16. *Letters of Henry Adams (1892–1918)*, ed. Worthington Chauncey Ford (Boston: Houghton, Mifflin, 1938), II. 495.

17. Barnes, 'The Follies of Writer Worship', *New York Times Book Review*, 17 Feb. 1985, 16; *Flaubert's Parrot* was published in London by Jonathan Cape in 1984.

18. Frayn, *The Trick of It* (London: Viking, 1989).

19. Simone de Beauvoir, *Lettres à Sartre*, ed. Sylvie Le Bon de Beauvoir (Paris: Gallimard, 1990), 10; Diane Middlebrook, 'Method in the Madness: Anne Sexton and the Literary Uses of Psychotherapy', *The Times Literary Supplement*, 18 Oct. 1991, 13–14; Marr, *Patrick White: A Life* (London: Jonathan Cape, 1991), 646.

20. R. W. B. Lewis, *Edith Wharton: A Biography* (New York: Harper & Row, 1975), xi; Lubbock, *Portrait of Edith Wharton* (London: Jonathan Cape, 1947). Lewis calls the *Portrait* 'subtly denigrating' (297) and observes that since Wharton had broken off her friendship with Lubbock by the time of her death it is remarkable that he should have been invited by her executor, Gaillard Lapsley, to undertake the memoir at all (515–16).

21. See, for example, Quentin Anderson, introd., *Walt Whitman's Autograph Revision of the Analysis of Leaves of Grass (for Dr. R. M. Bucke's Walt Whitman)* (New York: New York Univ. Press, 1974).

22. Gosse, 'A Note on Walt Whitman', *New Review*, 10 (April 1894), 451; quoted in Gosse, *Portraits from Life*, ed. Ann Thwaite (Aldershot: Scolar Press, 1991), 92. See also John C. Brodrick, 'The Greatest Whitman Collector and the Greatest Whitman Collection', *Library of Congress Quarterly Journal*, 27 (April 1970), 109–28, not least for its confirmatory photograph (110) of the bedroom itself.

23. Justin Kaplan, *Walt Whitman: A Life* (New York: Simon & Schuster, 1980), 19.

24. *Boswell's Life of Johnson*, ed. George Birkbeck Hill, rev. L. F. Powell, 6 vols. (Oxford: at the Clarendon Press, 1934–50), IV. 404–5. More recent commentators have suggested that Johnson well knew what he was doing, especially in so far as his diary was concerned.

25. Hilary Spurling, *Ivy: The Life of I. Compton-Burnett* (New York: Columbia Univ. Press, 1986), xii. This is a reprinting in one volume of the two volumes separately published in England in 1974 and 1984.

26. See Peter Ackroyd, *T. S. Eliot: A Life* (New York: Simon & Schuster,

1984), 10: 'I am forbidden by the Eliot estate to quote from Eliot's published work, except for purposes of fair comment in a critical context, or to quote from Eliot's unpublished work or correspondence.'

27. The situation is described in some detail in *The Letters of T. S. Eliot. Volume I: 1898–1922*, ed. Valerie Eliot (San Diego: Harcourt Brace Jovanovich, 1988), xvi–xvii.

28. The request was not, however, incorporated into his will: see Humphrey Carpenter, *W. H. Auden: A Biography* (London: George Allen & Unwin, 1981), 435.

29. Will, dated 29 Apr. 1943; copy kindly provided by Professor James Woodress.

30. James Woodress, *Willa Cather: A Literary Life* (Lincoln: Univ. of Nebraska Press, 1987), xiv.

31. Ibid.

32. Quoted at the conclusion of the second volume of Brian Boyd's fine biography, *Vladimir Nabokov: The American Years* (Princeton, NJ: Princeton Univ. Press, 1991), 663.

33. *Essays, Speeches*, 114, 206.

34. See, e.g., *Lion in the Garden*, 238, 253, 227.

35. Whitman, *Complete Poetry and Collected Prose* (New York: Library of America, 1982), 639.

36. Benjamin, *Illuminations*, ed. Hannah Arendt (New York: Harcourt, Brace & World, 1968), 94.

37. Matthew 26: 28; Mark 14: 24; Luke 22: 20.

38. *OED*.

39. *The Letters of John Keats 1814–21*, ed. Hyder Edward Rollins, 2 vols. (Cambridge: at the University Press, 1958), II. 319.

40. Morson, 'Tolstoy's Absolute Language', in Morson, ed., *Bakhtin: Essays and Dialogues on His Work* (Chicago: Univ. of Chicago Press, 1986), 136–7. For the domestic turbulence surrounding Tolstoy's final will see Ernest J. Simmons, *Leo Tolstoy* (Boston: Little, Brown, 1946), 746–50.

41. Willis typescript, 'Copied from pencil notebook' (Boatwright Library, Univ. of Richmond).

42. He is said to have had 1,200 copies printed at his own cost and stored away in advance of his death: Ernest Newman, foreword to *Memoirs of Hector Berlioz from 1803 to 1865* (1932; New York: Dover Publications, 1966), vii.

43. *Boswell's Life of Johnson*, IV. 413.

44. *Boswell's Life of Johnson*, IV. 402, n. 2.

45. Details of Charlotte Shaw's will from Janet Dunbar, *Mrs G.B.S.: A Biographical Portrait of Charlotte Shaw* (London: George G. Harrap, 1963), 314–16; other wills from Somerset House.

46. See William M. Clarke, *The Secret Life of Wilkie Collins* (London: W. H. Allen, 1988).

47. Review of 'Bookmark' (BBC2 programme), *The Times Literary Supplement*, 19–25 Oct. 1990, 1129; will (Somerset House); and Spurling, *Ivy*, 544.

48. See Robert Lucas, *Frieda Lawrence: The Story of Frieda von Richthofen and D. H. Lawrence*, trans. Geoffrey Skelton (New York: Viking Press, 1973), 260–1, and *The Times*, 4 Nov. 1932, 4. Frieda Lawrence's solicitor, the 'famous lawyer' of her semi-fictionalized reminiscence of the affair, was the same Charles Douglas Medley on whom Florence Hardy learned to depend: see Frieda Lawrence, *The Memoirs and Correspondence*, ed. E. W. Tedlock, Jr (New York: Alfred A. Knopf, 1964), 113–19, 243 n.

49. Rose, *The Haunting of Sylvia Plath* (London: Virago Press, 1991), 65–113.

50. See, for example, *Selected Letters of William Faulkner*, ed. Joseph Blotner (New York: Random House, 1977), 362–4.

51. In *The Journals of Sylvia Plath* (New York: Dial Press, 1982) Frances McCullough is named as editor and Hughes as consulting editor. In the overall management of the estate Hughes has acted as executor, his sister, Olwyn Hughes, as literary executor.

52. Chester Kallman, Auden's literary executor and sole legatee, died some 16 months later without altering the will in which he had left everything to Auden. Since that will was now invalid the estate, including Auden's copyrights and royalties, passed to Kallman's next-of-kin, his octogenarian father, who then married a woman considerably younger than himself (Carpenter, *Auden*, 453–4). For the somewhat analogous long-term consequences of a single, perhaps little-considered, provision in Samuel L. Clemens's will, see two articles by Isabelle Budd, 'Twain's Will Be Done', *Mark Twain Journal*, 22 (Spring 1984), 34–9, and 'Clara Samossoud's Will', *Mark Twain Journal*, 25 (Spring 1987), 17–30.

53. *Henry James Letters*, ed. Leon Edel, 4 vols. (Cambridge, MA: Harvard Univ. Press, 1974–84), III. 499. James does, however, imply that he might have been willing to act as a literary executor.

54. Tim Hilton, 'Problem Parent', *The Times Literary Supplement*, 5 Apr. 1991, 20. The memoir itself was written by Guston's daughter.

55. Will, dated 17 July 1985 (Somerset House). See clause 7.ii ('shall be destroyed unread') in relation to clauses 7.i and 7.iv.

56. See, e.g., Nicolette Jones, 'Looking for Larkin', *Sunday Times*, 17 Feb. 1991, 'Books' section, 7, and Anthony Thwaite's introduction

to Larkin's *Collected Poems* (London: Marvell Press and Faber & Faber, 1988), xxii.

57. See Thomas Pinney, 'Kipling in the Libraries', *English Literature in Transition 1880–1920*, 29, i (1986), 89, and Barbara Rosenbaum, *Index of English Literary Manuscripts. Volume IV: 1800–1900, Part 2: Hardy–Lamb* (London: Mansell, 1990), 412–15. The manuscript of *Kim o' the 'Rishti*, for example, presented to the British Museum by Kipling himself in October 1925, is currently (in the British Library) accompanied by the statement: 'Under the terms of gift collation of the contents of this MS. is not allowed, nor may any photograph of it be taken.' According to Rosenbaum, *Index*, 414–15, the restrictions placed by Kipling's widow on her gift of the MS of *Stalky & Co.* to the Imperial Service College (now Haileybury School) have been judged to forbid access entirely.

58. James Anthony Froude, *Thomas Carlyle: A History of His Life in London, 1834–1881*, 2 vols. (New York: Charles Scribner's Sons, 1884), II. 403.

59. Froude, *Thomas Carlyle*, II. 404–5; see also Fred Kaplan, *Thomas Carlyle: A Biography* (Ithaca, NY: Cornell Univ. Press, 1983), 553–5. Froude's biography (of which the first part, also in two volumes, was published in 1882) has itself been a controversial document: see, e.g., David J. DeLaura, 'Thomas Carlyle', in DeLaura, ed., *Victorian Prose: A Guide to Research* (New York: Modern Language Association of America, 1973), 45–7, 51–4, and K. J. Fielding, 'Froude and Carlyle: Some New Considerations', in K. J. Fielding and Rodger L. Tarr, eds., *Carlyle Past and Present: A Collection of New Essays* (London: Vision Press, 1976), 239–69.

60. Will (Somerset House).

61. J. Kaplan, *Walt Whitman*, 49–52, 53–4; for a photograph see opp. 321.

62. J. Kaplan, *Walt Whitman*, 49–50. Whitman's letter to Bucke of 25–6 Dec. 1889 refers to the tomb as 'a plain massive stone temple' and indicates that the burial lot (20 ft. by 30 ft.) was a presentation to Whitman by the cemetery itself, then newly opened: Whitman, *The Correspondence. Volume IV: 1886–1889*, ed. Edwin Haviland Miller (New York: New York Univ. Press, 1969), 408.

63. Schorer, *Sinclair Lewis: An American Life* (New York: McGraw-Hill, 1961), 809.

64. W. A. Swanberg, *Dreiser* (New York: Charles Scribner's Sons, 1965), 524–5.

65. For the fate of Shelley's body—drowned, buried in quicklime, disinterred, cremated, the ashes buried and then reburied—see Newman Ivey White, *Shelley*, 2 vols. (New York: Alfred A. Knopf,

1940), II. 381–4; for the fate of his heart, see *The Letters of Mary Wollstonecraft Shelley*, ed. Betty T. Bennett, 3 vols. (Baltimore: Johns Hopkins Univ. Press, 1980–8), I. 255–6.

66. See A. Norman Jeffares, *W. B. Yeats: A New Biography* (London: Hutchinson, 1988), 364, n. 43; for the questions themselves see Diana Souhami, *Gluck, 1895–1978* (London: Pandora, 1988), 228–38.

67. See Harry T. Moore, *The Intelligent Heart: The Story of D. H. Lawrence* (New York: Farrar, Straus & Young, 1954), 440–1; Frieda Lawrence, *Memoirs*, 113; and esp. Lucas, *Frieda Lawrence*, 267–70. According to Lucas (270), Lawrence's ashes were actually mixed in with the sand and cement from which the altar was constructed, Mabel Dodge Luhan having threatened to scatter them once Frieda was dead.

68. In rather a different category were the two identical plaques recalling the birth of Thomas Arnold of Rugby long visible in and near Cowes, Isle of Wight, one on the house itself, the other on the brickworks where the plaques were fired.

69. *Lincoln Leader*, 22 July 1905, 8.

70. Sylvia Townsend Warner, *Letters*, ed. William Maxwell (London: Chatto & Windus, 1982), 222.

71. See Arthur Hobson Quinn, *Edgar Allan Poe: A Critical Biography* (New York: Appleton-Century-Crofts, 1941), 642–95.

72. For Willis and Vernon Lee see above, pp. 169–70. For Curtis Brown's 'Personal Note' see Ted Morgan, *Maugham* (New York: Simon & Schuster, 1980), vii–viii; Morgan's biography proved in fact to be controversial, and a subsequent biographer, Robert Calder, has characterized it as revealing 'an essential distaste for its subject': Calder, *Willie: The Life of W. Somerset Maugham* (London: Heinemann, 1989), xvi. Calder, unlike Morgan, was not permitted to quote from Maugham's correspondence, the current executor of the estate, the Royal Literary Fund, having decided that, as a beneficiary under Maugham's will, it has an obligation to observe that prohibition against the use of previously unpublished materials which Curtis Brown allowed Morgan to infringe (Calder, *Willie*, xvii–xviii).

73. Brod, 'Postscript to the First Edition' (1925), reprinted in Kafka, *The Trial* (New York: Alfred A. Knopf, 1957), 326–35.

74. It was perhaps a fear of damaging her specifically literary reputation which prompted Cather to include an absolute prohibition against the dramatization of any of her works for the theatre, radio, film, television, or any method of mechanical reproduction, whether 'now in existence or which may hereafter be discovered or perfected'.

75. Will (Somerset House); Shaw, making his will after his wife's death, named the Public Trustee as his first and sole executor.
76. See especially Richard J. Finneran, *Editing Yeats's Poems* (London: Macmillan, 1983) and *Editing Yeats's Poems: A Reconsideration* (Basingstoke: Macmillan, 1990); Warwick Gould, 'The Editor Takes Possession', *The Times Literary Supplement*, 29 June 1984, 731–3, together with the subsequent correspondence, beginning 3 Aug. 1984; and Gould's appendix to *Yeats's Poems*, ed. A. Norman Jeffares (London: Macmillan, 1989), 706–49.
77. Will (Somerset House).
78. Gill, *William Wordsworth: A Life* (Oxford: Clarendon Press, 1989), 389, 390; *The Letters of William and Dorothy Wordsworth*, ed. Ernest de Sélincourt: *The Later Years*, revised Alan G. Hill, 4 vols. (Oxford: Clarendon Press, 1978–88), III. 353. The letter shows the sureness of Wordsworth's bibliographical as well as textual control over his individual works.
79. Whitman, *Leaves of Grass* (Philadelphia: David McKay, 1891–2), 2. The 1891–2 *Leaves*, the end-point of a long developmental process, was not a true edition but a slightly modified impression of the 1881 edition supplemented by 'annexes' of additional poems and other materials.
80. Greg's influential essay, 'The Rationale of Copy-Text', is in W. W. Greg, *Collected Papers*, ed. J. C. Maxwell (Oxford: at the Clarendon Press, 1966), 374–91; for the development of policies derived from Greg, see G. Thomas Tanselle, 'Greg's Theory of Copy-Text and the Editing of American Literature', *Studies in Bibliography*, 28 (1975), 167–229. See also the convenient epitomization of Bowers's central tenets (as of the early 1960s) in his 'Textual Criticism', in James Thorpe, ed., *The Aims and Methods of Scholarship in Modern Languages and Literatures* (New York: Modern Language Association of America, 1963), 23–42, and the particularly accessible account of Tanselle's position in his *A Rationale of Textual Criticism* (Philadelphia: Univ. of Pennsylvania Press, 1989).
81. McLaverty, 'The Concept of Authorial Intention in Textual Criticism', *The Library*, 6th series, 6 (June 1984), 132.
82. Jerome J. McGann, Hershel Parker, and D. F. McKenzie have figured prominently among recent critics of the Greg–Bowers–Tanselle position, Tanselle himself and, more recently, T. H. Howard-Hill among its defenders: see, e.g., McGann, *A Critique of Modern Textual Criticism* (Chicago: Univ. of Chicago Press, 1983) and 'What Is Critical Editing?', in D. C. Greetham and W. Speed Hill, eds., *Text (Transactions of the Society for Textual Scholarship)* 5 (New York: AMS Press, 1991), 15–29; Parker, *Flawed Texts and Verbal Icons:*

Literary Authority in American Fiction (Evanston: Northwestern Univ. Press, 1984); McKenzie, *Bibliography and the Sociology of Texts* (London: The British Library, 1986); Tanselle, 'Historicism and Critical Editing', *Studies in Bibliography*, 39 (1986), 1–46, and 'Textual Criticism and Literary Sociology', *Studies in Bibliography*, 44 (1991), 83–143; and Howard-Hill, 'Theory and Praxis in the Social Approach to Editing', *Text* 5, 31–48.

83. Whitman, note to (first) 'Good-Bye my Fancy', *Complete Poetry and Collected Prose*, 639.

84. For some relevant observations see Simon Gatrell, *Hardy the Creator: A Textual Biography* (Oxford: Clarendon Press, 1988), 220–1.

85. *Studies in Bibliography*, 29 (1976), 195.

86. *The English Auden: Poems, Essays, and Dramatic Writings, 1927–1939*, ed. Edward Mendelson (New York: Random House, 1977), 241.

87. *In the Shadow of the Giant: Thomas Wolfe. Correspondence of Edward C. Aswell and Elizabeth Nowell 1949–1958*, ed. Mary Aswell Doll and Clara Stites (Athens, OH: Ohio Univ. Press, 1988), xi. For another study along somewhat similar lines see Michael Squires, ed., *D. H. Lawrence's Manuscripts: The Correspondence of Frieda Lawrence, Jake Zeitlin and Others* (New York: St Martin's Press, 1991).

88. James E. Miller, Jr, in a volume of essays devoted to the role of psychoanalysis in biography, speaks specifically of the intimacy, 'closer perhaps than a family relationship', that must have developed between Leon Edel and Henry James: Miller, 'The Biographer with the Blue Guitar', in George Moraitis and George H. Pollock, eds., *Psychoanalytic Studies of Biography* (Madison, CT: International Universities Press, 1987), 44–5. Edel himself speaks in the same volume ('Confessions of a Biographer', 3) of his life *with* James, of their living together over many years much as Boswell lived with Johnson.

89. See Coburn, *In Pursuit of Coleridge* (London: Bodley Head, 1977), and David Buchanan, *The Treasure of Auchinleck: The Story of the Boswell Papers* (New York: McGraw-Hill, 1974).

90. Reed, *Hilda Tablet and Others: Four Pieces for Radio* (London: British Broadcasting Corporation, 1971), 9–51; as noted earlier, the play owes much to Reed's own experience of working towards a never-completed biography of Thomas Hardy.

91. Charles Carrington, *Rudyard Kipling: His Life and Work* (London: Macmillan, 1955), vi. Anne Stevenson makes a similar acknowledgement ('almost a work of dual authorship') of Olwyn Hughes, as

Plath's literary executor, in her *Bitter Fame: A Life of Sylvia Plath* (Boston: Houghton Mifflin, 1989), ix, although the two situations are not precisely comparable.

92. See Nathaniel Hawthorne, *The American Notebooks*, ed. Claude M. Simpson (Columbus, OH: Ohio State Univ. Press, 1972), 686–90.

93. Rosenbaum, *Index*, 416; and see p. 422 for Elsie Bambridge's possible role in the disappearance of letters from Kipling to his wife.

94. For an amusing instance, see Mina Curtiss's account of her negotiations with Prince Antoine Bibesco for access to the letters he had received from Marcel Proust: *Other People's Letters: A Memoir* (Boston: Houghton, Mifflin, 1978), 83–9, 93–4, 126–30, 133–4.

95. James, *The Aspern Papers* (New York: Charles Scribner's Sons, 1908) [New York Edition XII], 118.

96. Larkin, *Required Writing: Miscellaneous Pieces 1955–1982* (London: Faber & Faber, 1983), 99, 101.

97. *Sunday Times* (London), 27 Aug. 1989, 'Books', G4.

98. Michael Burn, *Mary and Richard: The Story of Richard Hillary and Mary Booker* (London: André Deutsch, 1988), 193; Mary Booker was in fact divorced.

99. See D. Anthony Bischoff, 'The Manuscripts of Gerard Manley Hopkins', *Thought*, 26 (Winter 1951–2), 551–7; the subject is well surveyed in Rosenbaum, *Index*, 259–73, esp. 260, 263–4. For another remarkable instance of the recovery of documents initially neglected see David Gilmour, *The Last Leopard: A Life of Giuseppe di Lampedusa* (London: Quartet Books, 1988).

100. F. Hardy to Cockerell, 27 Dec. 1919 (Beinecke), extracted in *Friends of a Lifetime: Letters to Sydney Carlyle Cockerell*, ed. Viola Meynell (London: Jonathan Cape, 1940), 305–6. See also Margaret Atwood, 'Biographobia', in Laurence S. Lockridge, John Maynard, and Donald D. Stone, eds., *Nineteenth-Century Lives: Essays Presented to Jerome Hamilton Buckley* (Cambridge: Cambridge Univ. Press, 1989), 7.

101. Froude, *Thomas Carlyle*, II. 357.

102. Zdzislaw Najder, *Joseph Conrad: A Chronicle*, trans. Halina Carroll-Najder (New Brunswick, NJ: Rutgers Univ. Press, 1983), 39; Grove's deceptions were first fully explored in Douglas O. Spettigue, *Frederick Philip Grove* (Toronto: Copp Clark, 1969).

Index

Gilmour, David 262 n. 99
Ginevra (housekeeper to Pen Browning)
     31, 211 n. 93, 215 n. 124
Gittings, Robert 246 n. 17
Gladstone, William Ewart 42, 46
Goethe, Johann Wolfgang von 177,
     205
Gosse, Edmund: and Browning 7, 15,
     20, 31, 210 n. 49, 212 n. 71; and
     Hardy 7, 129, 140, 142, 146, 148,
     149, 245 n. 10; and James 78, 97,
     100, 104, 233 n. 56; and Tennyson
     46, 55, 221 nn. 53 & 56, 224 n. 99;
     and Whitman 182–3
Gould, Warwick 260 n. 76
Granville-Barker, Harley 148, 150
Greene, Graham 3, 182, 196, 203, 205
Greer, Louise 210 n. 44
Greg, (Sir) Walter Wilson 197, 260 nn.
     80 & 82
Griffin, Susan M. 236 n. 99
Griffin, W. Hall 26, 28–9, 31
Griswold, Rufus 192, 230 n. 19
Grove, Frederick Philip 205
Grove, (Sir) George 20
Gunn, Peter 170
Guston, Philip 189

Habegger, Alfred 235 n. 97
Hagen, June Steffensen 219 n. 14
Hahn, Stephen 254 n. 13
Hale, Emily 183
Hallam, Arthur Henry 41, 55, 70, 224
     n. 98
Hanbury, Cecil 149
Hardy, Charles Meech 154
Hardy, Emma Lavinia (*née* Gifford)
     114 ('widow'), 115, 132, 133, 137,
     154, 164; death 122, 131;
     tomb 143, 144
HARDY, FLORENCE EMILY (*née*
     Dugdale) 139–74; 131, 135–6, 180,
     204; and Barrie 140–1, 154, 162–3,
     246 n. 17; and composition of Hardy
     'Life' 122–7, 161–4, 201; as
     custodian of Max Gate 168–9, 170,
     175; and Hardy's death and funerals
     139–46, 147, 246 n. 29, 247 nn. 41
     & 45; as Hardy's literary executor 4,
     140, 141, 159–61, 165–8, 189, 190,
     194, 200, 249 n. 91, 250 n. 98; and
     Hardy memorials 147–52, 171–2,
     248 nn. 58 & 76, 249 nn. 80 & 84;

and Hardy's will 153–9; relationship
     with S. Cockerell 140–1, 143–5,
     147–51, 156, 160–1, 162, 163,
     165–8, 245 n. 15, 252 n. 146;
     will 170–1, 186
  WORKS: *Early Life of Thomas
     Hardy* 122–7, 163–4, 165, 242 n.
     46, *see also* Hardy, T., Prose: *Life and
     Work*; *Later Years of Thomas Hardy*
     122–7, 139, 163–4, 242 n. 46, *see
     also* Hardy, T., Prose: *Life and Work*
Hardy, Henry: and brother's death and
     funerals 139, 143, 144, 145, 146;
     and brother's will 154, 249 n. 91,
     250 n. 98; and memorial to brother
     149
Hardy, Jemima 136, 137, 143, 144
Hardy, Katharine ('Kate'): and
     brother's death and funerals 139,
     143, 144, 145, 146, 147, 247 n. 36;
     and brother's will 154, 249 n. 91,
     250 n. 98, 253 n. 165; and Max Gate
     155, 170; and memorials to brother
     149–50, 152, 171, 248 nn. 62 & 76,
     249 n. 80
Hardy, Mary 137, 155
Hardy, Teresa 145, 247 nn. 38 & 45
HARDY, THOMAS 110–38; 3, 8, 18–
     19, 61, 212 n. 70, 250 n. 96; and
     Brownings 7, 27, 36, 207 n. 7, 208 n.
     17, 215 n. 119; death and
     funerals 139, 141–7, 170, 180, 184,
     190, 191, 246 nn. 28 & 29, 247 n.
     41; dispersal of library 158, 159,
     170, 171–3, 250 n. 100, 253 nn. 176
     & 181; disposal of papers 120, 124–
     5, 134–5, 157–61, 170–1, 250 n.
     107, 253 n. 170; and memorials 144,
     147–52, 157, 171–2, 173–4, 192,
     246 n. 32; and memory 131–8; and
     old age 110, 127–31, 135–8, 175–
     6, 177–8; and 'posthumousness'
     126–7, 243 n. 67, 244 n. 106; and
     privacy 122–7, 158–60, 161–4, *see
     also under* Prose *below*, *Life and
     Work*; and Tennysons 40, 46–7, 55,
     222 n. 59, 225 n. 119; will 140, 141,
     147, 153–61, 167, 249 n. 91, 250 nn.
     98, 100, & 101
  WORKS: collected editions 115,
     116, 134, 195, 240 n. 11; Mellstock
     edition 121, 131, 175; Wessex
     edition 116–21, 122, 196, 221 n. 38,